D1094760

RECENT HISTORY ATLAS

Also by Martin Gilbert

The Appeasers (*with Richard Gott*)
Britain and Germany Between the Wars
The European Powers 1900–45
Plough My Own Furrow: The Life of Lord Allen of Hurtwood
Winston Churchill (Clarendon Biographies)
Servant of India
The Roots of Appeasement

RECENT HISTORY ATLAS

1870 TO THE PRESENT DAY

MARTIN GILBERT

Fellow of Merton College, Oxford

Cartography by JOHN R. FLOWER

The Macmillan Company

Library of Congress Catalog Card Number: 69-17102

First American Edition 1969

Recent History Atlas *was first published in Great Britain in 1966 by Weidenfeld and Nicolson, London*

The Macmillan Company

Printed in the United States of America

Preface

The maps in this atlas aim to present the main historical developments of the last hundred years. Each map has been specially designed to help explain some important episode in recent history. Each continent is given as much importance as the events determine; not only wars and battles, but also treaties, alliances, population problems and political confrontations are the subject of these maps. I have consulted a wide range of existing atlases, reference books, newspaper files, and specialized historical works. These sources have provided the statistical and factual information which can be usefully brought together on a map. My aim has been to help the reader grasp at once a wide range of relevant historical points, as clearly and accurately as possible.

My thanks go to all those who have helped improve the maps by their suggestions; in particular to Mr. John Emerson, Miss Joanna Kaye, Mr. Michael Perman, Dr. John Roberts, and Miss Maureen Turnbull.

I should also like to thank those who have sent me corrections since the first English edition was published in August 1966, and have thereby greatly improved the accuracy of the Atlas:
Mr. John M. Austen, Mr. T. F. R. G. Braun, Mr. Lance Brown, Mr. Frank Gannon, Mr. I. M. Gillies, Mr. Tosco Fyvel, Professor Michael Roberts, Lieutenant Commander A. G. Thomas, R.N., Mr. Alexander Werth, Sir John Wheeler-Bennett and Mr. Michael St. J. Wright.

I should welcome any further corrections for future editions.

MARTIN GILBERT
Merton College, Oxford

1967

List of Maps

	GREAT BRITAIN	GERMANY	FRANCE	ITALY	U. S. A.	RUSSIA	OTHER NATIONS
1860	1867 Occupies Bahrein MAP 12 1869 Occupies Nicobar Islands MAP 19	1866 Defeats Austria MAP 4	1860 Gains Nice and Savoy MAP 3 1863 Gains Cambodia MAP 17 & 119	1860 Garibaldi enters Palermo MAP 3 1866 Fleet destroyed by Austria MAP 3 1866 Gains Venice MAP 5	1861 Civil War begins MAP 11 1865 Confederates surrender; Lincoln assassinated MAP 11	1860 Annexes Vladivostok MAP 17 1868 Occupies Samarkand MAP 12	1863 Greeks gain Corfu MAP 13 1866 Austria loses Venice MAP 5
1870	1874 Protectorate over Malaya MAP 17 1878 Occupies Cyprus MAP 7	1870 Besieges Paris MAP 2 1871 Annexes Alsace-Lorraine MAP 4	1870 Attacks Germany MAP 2 1871 Defeated by Germany MAP 2	1870 Final unification MAP 3 1871 Rome made capital MAP 3		1873 Occupies Khiva and Bukhara MAP 12 1877 Declares war on Turkey MAP 8 1878 Occupies Kars MAP 7 1878 Defeats Turks MAP 8	1876 Turks massacre Bulgarians MAP 8 1878 Austria occupies Bosnia MAP 5
1880	1882 Occupies Egypt MAP 7 1886 Occupies Upper Burma MAP 17	1884 Colony in South West Africa MAP 16	1881 Occupies Tunisia MAP 7 1884 Gains Annam MAP 17	1889 Colony in East Africa MAP 16		1887 Occupies Penjdeh MAP 12	
1890	1890 Occupies Quetta MAP 12 1898 Dervishes defeated at Omdurman MAP 20 1899 Protects Kuwait MAP 12 1899 Attacked by Boers MAP 15	1890 Colony in East Africa MAP 16	1893 Gains Laos MAP 17 & 119 1898 Sphere of influence in Siam MAP 17 & 119		1898 Gains Philippines from Spain MAP 17 1898 Occupies Cuba MAP 104		1895 Japan annexes Formosa MAP 17
1900	1902 Boers surrender MAP 15 1904 Defeats Tibetans MAP 12 1907 Extends influence over Persia MAP 12	1909 Plan to invade France through neutral Belgium MAP 26			1900 Decade of most intense immigration begins MAP 10 1909 Occupies Nicaragua MAP 104	1905 Defeated by Japan MAP 18 1907 Extends influence over Persia MAP 12	1905 Japan defeats Russia MAP 18
1910	1910 Churchill at German Army manoeuvres MAP 20 1914 Army helps France to resist German attack MAP 25 1915 Attempts to defeat Turkey at Dardanelles MAP 33 1916 Vast losses for tiny gains at Battle of the Somme MAP 28 1918 Defeats Germany MAP 30 1918 Intervenes in Russian Civil War MAP 39	1914 Vast expenditure on military preparations MAP 22 1914 Attacks Belgium and France MAP 25 1914 Defeats Russians at Tannenberg MAP 31 1916 Fleet checked at Jutland MAP 38 1918 Defeated MAP 30 1918 War Deaths MAP 38	1915 Trench warfare across Eastern France MAP 27 1917 Relief force sent to help Italy MAP 29 1918 Regains Alsace-Lorraine MAP 30	1912 Conquers Libya MAP 7 1914 Neutral on outbreak of War MAP 24 1917 Defeated by Austria at Caporetto MAP 29 1919 Gains Istria and Tyrol MAP 3	1916 Occupies Dominican Republic MAP 104 1917 Enters World War MAP 23 1918 Troops active against Germany MAP 30 1918 Intervenes in Russian Civil War MAP 39	1914 Initial victory against Germany MAP 31 1915 Driven back by Germany MAP 32 1917 Cedes territory to Germany MAP 37 1917 High number of War deaths MAP 38 1918 Civil War MAP 39	1913 Turks driven from Balkans MAP 13 1914 Liberia and Abyssinia only two Independent African States MAP 14 1914 Austrians driven back by Russians MAP 31 1915 Serbia defeated MAP 32 1917 China and Brazil join World War MAP 23 1917 Austria advances towards Venice MAP 29 1918 Turkey defeated MAP 35 1918 Bulgaria defeated MAP 36
1920							

	GREAT BRITAIN	GERMANY	FRANCE	ITALY	U. S. A.	RUSSIA	OTHER NATIONS
1920		1920 Loses large part of Silesia MAP 44 1922 Retains East Prussia MAP 62 1923 Hitler fails to seize power in Munich MAP 49		1921 Becomes dictatorship MAP 48	1926 Occupies Nicaragua MAP 104	1920 Fails to conquer Poland MAP 40	1920 Poles drive Russians back from Warsaw MAP 40 1920 Poland a State with many minorities MAP 61 1922 Turks defeat Greeks MAP 42 1926 Poland becomes dictatorship MAP 48
1930	1935 Plan to partition Abyssinia MAP 51 1939 Guarantees Poland, Greece, Rumania & Turkey MAP 65	1930 First Nazi election successes MAP 49 1935 Gains Saar by Plebiscite MAP 50 1938 Annexes Austria MAP 50 1938 Gains territory from Czechoslovakia MAP 53 1939 Air Force largest in the World MAP 63 1939 Invades Poland MAP 64		1935 Invades Abyssinia MAP 51 1936 Pact of Steel with Germany MAP 65 1939 Occupies Albania MAP 56		1939 Non-aggression pact with Germany MAP 65 1939 Occupies Eastern Poland MAP 64 1939 Expelled from League of Nations MAP 47	1931 Japan invades Manchuria MAP 52 1936 Spanish Civil War begins MAP 55 1937 Japan occupies Peking MAP 52 1938 Hungary gains Czechoslovak territory MAP 46 1938 Czechoslovakia loses vital industry & defences MAP 54 1939 Poland partitioned MAP 59 1939 Russia invades Finland MAP 66
1940	1940 Driven from Norway by Germans MAP 67 1940 Bombed by Germans MAP 69 1941 Attempts to resist Germans in Greece MAP 70 1943 invades Italy MAP 79 1944 Plans invasion of Hitlers Europe MAP 82 1944 Normandy Landings MAP 83 1945 Churchill crosses the Rhine MAP 92 1947 Leaves India MAP 100 1948 Leaves Palestine MAP 102	1940 Occupies Paris MAP 68 1941 Occupies parts of Slovenia & Serbia MAP 56 1941 Invades Greece MAP 70 1941-1945 Murders Jews MAP 86 1942 Reaches Stalingrad MAP 72 1943-1945 Cities bombed MAP 84 1945 Dresden destroyed MAP 85 1945 Surrenders MAP 87 1945 Germans expelled from Central Europe MAP 89 1945 Occupied by victors MAP 94 1945 Berlin partitioned MAP 117 & 118	1940 Defeated by Germany MAP 68 1943 Resistance Movement in Corsica MAP 79 1945 Paris liberated MAP 87 1949 A member of NATO MAP 116	1941 Invades Greece MAP 56 1943 Surrenders to allied nations MAP 79	1940 Leases British bases in return for bombers MAP 73 1941 Sends Lend-Lease to allied nations MAP 75 1941 Attacked by Japan MAP 52 1942 Naval victories against Japan MAP 90 1943 Invades Italy MAP 79 1944 Normandy Landings MAP 83 1945 Defeats Japan MAP 91 1945 Occupies Japan MAP 101	1941 Invaded by Germany MAP 71 1941 Leningrad besieged MAP 80 1942 Drives out Germans MAP 81 1945 Immense toll of war MAP 93 1945 Gains Bessarabia MAP 58 1945 Annexes Eastern Poland MAP 60 1946 Establishes economic block in Eastern Europe MAP 111	1940 Germany invades Holland, Belgium and France MAP 68 1941 Germany invades Yugoslavia and Greece MAP 70 1941 Hungary gains Rumanian territory MAP 46 1941 Japan attacks British, French & U.S. territory in the Pacific MAP 52 1941 Britain liberates Abyssinia MAP 77 1942 Japan occupies Singapore MAP 90 1945 The immense toll of the war MAP 93 1945-1948 Advance of communism in Eastern Europe MAP 94 1947 Civil war between India and Pakistan MAP 100 1948 Arab-Jewish War MAP 102
1950	1956 Attacks Suez Canal MAP 103		1954 Defeated in Indo-China MAP 119	1954 Retains Trieste but not Istria MAP 99	1950 Main United Nations participant in Korean War MAP 106 & 107	1955 Establishes defensive Warsaw Pact MAP 116	1950 Communist Revolution in China MAP 101 1950 Korean War MAP 106 & 107 1956 United Nations intervenes after Suez War MAP 103 1957 European Common Market established MAP 111
1960	1961 Oil interests in Middle East MAP 112	1960 Divided Germany an area of east-west conflict MAP 116			1960 Negroes MAP 109 1962 Blockades Cuba MAP 105 1963 Signs Test Ban Treaty MAP 110 1964 New York's population MAP 114 1965 Active in Vietnam War MAP 120	1960 Shoots down U.S. spy plane over central Russia MAP 121 1962 Establishes missile bases in Cuba MAP 105 1964 Chinese claim territory from MAP 108	1960 The rapid spread of African independence MAP 98 1960 United Nations active in the Congo MAP 97 1953 Nuclear Test Ban Treaty signed in Moscow MAP 110 1964 China explodes her first atomic device MAP 108 1965 War between India and Pakistan MAP 116
1970							

The EUROPEAN EMPIRES in 1870

Before the Franco Prussian war

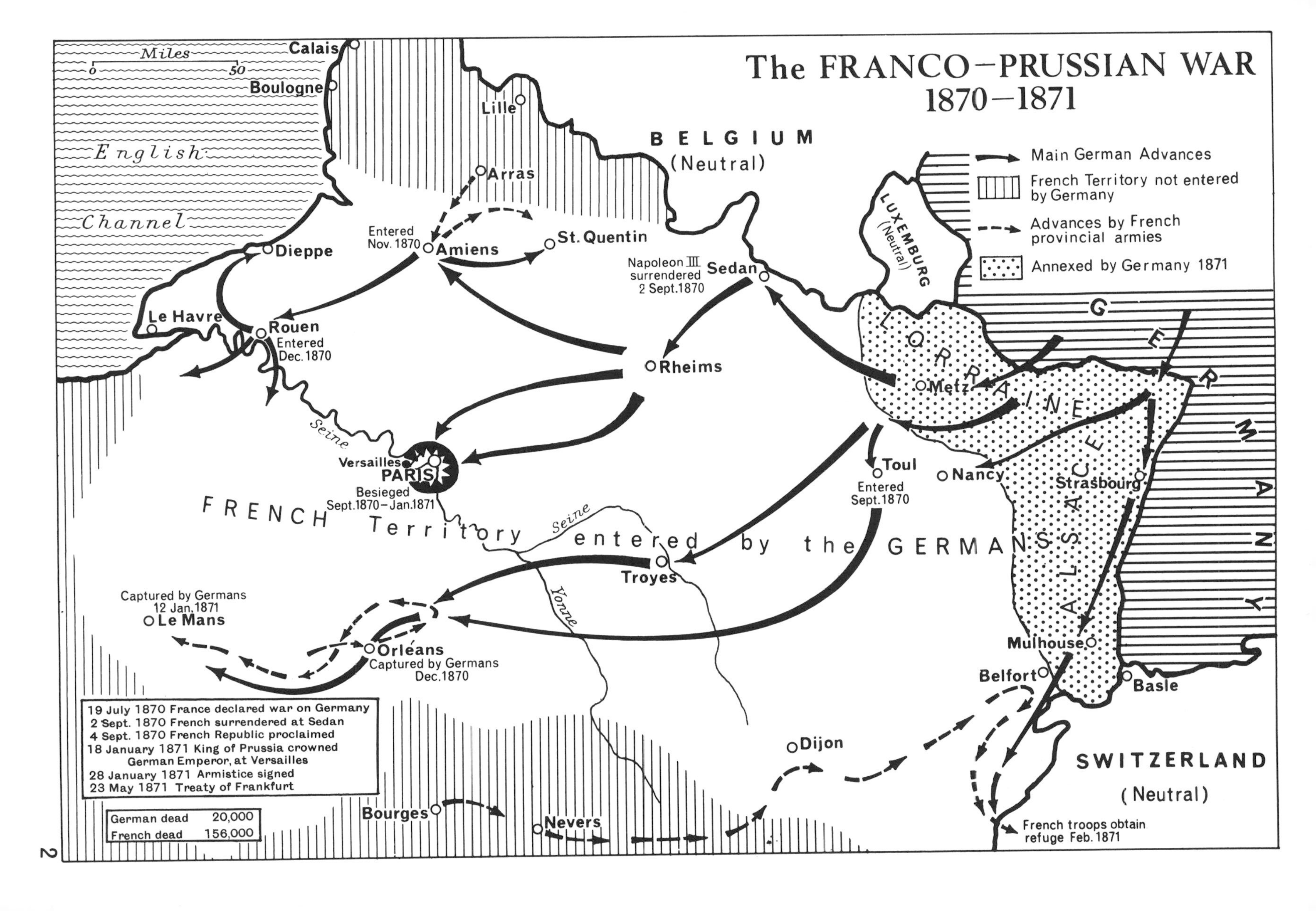
The FRANCO–PRUSSIAN WAR
1870–1871
Main German Advances
French Territory not entered by Germany
Advances by French provincial armies
Annexed by Germany 1871
Miles
0
50
English Channel
Calais
Boulogne
Lille
Arras
BELGIUM
(Neutral)
LUXEMBURG
(Neutral)
Entered Nov. 1870
Amiens
St. Quentin
Dieppe
Le Havre
Rouen
Entered Dec. 1870
Napoleon III surrendered 2 Sept. 1870
Sedan
Rheims
Metz
LORRAINE
GERMANY
ALSACE
Strasbourg
Nancy
Toul
Entered Sept. 1870
Seine
Versailles
PARIS
Besieged Sept. 1870 – Jan. 1871
FRENCH Territory entered by the GERMANS
Troyes
Yonne
Captured by Germans 12 Jan. 1871
Le Mans
Orléans
Captured by Germans Dec. 1870
Mulhouse
Belfort
Basle
Dijon
SWITZERLAND
(Neutral)
French troops obtain refuge Feb. 1871
Bourges
Nevers
19 July 1870 France declared war on Germany
2 Sept. 1870 French surrendered at Sedan
4 Sept. 1870 French Republic proclaimed
18 January 1871 King of Prussia crowned German Emperor, at Versailles
28 January 1871 Armistice signed
23 May 1871 Treaty of Frankfurt
German dead 20,000
French dead 156,000

Germany
France
Switzerland
Austria - Hungary
TYROL
SAVOY
(to France)
1860
KINGDOM OF SARDINIA
LOMBARDY
1859
VENETIA
1866
Trieste
ISTRIA
Fiume
Magenta
1859
Milan
Solferino
1859
Custozza
1866
Verona
Venice
Turin
PIEDMONT
R. Po
PARMA
1860
MODENA
1860
ROMAGNA
1860
Genoa
Ottoman Empire
Dalmatia
NICE
(to France)
1860
MONACO Independent,
Sardinian Protection
1815-1860.
French Protection since
1861.
(PIEDMONT)
SAN MARINO
(Ind. Rep.)
Florence
Capital of Italy
1864-1871
TUSCANY
1860
MARCHES
1860
Castelfidardo
1860
Adriatic Sea
PAPAL STATES
UMBRIA
1860
Lissa
1866
Austrians destroy
Italian fleet
Lagosta
(Italian until
1945)
Elba
Corsica
(French)
THE PATRIMONY
1870
Mentana
Garibaldi defeated
by the French
3 November
1867
ROME
Entered by
Italians 1870.
Made Italian Capital
1871.
Gaeta
1861
BENEVENTO
(Papal
to 1860)
NAPLES
Naples
Entered by Garibaldi
7 September 1860
Tyrrhenian Sea
SARDINIA
KINGDOM
OF THE
TWO SICILIES
1860
1852 Cavour, Premier
of Piedmont.
1861 Victor Emmanuel
King of Italy.
Entered by Garibaldi
6 June 1860
Palermo
Aspromonte
Garibaldi captured
29 August 1862
SICILY
Mediterranean Sea
TUNISIA
(Part of OTTOMAN
EMPIRE)
Miles
0
50
100
Dates refer to
Union with Piedmont
Italian gains in 1919
The
UNIFICATION of ITALY
1859–1870
with gains of 1919

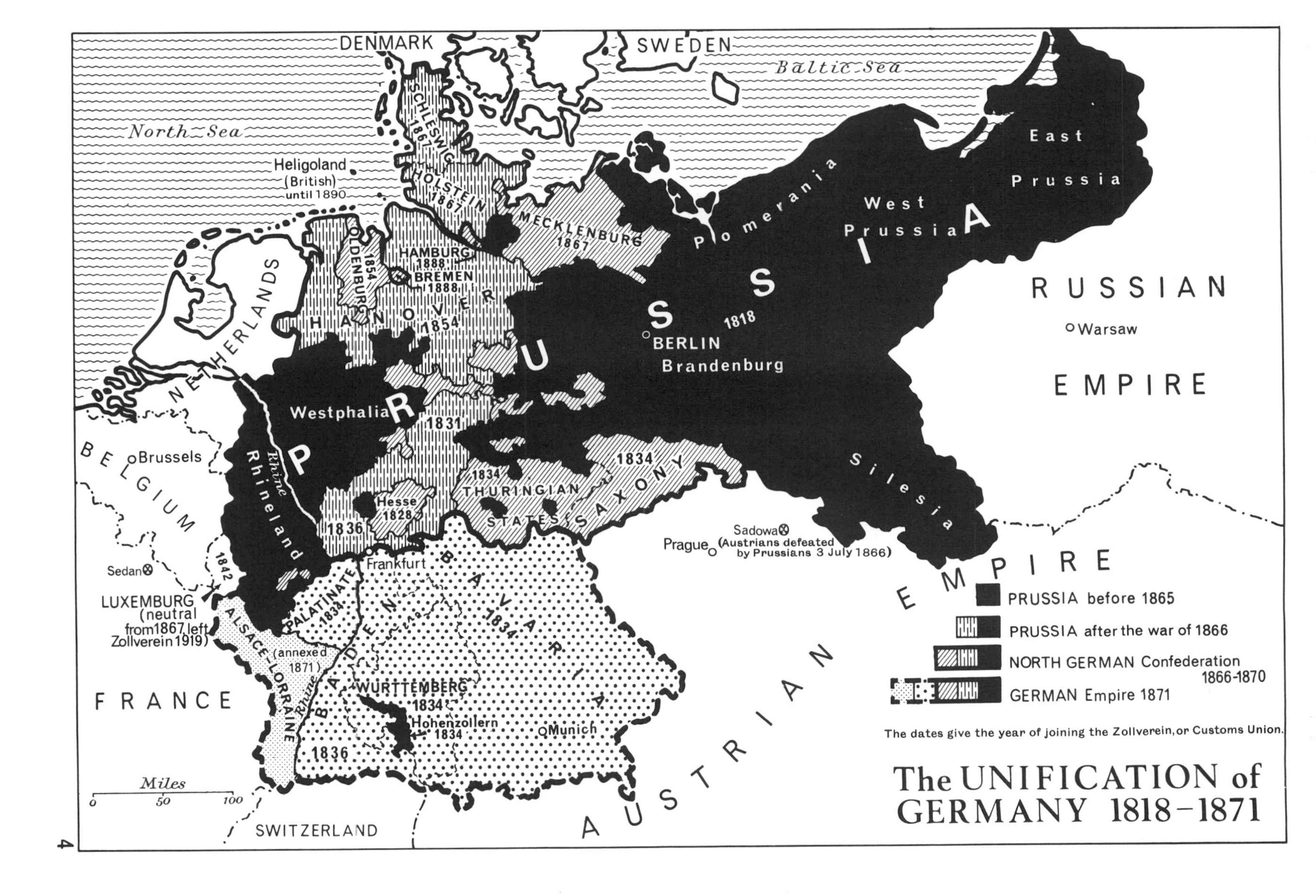
The UNIFICATION of GERMANY 1818–1871
PRUSSIA before 1865
PRUSSIA after the war of 1866
NORTH GERMAN Confederation 1866-1870
GERMAN Empire 1871
The dates give the year of joining the Zollverein, or Customs Union.
DENMARK
SWEDEN
Baltic Sea
North Sea
Heligoland (British) until 1890
SCHLESWIG 1867
HOLSTEIN 1867
MECKLENBURG 1867
HAMBURG 1888
BREMEN 1888
OLDENBURG 1854
HANOVER 1854
NETHERLANDS
PRUSSIA
Pomerania
West Prussia
East Prussia
BERLIN
Brandenburg
1818
RUSSIAN EMPIRE
Warsaw
Westphalia
1831
Rhine
Rhineland
BELGIUM
Brussels
Sedan
1842
LUXEMBURG (neutral from 1867, left Zollverein 1919)
Hesse 1828
1836
Frankfurt
1834
THURINGIAN STATES
1834
SAXONY
Silesia
Sadowa
Prague (Austrians defeated by Prussians 3 July 1866)
AUSTRIAN EMPIRE
PALATINATE 1834
ALSACE-LORRAINE (annexed 1871)
Rhine
BADEN
1836
WÜRTTEMBERG 1834
Hohenzollern 1834
BAVARIA 1834
Munich
FRANCE
SWITZERLAND
Miles
0
50
100

THE HABSBURG EMPIRE 1867–1918 (POLITICAL)

5

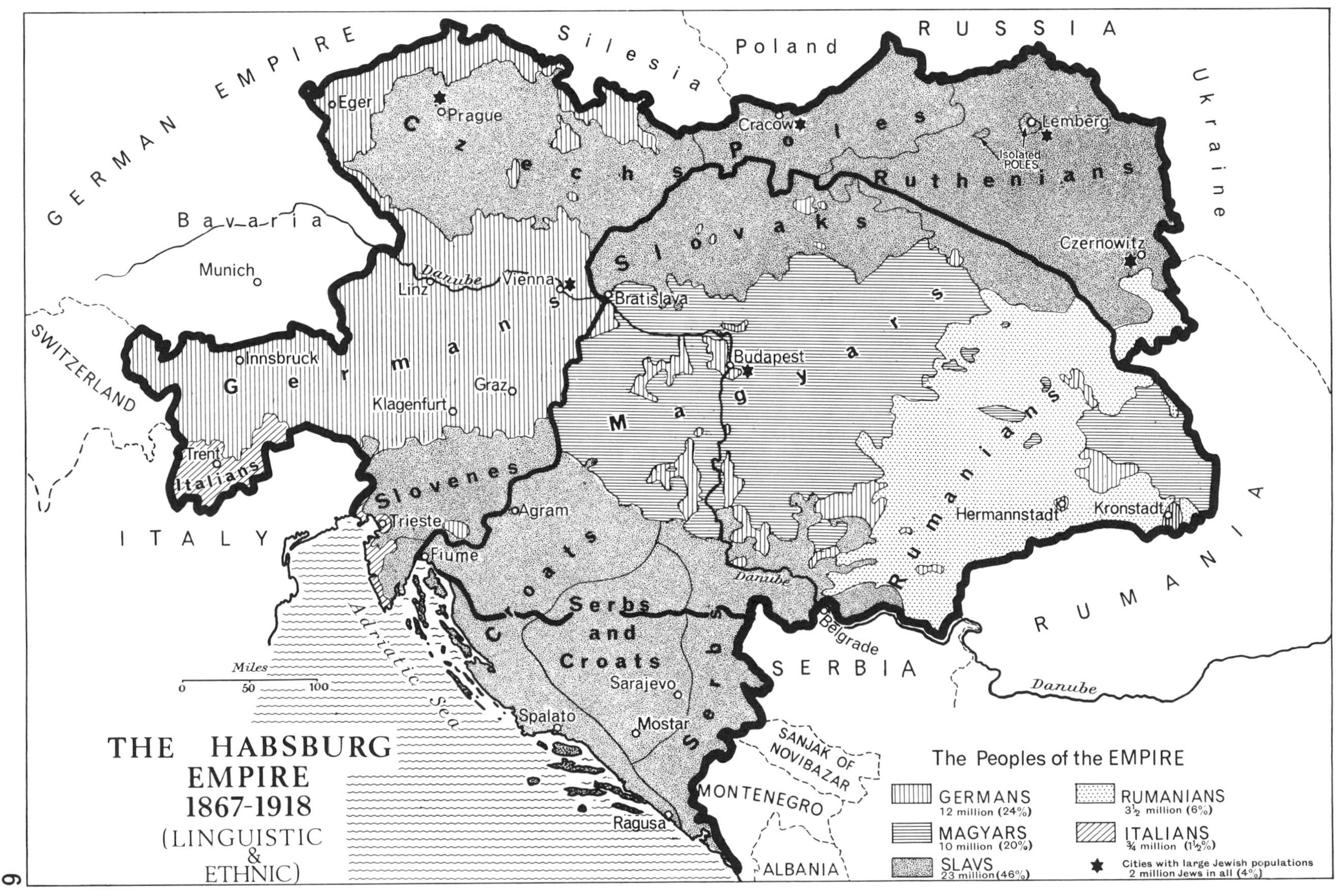
THE HABSBURG EMPIRE 1867-1918
(LINGUISTIC & ETHNIC)
The Peoples of the EMPIRE
GERMANS
12 million (24%)
MAGYARS
10 million (20%)
SLAVS
23 million (46%)
RUMANIANS
3½ million (6%)
ITALIANS
¾ million (1½%)
Cities with large Jewish populations
2 million Jews in all (4%)
Miles
0
50
100
GERMAN EMPIRE
Silesia
Poland
RUSSIA
Ukraine
Bavaria
Munich
SWITZERLAND
ITALY
RUMANIA
SERBIA
SANJAK OF NOVIBAZAR
MONTENEGRO
ALBANIA
Adriatic Sea
Danube
Czechs
Poles
Ruthenians
Slovaks
Germans
Magyars
Rumanians
Italians
Slovenes
Croats
Serbs and Croats
Serbs
Eger
Prague
Cracow
Lemberg
Isolated POLES
Czernowitz
Linz
Vienna
Bratislava
Budapest
Innsbruck
Graz
Klagenfurt
Trent
Trieste
Agram
Fiume
Hermannstadt
Kronstadt
Belgrade
Sarajevo
Spalato
Mostar
Ragusa

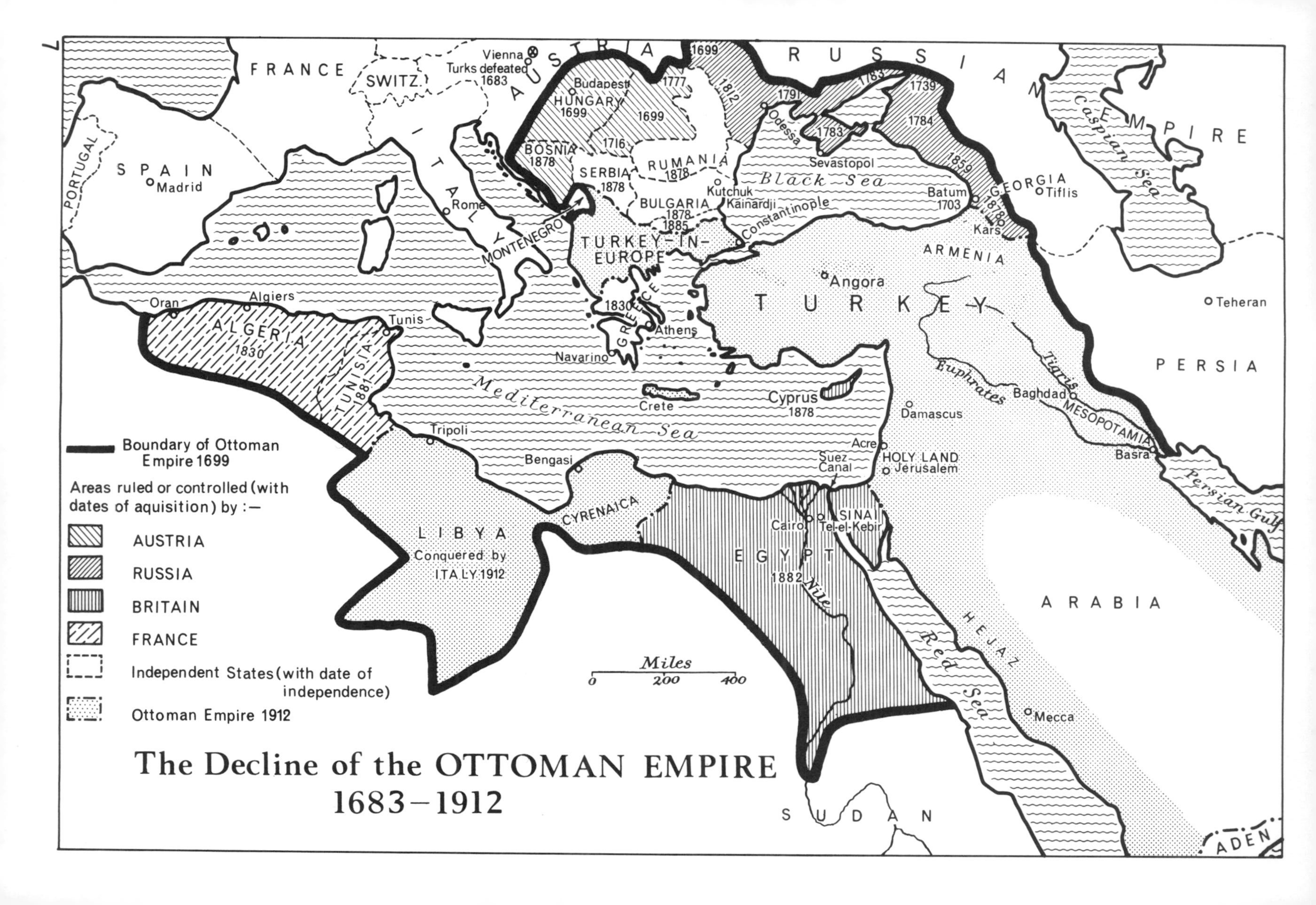

The Decline of the OTTOMAN EMPIRE 1683–1912

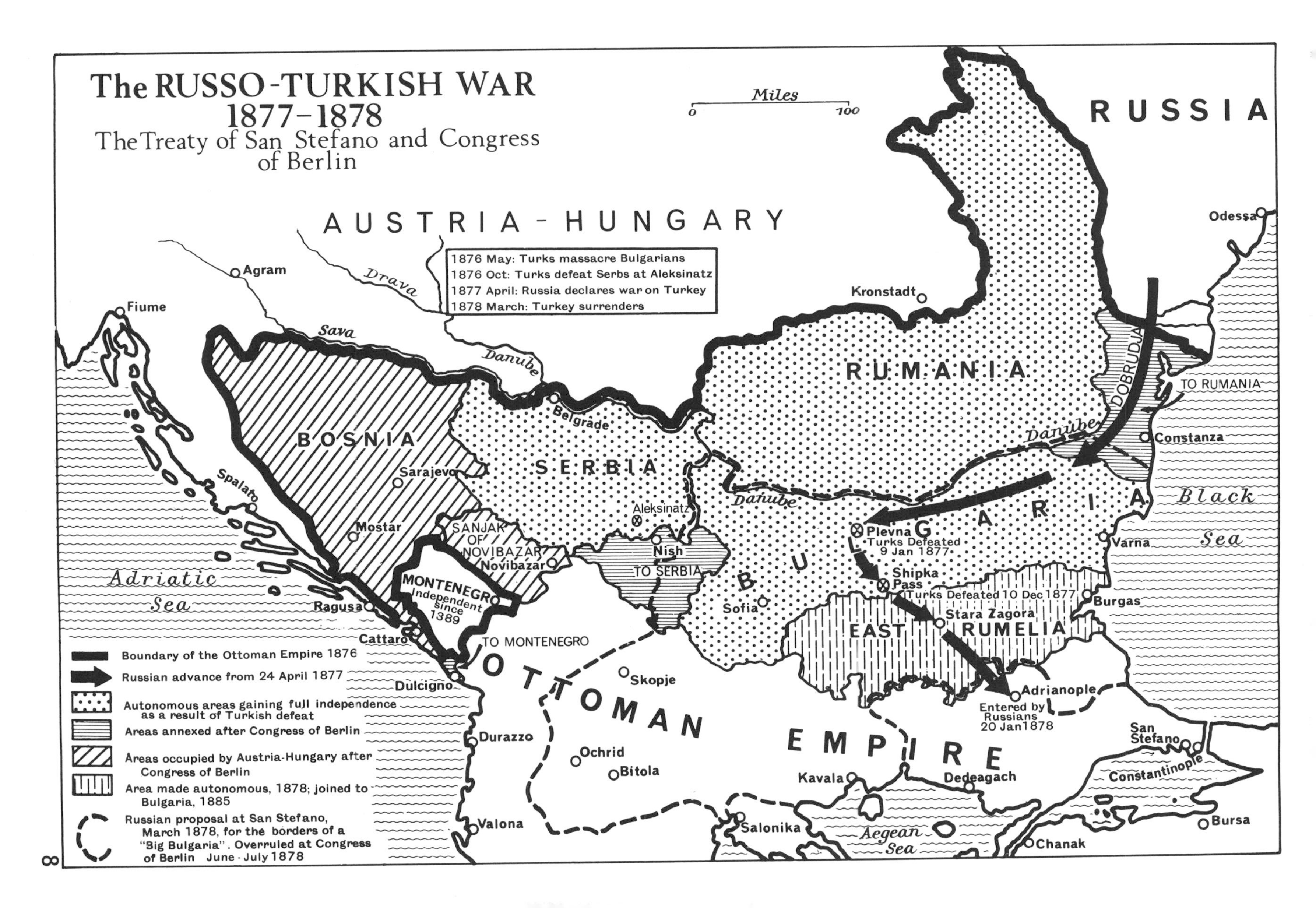

The RUSSO-TURKISH WAR
1877–1878
The Treaty of San Stefano and Congress of Berlin
Miles
0
100
RUSSIA
AUSTRIA-HUNGARY
1876 May: Turks massacre Bulgarians
1876 Oct: Turks defeat Serbs at Aleksinatz
1877 April: Russia declares war on Turkey
1878 March: Turkey surrenders
Odessa
Agram
Drava
Kronstadt
Fiume
Sava
Danube
RUMANIA
DOBRUDJA
TO RUMANIA
Constanza
Belgrade
BOSNIA
SERBIA
Sarajevo
Spalato
Mostar
Aleksinatz
Black Sea
SANJAK OF NOVIBAZAR
Novibazar
Nish
TO SERBIA
Plevna
Turks Defeated 9 Jan 1877
BULGARIA
Varna
Shipka Pass
Turks Defeated 10 Dec 1877
Burgas
Adriatic Sea
MONTENEGRO
Independent since 1389
Ragusa
Sofia
Stara Zagora
EAST RUMELIA
Cattaro
TO MONTENEGRO
OTTOMAN EMPIRE
Skopje
Dulcigno
Adrianople
Entered by Russians 20 Jan 1878
Durazzo
Ochrid
Bitola
San Stefano
Constantinople
Kavala
Dedeagach
Valona
Salonika
Aegean Sea
Chanak
Bursa
Boundary of the Ottoman Empire 1876
Russian advance from 24 April 1877
Autonomous areas gaining full independence as a result of Turkish defeat
Areas annexed after Congress of Berlin
Areas occupied by Austria-Hungary after Congress of Berlin
Area made autonomous, 1878; joined to Bulgaria, 1885
Russian proposal at San Stefano, March 1878, for the borders of a "Big Bulgaria". Overruled at Congress of Berlin June-July 1878

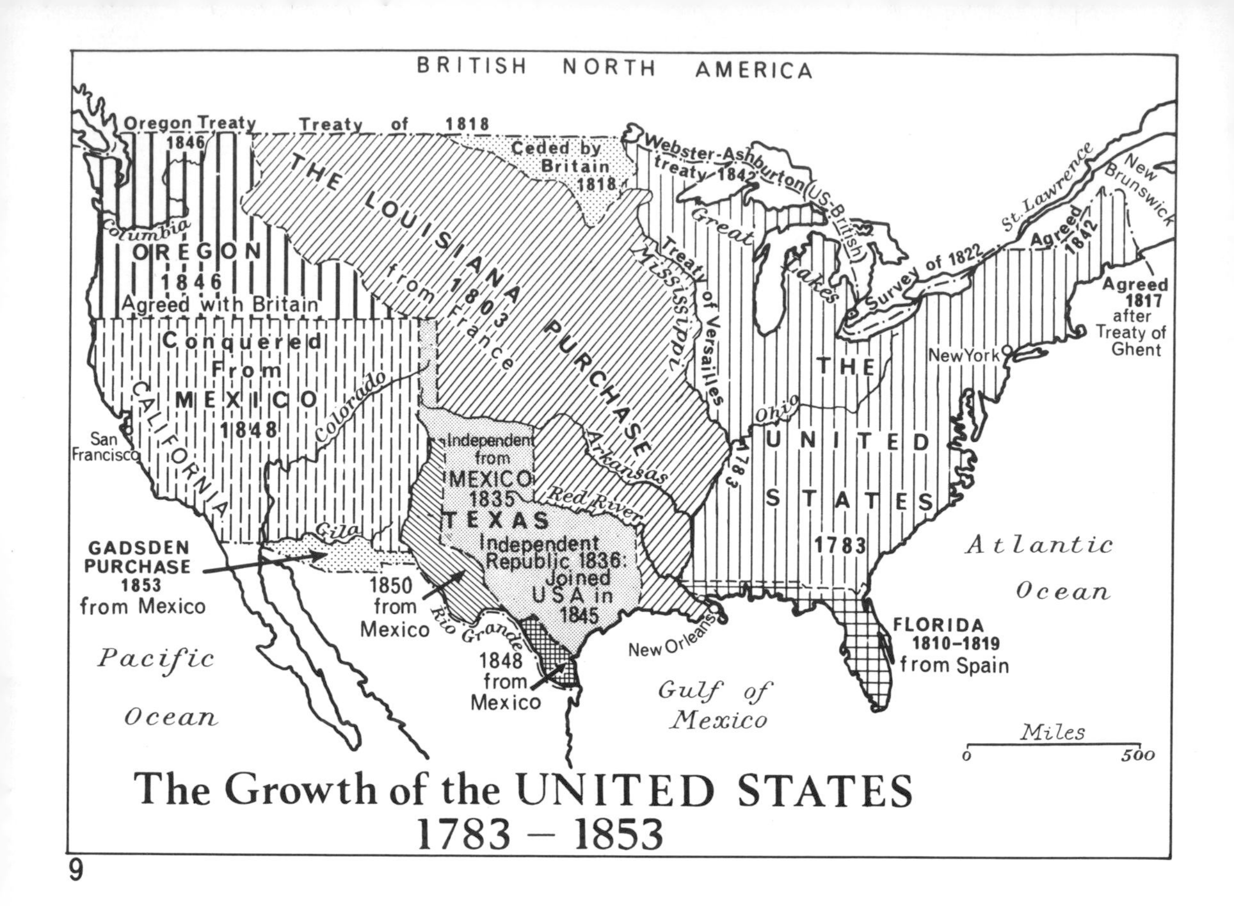

The Growth of the UNITED STATES 1783 – 1853

9

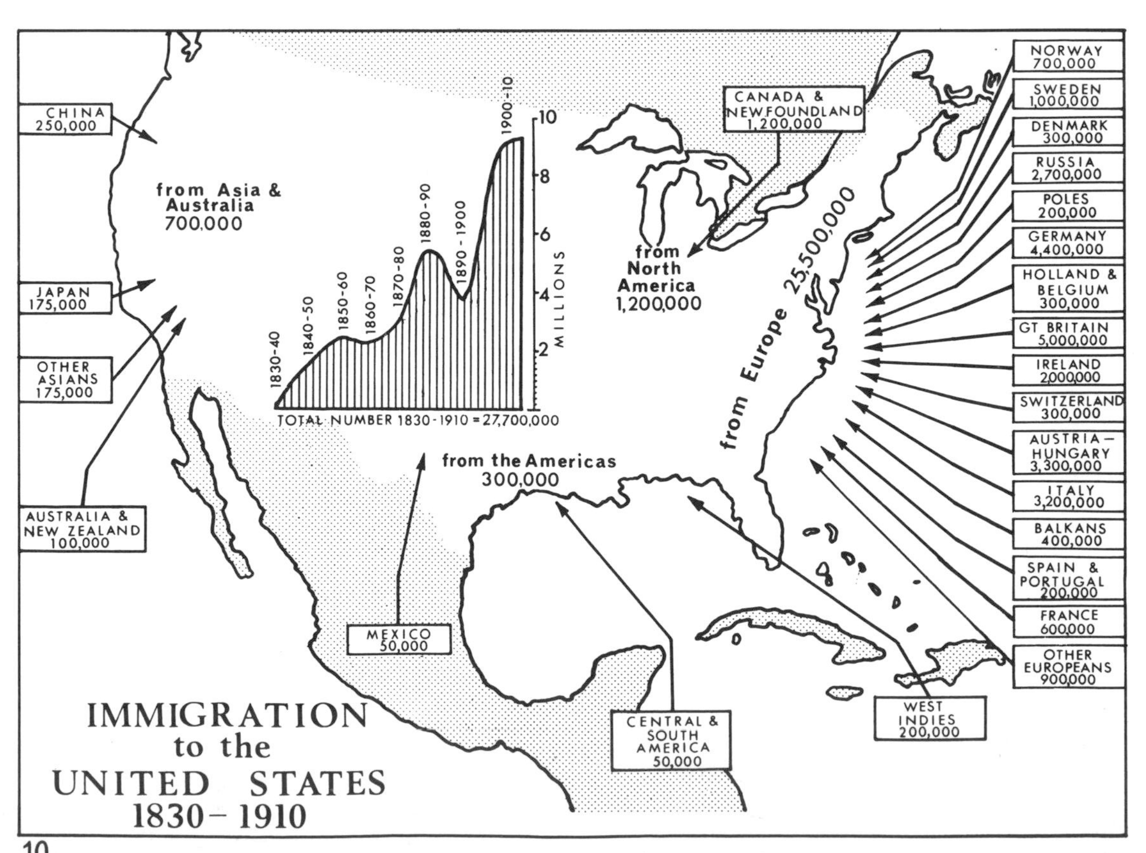

IMMIGRATION to the UNITED STATES 1830–1910

10

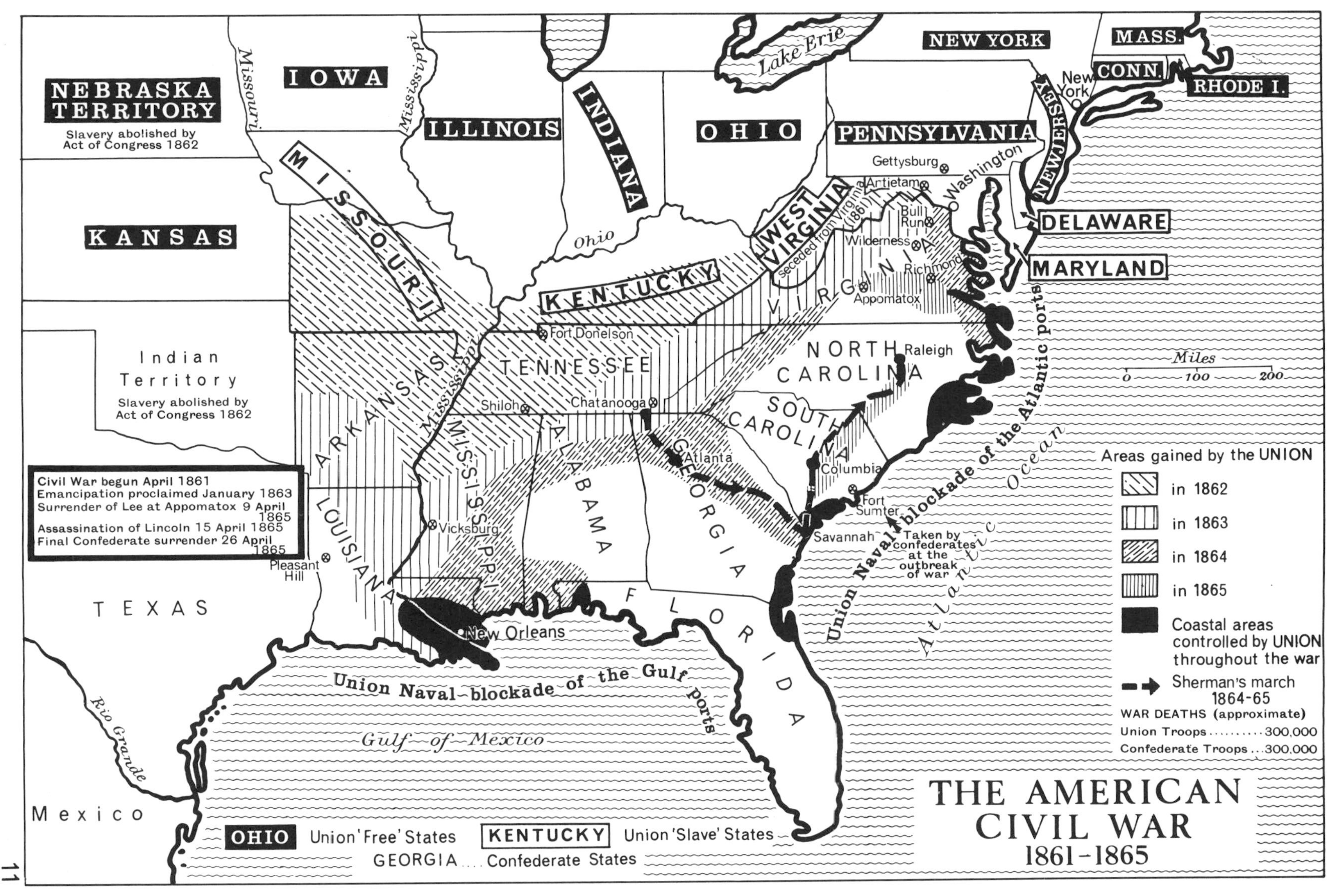
THE AMERICAN CIVIL WAR 1861-1865
Areas gained by the UNION
in 1862
in 1863
in 1864
in 1865
Coastal areas controlled by UNION throughout the war
Sherman's march 1864-65
WAR DEATHS (approximate)
Union Troops 300,000
Confederate Troops ... 300,000
OHIO Union 'Free' States
KENTUCKY Union 'Slave' States
GEORGIA .... Confederate States
Civil War begun April 1861
Emancipation proclaimed January 1863
Surrender of Lee at Appomatox 9 April 1865
Assassination of Lincoln 15 April 1865
Final Confederate surrender 26 April 1865
NEBRASKA TERRITORY
Slavery abolished by Act of Congress 1862
KANSAS
Indian Territory
Slavery abolished by Act of Congress 1862
TEXAS
Mexico
Rio Grande
IOWA
ILLINOIS
INDIANA
OHIO
PENNSYLVANIA
NEW YORK
MASS.
CONN.
RHODE I.
NEW JERSEY
New York
DELAWARE
MARYLAND
Washington
Gettysburg
Antietam
Bull Run
Wilderness
Richmond
Appomatox
WEST VIRGINIA
Seceded from Virginia (1861)
VIRGINIA
KENTUCKY
MISSOURI
Missouri
Mississippi
Ohio
Lake Erie
Fort Donelson
TENNESSEE
Shiloh
Chatanooga
ARKANSAS
MISSISSIPPI
Vicksburg
LOUISIANA
Pleasant Hill
New Orleans
ALABAMA
GEORGIA
Atlanta
FLORIDA
NORTH CAROLINA
Raleigh
SOUTH CAROLINA
Columbia
Fort Sumter
Taken by confederates at the outbreak of war
Savannah
Union Naval blockade of the Atlantic ports
Atlantic Ocean
Union Naval blockade of the Gulf ports
Gulf of Mexico
Miles
0 100 200

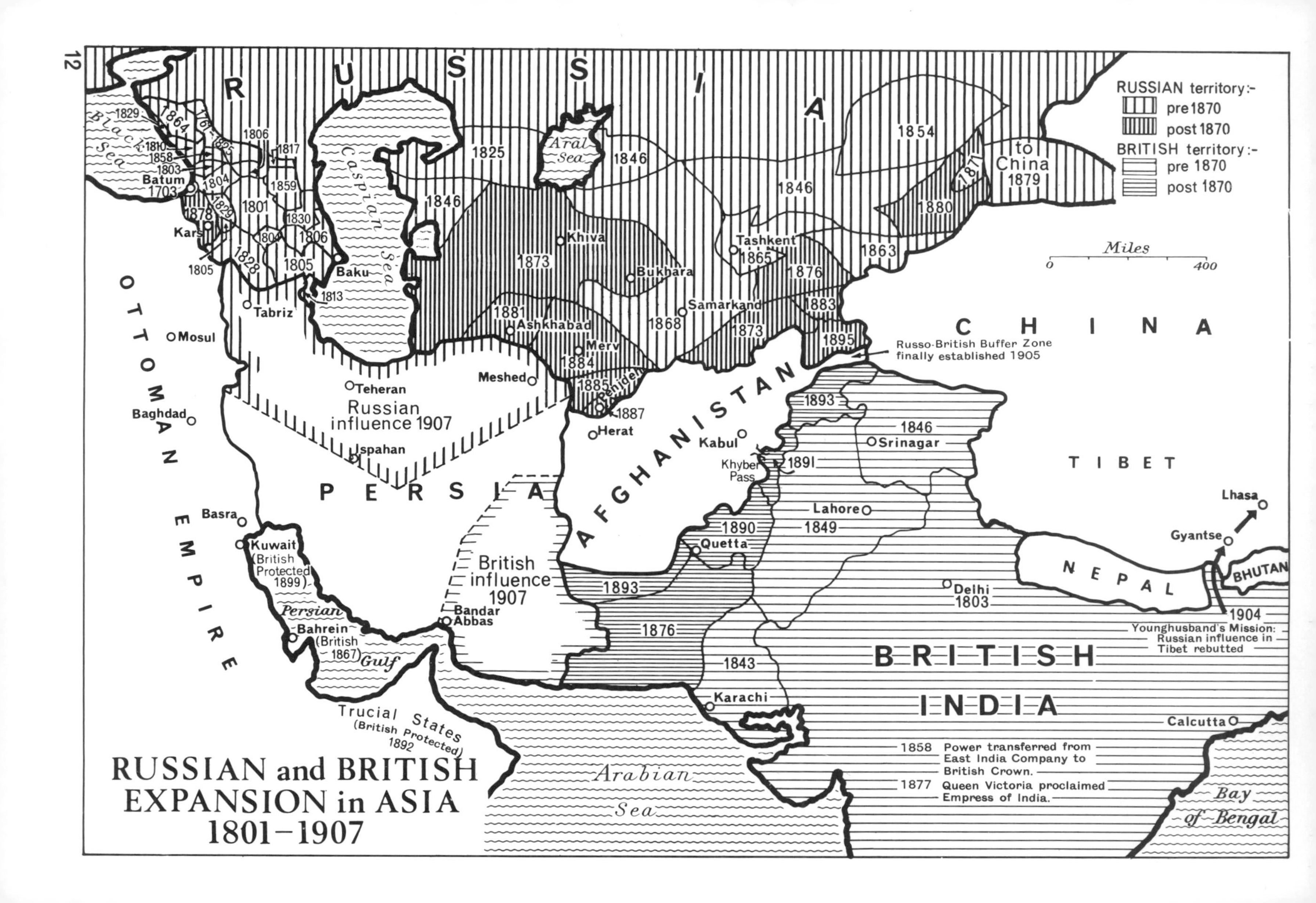
RUSSIA
RUSSIAN territory:-
pre 1870
post 1870
BRITISH territory:-
pre 1870
post 1870
Miles
0
400
CHINA
to China 1879
1854
1871
1880
1863
1846
1825
1876
1883
1895
1873
1868
1881
1884
1885
1887
Aral Sea
Caspian Sea
Black Sea
Tashkent
1865
Samarkand
Bukhara
Khiva
Ashkhabad
Merv
Meshed
Herat
Kabul
Khyber Pass
Russo-British Buffer Zone finally established 1905
AFGHANISTAN
TIBET
Lhasa
Gyantse
BHUTAN
NEPAL
1904
Younghusband's Mission: Russian influence in Tibet rebutted
Srinagar
1846
1893
1891
Lahore
1849
1890
Quetta
Delhi
1803
1893
1876
1843
Karachi
Calcutta
BRITISH INDIA
1858 Power transferred from East India Company to British Crown.
1877 Queen Victoria proclaimed Empress of India.
Bay of Bengal
Arabian Sea
PERSIA
Teheran
Russian influence 1907
Ispahan
British influence 1907
Bandar Abbas
Tabriz
Baku
1813
1806
1817
1859
1830
1801
1804
1805
1828
1829
1878
1864
1829
1810
1858
1803
Batum
1703
Kars
Mosul
Baghdad
Basra
Kuwait (British Protected 1899)
Persian Gulf
Bahrein (British 1867)
Trucial States (British Protected) 1892
OTTOMAN EMPIRE
RUSSIAN and BRITISH EXPANSION in ASIA 1801–1907

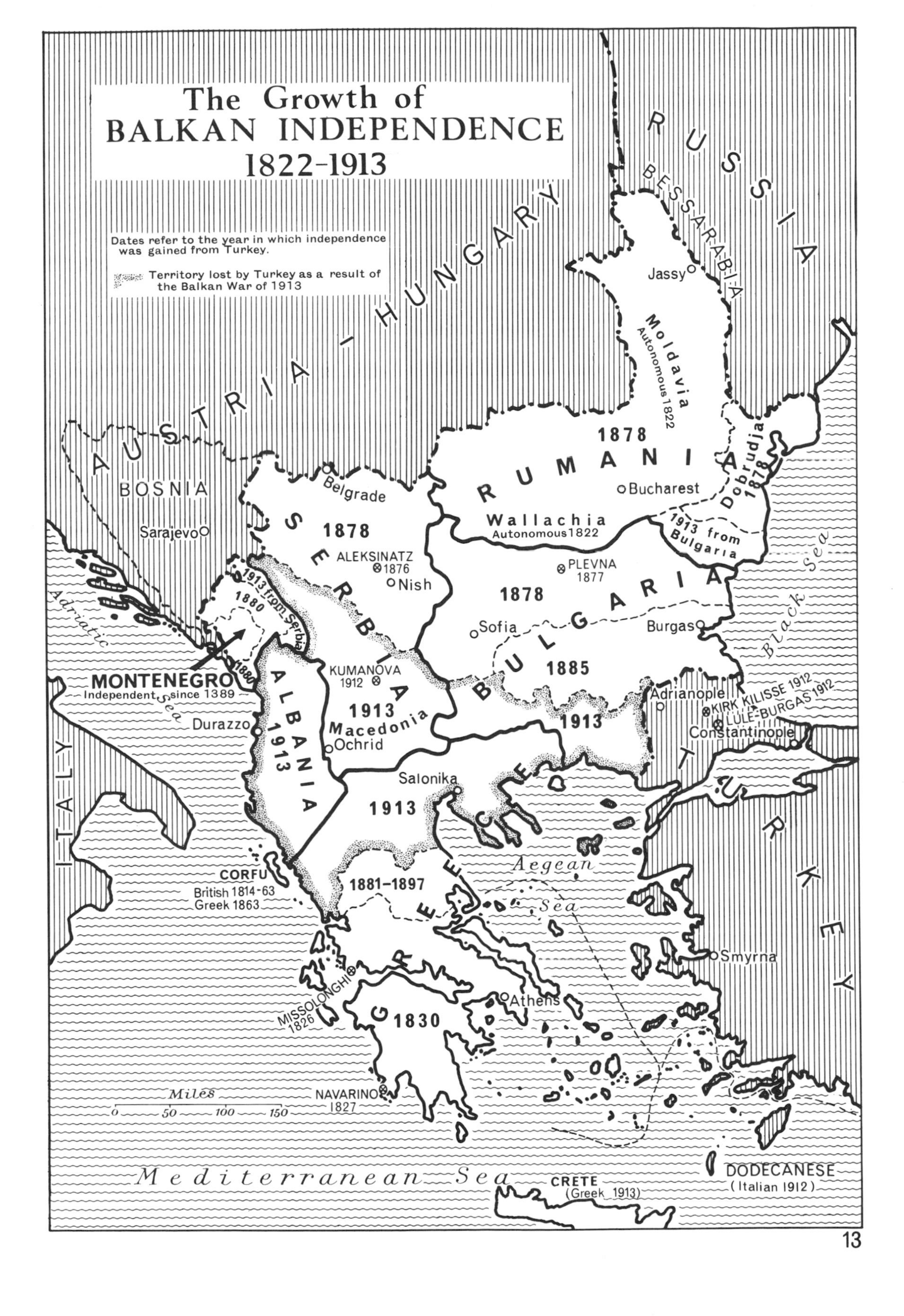

The Growth of
BALKAN INDEPENDENCE
1822-1913
Dates refer to the year in which independence was gained from Turkey.
Territory lost by Turkey as a result of the Balkan War of 1913
AUSTRIA - HUNGARY
RUSSIA
BESSARABIA
Jassy
Moldavia
Autonomous 1822
1878
RUMANIA
Bucharest
Wallachia
Autonomous 1822
Dobrudja 1878
1913 from Bulgaria
BOSNIA
Sarajevo
Belgrade
SERBIA
1878
ALEKSINATZ
1876
Nish
PLEVNA
1877
1878
BULGARIA
Sofia
Burgas
1885
Black Sea
Adriatic Sea
1913 from Serbia
1880
1880
MONTENEGRO
Independent since 1389
Durazzo
ALBANIA 1913
KUMANOVA
1912
1913
Macedonia
Ochrid
Adrianople
KIRK KILISSE 1912
LULE-BURGAS 1912
Constantinople
1913
Salonika
1913
GREECE
TURKEY
ITALY
CORFU
British 1814-63
Greek 1863
1881–1897
Aegean Sea
Smyrna
MISSOLONGHI
1826
Athens
1830
Miles
0 50 100 150
NAVARINO
1827
Mediterranean Sea
CRETE
(Greek 1913)
DODECANESE
(Italian 1912)

AFRICA and EUROPEAN EXPANSION to 1914

Coastal regions under European control before 1880
Boundaries in 1914, with dates of annexation by the European powers.

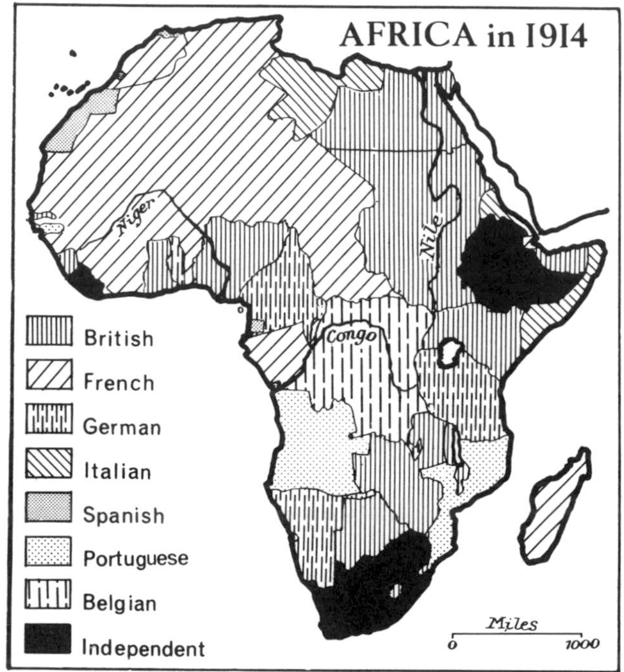

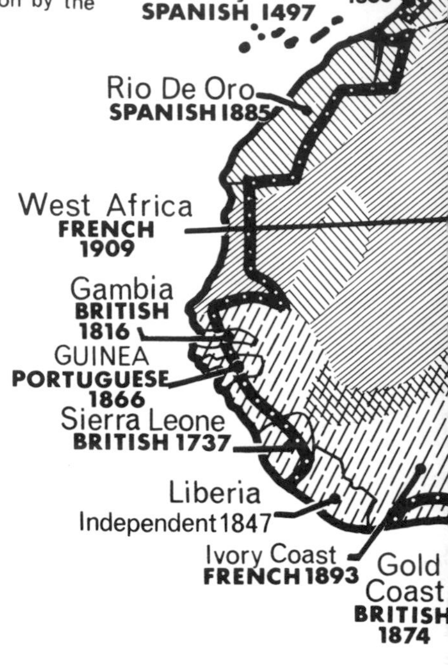

14

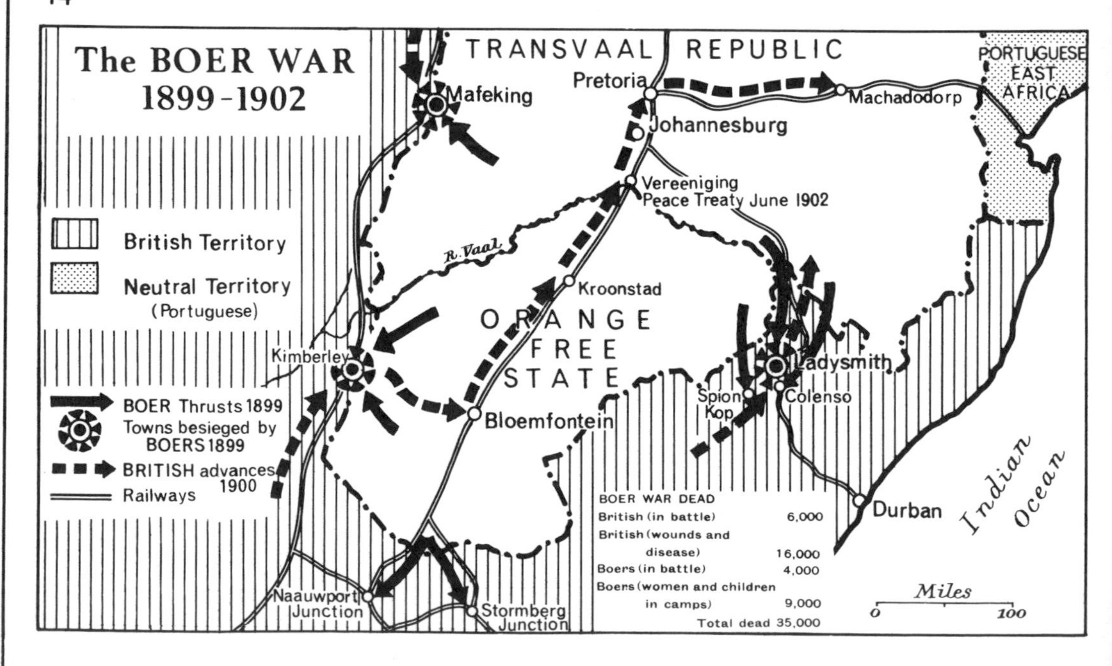

15

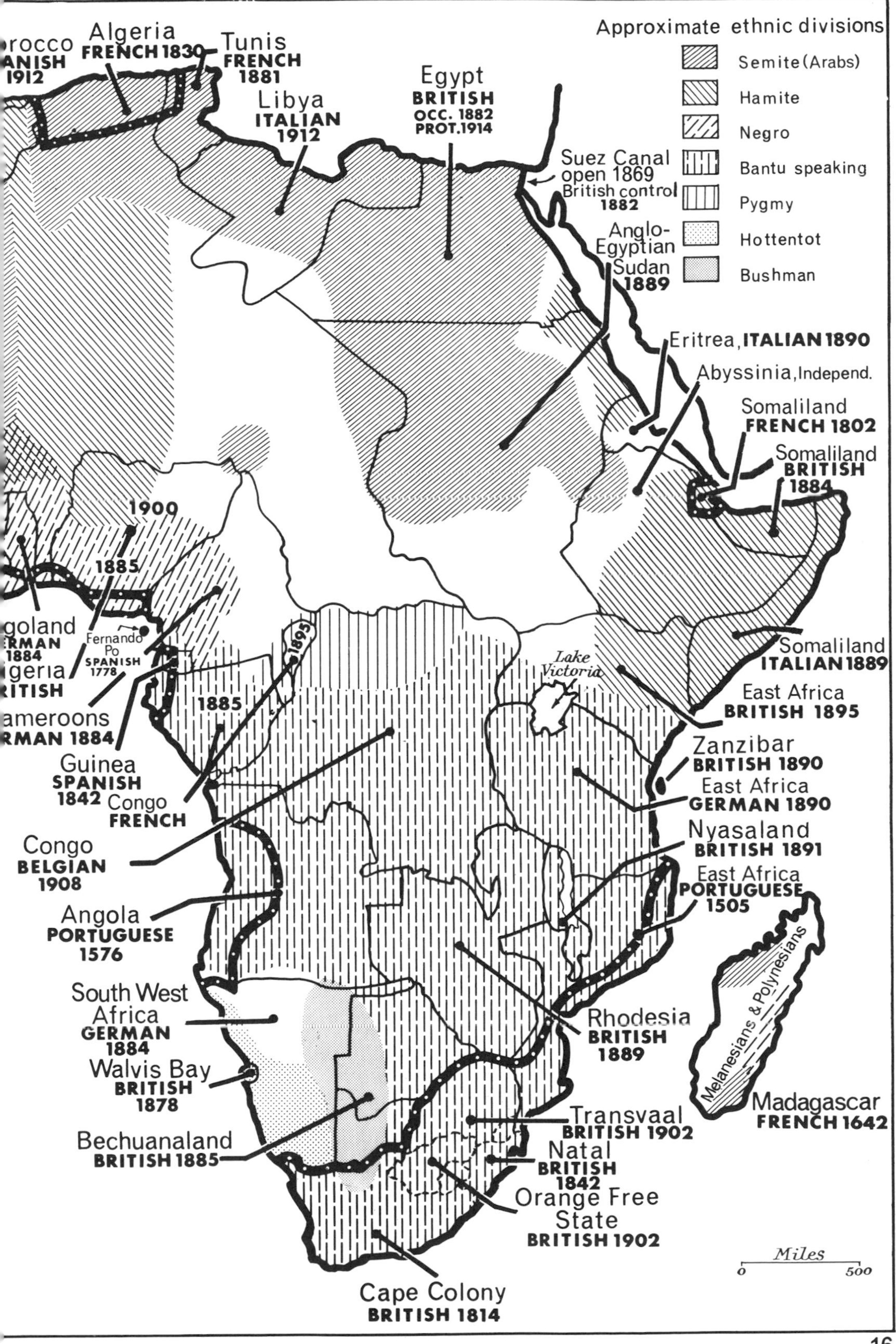
Algeria
FRENCH 1830
Tunis
FRENCH
1881
Egypt
BRITISH
OCC. 1882
PROT.1914
Libya
ITALIAN
1912
Approximate ethnic divisions
Semite (Arabs)
Hamite
Negro
Bantu speaking
Pygmy
Hottentot
Bushman
Suez Canal
open 1869
British control
1882
Anglo-
Egyptian
Sudan
1889
Eritrea, ITALIAN 1890
Abyssinia, Independ.
Somaliland
FRENCH 1802
Somaliland
BRITISH
1884
1900
1885
Fernando
Po
SPANISH
1778
1895
1885
Somaliland
ITALIAN 1889
Lake
Victoria
East Africa
BRITISH 1895
Cameroons
Guinea
SPANISH
1842
Congo
FRENCH
Zanzibar
BRITISH 1890
East Africa
GERMAN 1890
Congo
BELGIAN
1908
Nyasaland
BRITISH 1891
East Africa
PORTUGUESE
1505
Angola
PORTUGUESE
1576
Melanesians & Polynesians
South West
Africa
GERMAN
1884
Rhodesia
BRITISH
1889
Walvis Bay
BRITISH
1878
Madagascar
FRENCH 1642
Bechuanaland
BRITISH 1885
Transvaal
BRITISH 1902
Natal
BRITISH
1842
Orange Free
State
BRITISH 1902
Miles
0
500
Cape Colony
BRITISH 1814

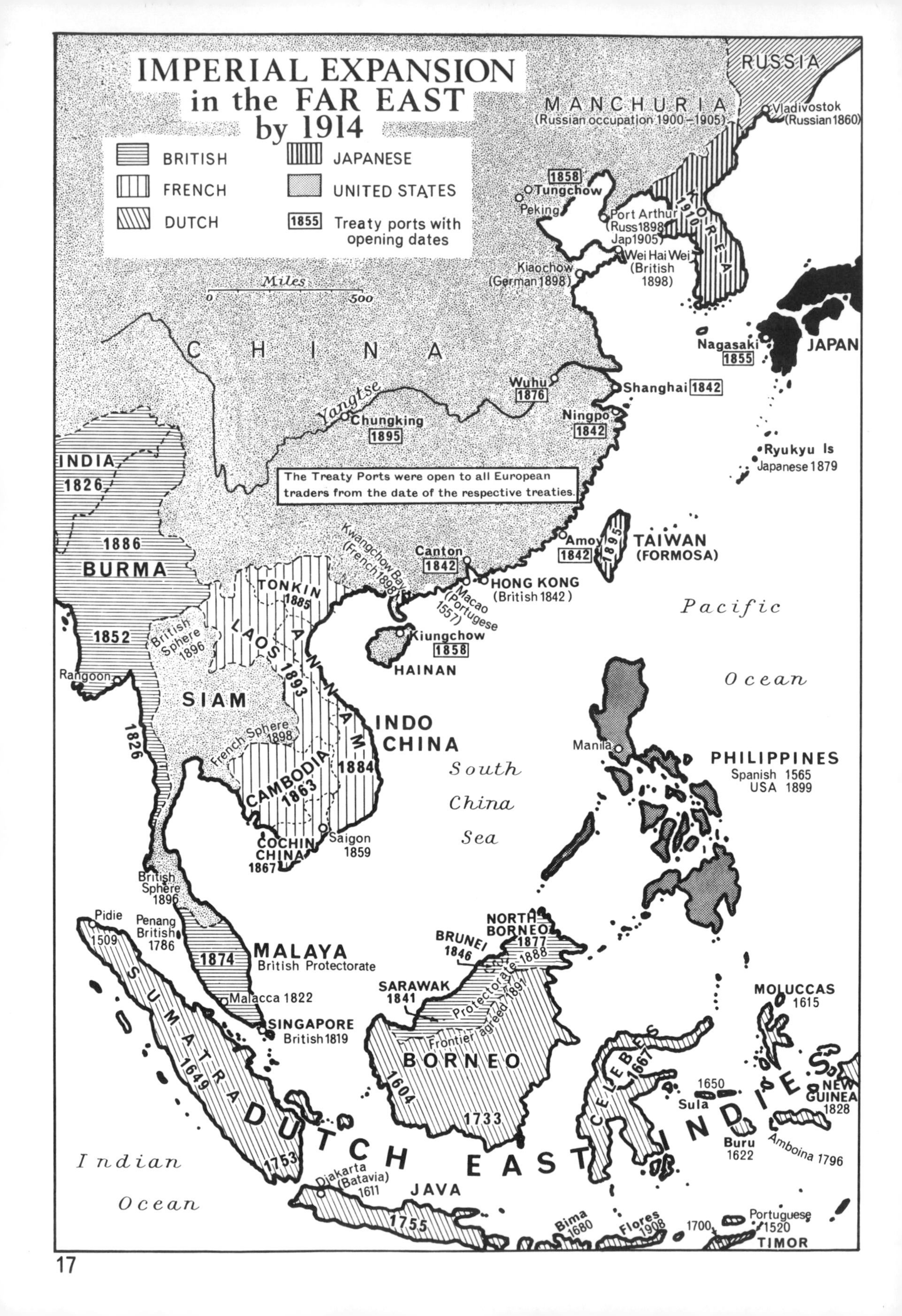
IMPERIAL EXPANSION in the FAR EAST by 1914
BRITISH
FRENCH
DUTCH
JAPANESE
UNITED STATES
1855 Treaty ports with opening dates
Miles
0
500
The Treaty Ports were open to all European traders from the date of the respective treaties.
RUSSIA
MANCHURIA (Russian occupation 1900–1905)
Vladivostok (Russian 1860)
1858 Tungchow
Peking
Port Arthur (Russ 1898 Jap 1905)
KOREA 1910
Wei Hai Wei (British 1898)
Kiaochow (German 1898)
Nagasaki 1855
JAPAN
CHINA
Yangtse
Wuhu 1876
Shanghai 1842
Chungking 1895
Ningpo 1842
Ryukyu Is Japanese 1879
INDIA 1826
1886
BURMA
1852
Rangoon
1826
Kwangchow Bay (French 1898)
Canton 1842
Amoy 1842
TAIWAN (FORMOSA)
1895
HONG KONG (British 1842)
Macao (Portugese 1557)
Kiungchow 1858
HAINAN
Pacific
Ocean
TONKIN 1885
LAOS
ANNAM 1893
British Sphere 1896
SIAM
French Sphere 1898
CAMBODIA 1863
1884
INDO CHINA
COCHIN CHINA 1867
Saigon 1859
South China Sea
Manila
PHILIPPINES Spanish 1565 USA 1899
British Sphere 1896
Pidie 1509
Penang British 1786
MALAYA British Protectorate
1874
Malacca 1822
SINGAPORE British 1819
NORTH BORNEO 1877
BRUNEI 1846
SARAWAK 1841
Protectorate 1888
Frontier agreed 1891
BORNEO
1604
1733
SUMATRA
1649
1753
CELEBES 1667
MOLUCCAS 1615
1650
Sula
Buru 1622
Amboina 1796
NEW GUINEA 1828
DUTCH EAST INDIES
Indian Ocean
Djakarta (Batavia) 1611
JAVA
1755
Bima 1680
Flores 1908
1700
Portuguese 1520
TIMOR

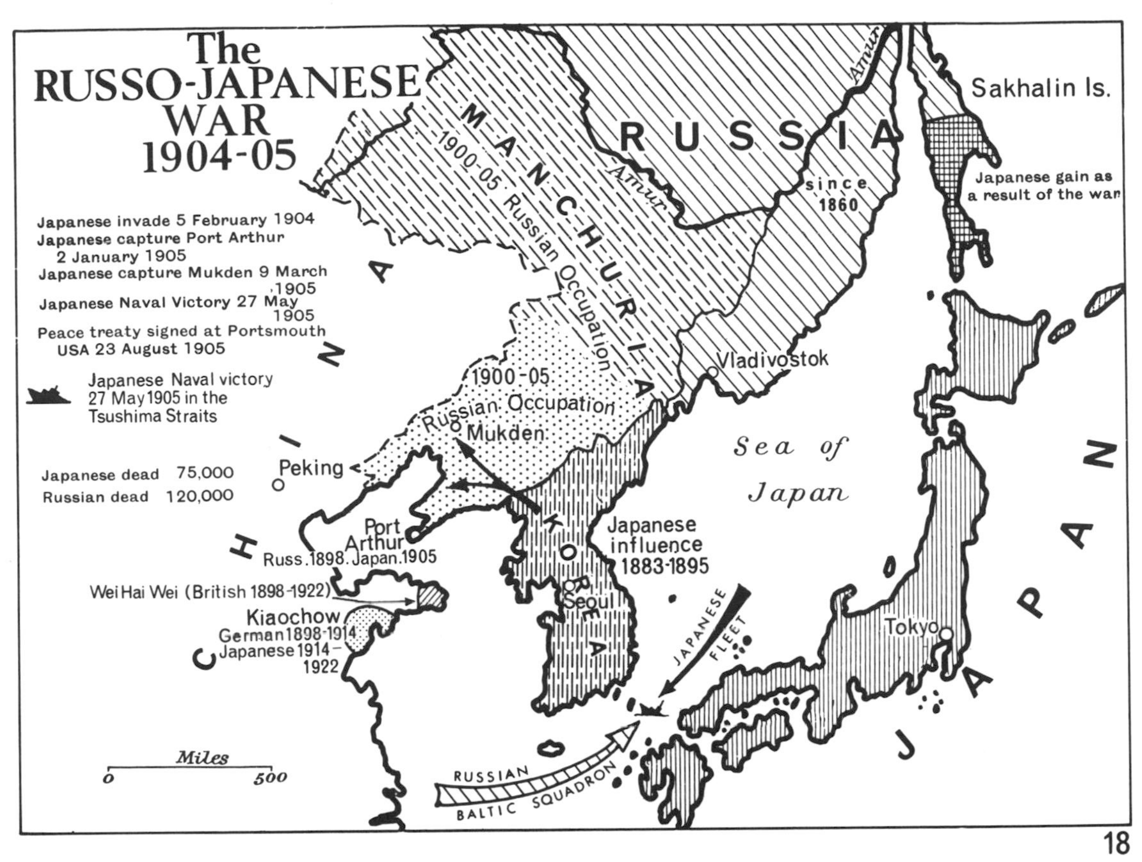
The RUSSO-JAPANESE WAR 1904-05
Japanese invade 5 February 1904
Japanese capture Port Arthur 2 January 1905
Japanese capture Mukden 9 March 1905
Japanese Naval Victory 27 May 1905
Peace treaty signed at Portsmouth USA 23 August 1905
Japanese Naval victory 27 May 1905 in the Tsushima Straits
Japanese dead 75,000
Russian dead 120,000
MANCHURIA
1900-05 Russian Occupation
RUSSIA
Amur
since 1860
Sakhalin Is.
Japanese gain as a result of the war
Vladivostok
1900-05 Russian Occupation
Mukden
Peking
Port Arthur
Russ. 1898. Japan. 1905
Wei Hai Wei (British 1898-1922)
Kiaochow
German 1898-1914
Japanese 1914-1922
CHINA
KOREA
Seoul
Japanese influence 1883-1895
Sea of Japan
JAPAN
Tokyo
JAPANESE FLEET
RUSSIAN BALTIC SQUADRON
Miles
0
500

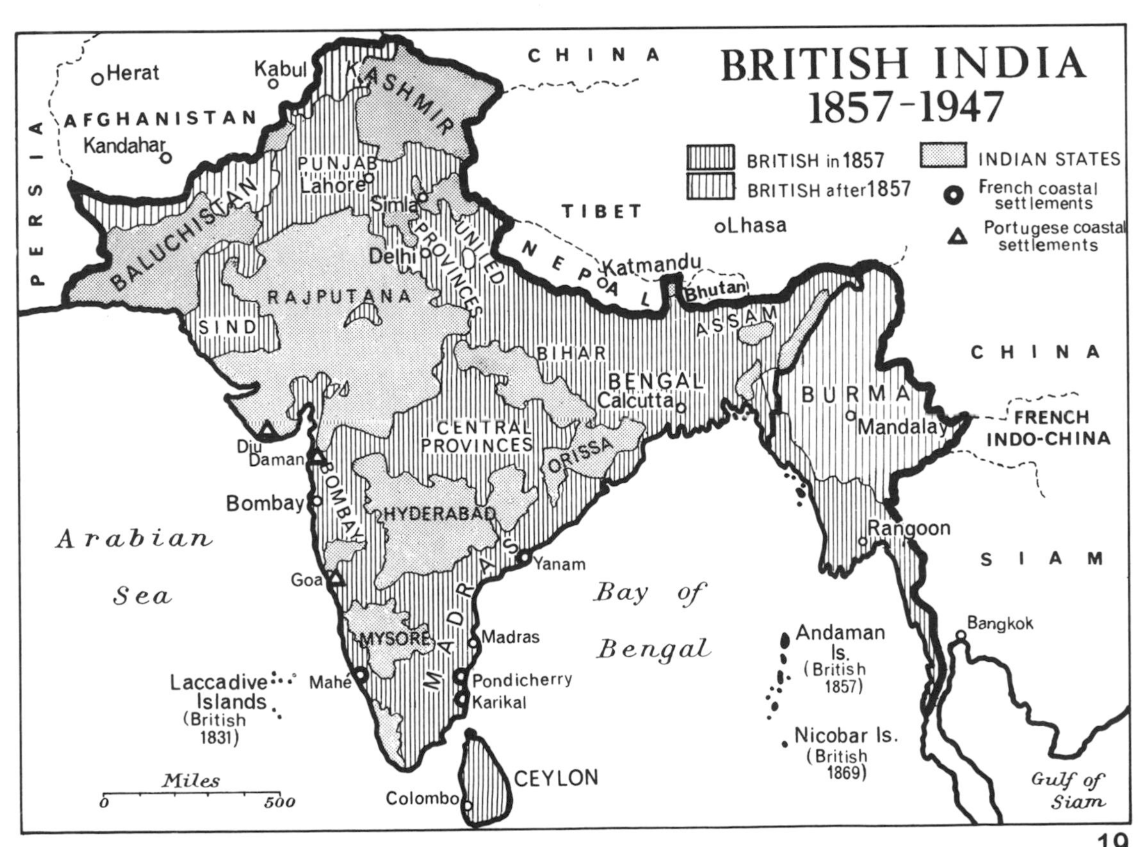
BRITISH INDIA 1857-1947
BRITISH in 1857
BRITISH after 1857
INDIAN STATES
French coastal settlements
Portugese coastal settlements
CHINA
Herat
Kabul
KASHMIR
AFGHANISTAN
Kandahar
PERSIA
BALUCHISTAN
PUNJAB
Lahore
Simla
UNITED PROVINCES
Delhi
TIBET
Lhasa
NEPAL
Katmandu
Bhutan
RAJPUTANA
SIND
ASSAM
BIHAR
BENGAL
Calcutta
BURMA
Mandalay
CHINA
FRENCH INDO-CHINA
CENTRAL PROVINCES
ORISSA
Diu
Daman
BOMBAY
Bombay
HYDERABAD
Arabian Sea
Rangoon
SIAM
MADRAS
Yanam
Goa
Bay of Bengal
MYSORE
Madras
Andaman Is. (British 1857)
Bangkok
Laccadive Islands (British 1831)
Mahé
Pondicherry
Karikal
Nicobar Is. (British 1869)
CEYLON
Colombo
Gulf of Siam
Miles
0
500

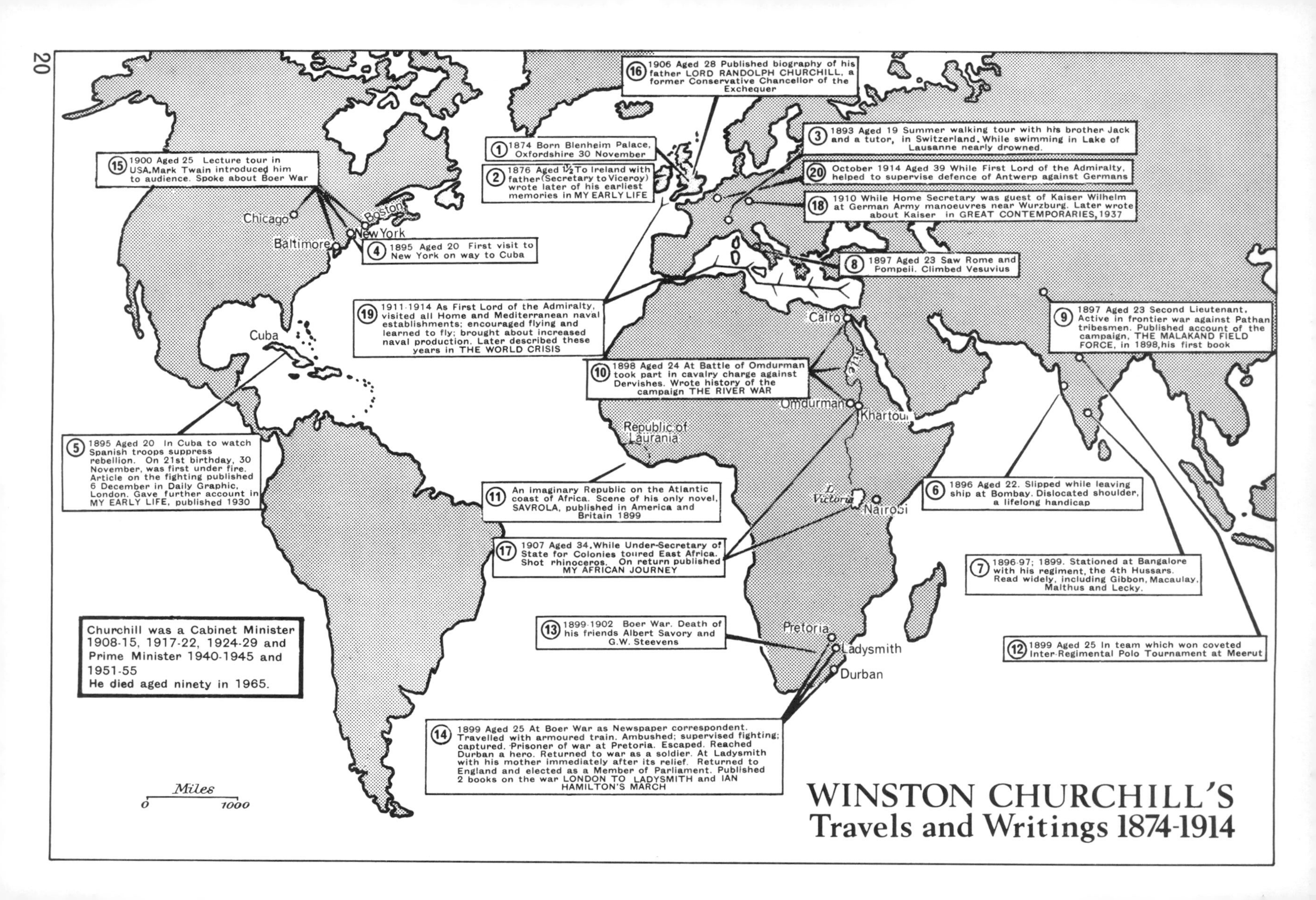
WINSTON CHURCHILL'S
Travels and Writings 1874-1914
1 1874 Born Blenheim Palace, Oxfordshire 30 November
2 1876 Aged 1½ To Ireland with father (Secretary to Viceroy) wrote later of his earliest memories in MY EARLY LIFE
3 1893 Aged 19 Summer walking tour with his brother Jack and a tutor, in Switzerland. While swimming in Lake of Lausanne nearly drowned.
4 1895 Aged 20 First visit to New York on way to Cuba
5 1895 Aged 20 In Cuba to watch Spanish troops suppress rebellion. On 21st birthday, 30 November, was first under fire. Article on the fighting published 6 December in Daily Graphic, London. Gave further account in MY EARLY LIFE, published 1930
6 1896 Aged 22. Slipped while leaving ship at Bombay. Dislocated shoulder, a lifelong handicap
7 1896-97; 1899. Stationed at Bangalore with his regiment, the 4th Hussars. Read widely, including Gibbon, Macaulay, Malthus and Lecky.
8 1897 Aged 23 Saw Rome and Pompeii. Climbed Vesuvius
9 1897 Aged 23 Second Lieutenant, Active in frontier war against Pathan tribesmen. Published account of the campaign, THE MALAKAND FIELD FORCE, in 1898, his first book
10 1898 Aged 24 At Battle of Omdurman took part in cavalry charge against Dervishes. Wrote history of the campaign THE RIVER WAR
11 An imaginary Republic on the Atlantic coast of Africa. Scene of his only novel, SAVROLA, published in America and Britain 1899
12 1899 Aged 25 In team which won coveted Inter-Regimental Polo Tournament at Meerut
13 1899-1902 Boer War. Death of his friends Albert Savory and G.W. Steevens
14 1899 Aged 25 At Boer War as Newspaper correspondent. Travelled with armoured train. Ambushed; supervised fighting; captured. Prisoner of war at Pretoria. Escaped. Reached Durban a hero. Returned to war as a soldier. At Ladysmith with his mother immediately after its relief. Returned to England and elected as a Member of Parliament. Published 2 books on the war LONDON TO LADYSMITH and IAN HAMILTON'S MARCH
15 1900 Aged 25 Lecture tour in USA. Mark Twain introduced him to audience. Spoke about Boer War
16 1906 Aged 28 Published biography of his father LORD RANDOLPH CHURCHILL, a former Conservative Chancellor of the Exchequer
17 1907 Aged 34. While Under-Secretary of State for Colonies toured East Africa. Shot rhinoceros. On return published MY AFRICAN JOURNEY
18 1910 While Home Secretary was guest of Kaiser Wilhelm at German Army manoeuvres near Wurzburg. Later wrote about Kaiser in GREAT CONTEMPORARIES, 1937
19 1911-1914 As First Lord of the Admiralty, visited all Home and Mediterranean naval establishments; encouraged flying and learned to fly; brought about increased naval production. Later described these years in THE WORLD CRISIS
20 October 1914 Aged 39 While First Lord of the Admiralty, helped to supervise defence of Antwerp against Germans
Chicago
Boston
New York
Baltimore
Cuba
Cairo
Nile
Omdurman
Khartoum
Republic of Laurania
L. Victoria
Nairobi
Pretoria
Ladysmith
Durban
Churchill was a Cabinet Minister 1908-15, 1917-22, 1924-29 and Prime Minister 1940-1945 and 1951-55
He died aged ninety in 1965.
Miles
0
1000

SOUTH AMERICA since 1800
PANAMA
Canal Zone USA1903 to1939
TRINIDAD British Independent 1962
BRITISH 1803 Independent 1966
DUTCH 1816
FRENCH 1818
Caracas
Georgetown
Paramaribo
Cayenne
VENEZUELA
War against Spain 1811-1821
Joined Columbia 1821-30
Then Independ.
GUIANA
Atlantic Ocean
Bogota
COLOMBIA
War against Spain 1811-1821.
Civil War 1831-1861
Secession of Panama 1903
Quito
ECUADOR
Joined Colombia 1822
Independ. 1830
1942
1934
Amazon
Belem
BRAZIL
Revolution against Portuguese rule 1820
Independent Empire 1822
War against Paraguay 1865-1870
Emancipation of 700,000 slaves 1888
Republic 1889
PERU
Independent from Spain 1821
Lima
War against Spain 1864-1866
1903
1867
Bahia
La Paz
Brasilia
BOLIVIA
War against Spain 1809-1825
Independent 1825
War against Chile 1879-1883
1929
CHACO 1938
1870
1870
PARAGUAY
Independent from Spain 1811
Asuncion
1874
1874
1884
Antofagasta
Rio de Janeiro
SAN FELIX Chile
Pacific Ocean
ARGENTINA
Independent from Spain 1810
War against Uruguay 1843-1851
War against Paraguay 1865-1870
URUGUAY
War against Portugal 1810-1830
Montevideo besieged by Argentina 1843-1851.
Valparaiso
Santiago
Montevideo
Buenos Aires
JUAN FERNANDEZ Chile
CHILE
Civil War 1810-18
Independent from Spain 1818
Atlantic Ocean
PATAGONIA 1881
1902
Miles
0
500
FALKLAND ISLANDS
British 1833
Claimed by Argentina
1881
Territory obtained after Independence, with date.

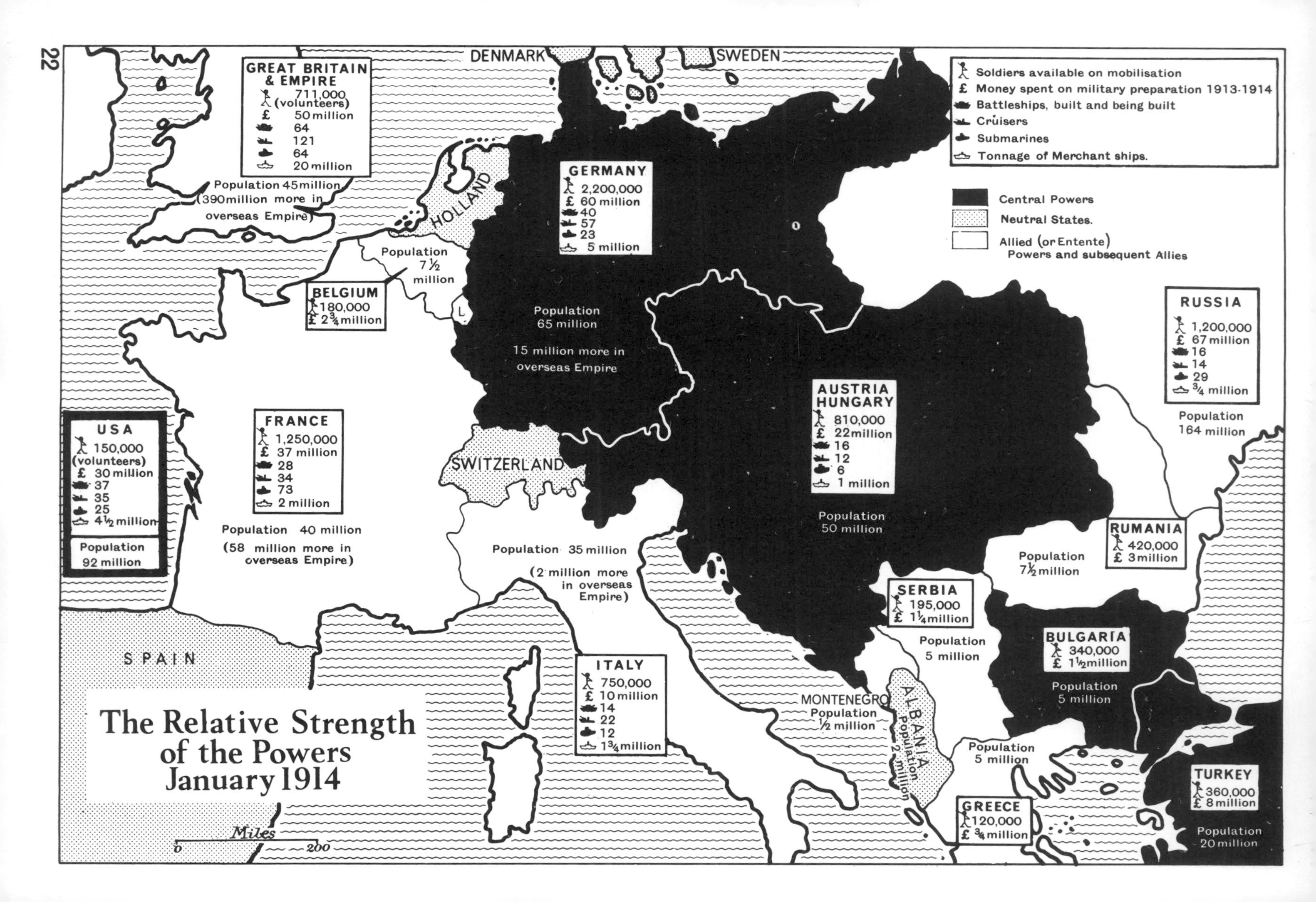

The Relative Strength of the Powers January 1914
Soldiers available on mobilisation
£ Money spent on military preparation 1913-1914
Battleships, built and being built
Cruisers
Submarines
Tonnage of Merchant ships.
Central Powers
Neutral States.
Allied (or Entente) Powers and subsequent Allies
GREAT BRITAIN & EMPIRE
711,000 (volunteers)
£ 50 million
64
121
64
20 million
Population 45 million (390 million more in overseas Empire)
DENMARK
SWEDEN
HOLLAND
GERMANY
2,200,000
£ 60 million
40
57
23
5 million
Population 65 million
15 million more in overseas Empire
Population 7½ million
BELGIUM
180,000
£ 2¾ million
L
USA
150,000 (volunteers)
£ 30 million
37
35
25
4½ million
Population 92 million
FRANCE
1,250,000
£ 37 million
28
34
73
2 million
Population 40 million
(58 million more in overseas Empire)
SWITZERLAND
Population 35 million
(2 million more in overseas Empire)
SPAIN
ITALY
750,000
£ 10 million
14
22
12
1¾ million
AUSTRIA HUNGARY
810,000
£ 22 million
16
12
6
1 million
Population 50 million
RUSSIA
1,200,000
£ 67 million
16
14
29
¾ million
Population 164 million
RUMANIA
420,000
£ 3 million
Population 7½ million
SERBIA
195,000
£ 1¼ million
Population 5 million
BULGARIA
340,000
£ 1½ million
Population 5 million
MONTENEGRO
Population ½ million
ALBANIA
Population 2 million
Population 5 million
GREECE
120,000
£ ¾ million
TURKEY
360,000
£ 8 million
Population 20 million
Miles
0
200

The FIRST WORLD WAR
1914-1918
Alaska (USA)
Canada
U S A
April 1917
Mexico
Cuba April 1917
Jamaica
1
2
3
4
5
Venezuela
Guianas
Colombia
Ecuador
Peru
Brazil
November 1917
Bolivia
Paraguay
Uruguay
Chile
Argentina
Falkland Is. (British)
1 Honduras July 1917.
2 Guatemala April 1918.
3 Nicaragua May 1918.
4 Costa Rica May 1918.
5 Panama April 1918.
Miles
0
1000
Neutral States.
States breaking diplomatic relations with Central Powers but not declaring war.
Dates refer to declaration of war of the non-European states
Sweden
Norway
Iceland & Denmark
Gt Britain
Germany
Austria-Hungary
Serbia
Rumania
Bulgaria
France
Spain
Portugal
Italy
Greece
Turkish Empire
Russian Empire
Afghanistan
Persia
Arabia
China
August 1917
Kiaochow (German)
Japan
August 1914
Indian Empire
Hong Kong (British)
Mariana Is. (German)
Philippines (USA)
Siam Aug 1917
Indo China
Caroline Is. (German)
Malay States
New Guinea (German)
Dutch East Indies
Australia
New Zealand
Spanish Rio de Oro
French Africa
Libya
Egypt
Sudan
Abyssiria
Liberia
Nigeria
Cameroon
Belgian Congo
British East Africa
German East Africa
Portugese Angola
German South West Africa
Madagascar
Portugese Mozambique
South Africa
ALLIED & ASSOCIATED POWERS
at war with
CENTRAL POWERS
British Empire.
French Empire.
Other European Powers and their Empires
Russian Empire.
Non-European states with dates of declaration of war
German Empire.
Austria-Hungary, Bulgaria & Turkey

GT. BRITAIN
DENMARK
SWEDEN
North Sea
Baltic Sea
King: George V
Prime Min: Asquith
For. Min: Grey
Ambassadors
French : Paul Cambon
Russian: Benckendorff
German: Lichnowsky
Austrian: Mensdorff
London
HOLLAND
BELGIUM
Attacked by Germany August 1914 Joined Entente Powers
Paris
LUXEMBURG
Kaiser Wilhelm II
Chancellor Bethman-Hollweg
For. Min: Jagow
Berlin
GERMANY
Ambassadors
British : Goschen
French : Jules Cambon
Russian: Sverbeev
Austrian: Szogyeny
Strasbourg
Munich
Königsberg
Warsaw
RUSSIA
Tsar: Nicolas II
For. Min: Sazonov
Ambassadors
British : Buchanan
French . Paléologue
German : Pourtales
Bolshevik Revolution November 1917
Armistice with Germany December 1917 and peace talks begun
Prague
Lemberg
Emperor: Franz Joseph
Prime Min: Tisza
For. Min. Berchtold
Vienna
AUSTRIA-HUNGARY
Budapest
Odessa
FRANCE
President: Poincaré
Premier: Viviani
For. Min: Viviani
Ambassadors
British : Bertie
Russian : Izvolsky
German : Schoen
Austrian : Szecsen
SWITZERLAND
Ambassadors
British : De Bunsen
French : Dumaine
Russian: Shebeko
German: Tschirsky
Kronstadt
RUMANIA
Neutral 1914-15 Treaty of London with Entente Powers 26 April 1915 Declared war on Austria-Hungary 23 May 1915
Trieste
Neutral 1914-1916 Declared war on Austria-Hungary August 1916
Black Sea
Belgrade
SERBIA
Sarajevo
Adriatic Sea
ITALY
SPAIN
CORSICA
BULGARIA
Neutral 1914-1915 Treaty with Central Powers 6 Sept 1915 Declared war on Serbia 12 Oct 1915
Constantinople
TURKEY
MONTENEGRO
ALBANIA
GREECE
Gallipoli
Secret Alliance with Germany 2 August 1914
Attacked Russian ships September 1914
Britain declared war on November 1914
Benevolent Neutrality in interest of Entente November 1915
Declared war on Bulgaria and Central Powers 29 June 1917
Aegean Sea
SARDINIA
Miles
0
200
Entente Powers 1914
Allies and associates of the Entente Powers
Neutral States 1914
Central Powers 1914
Allies of the Central Powers but declared neutrality on outbreak of war
EUROPEAN DIPLOMACY 1914

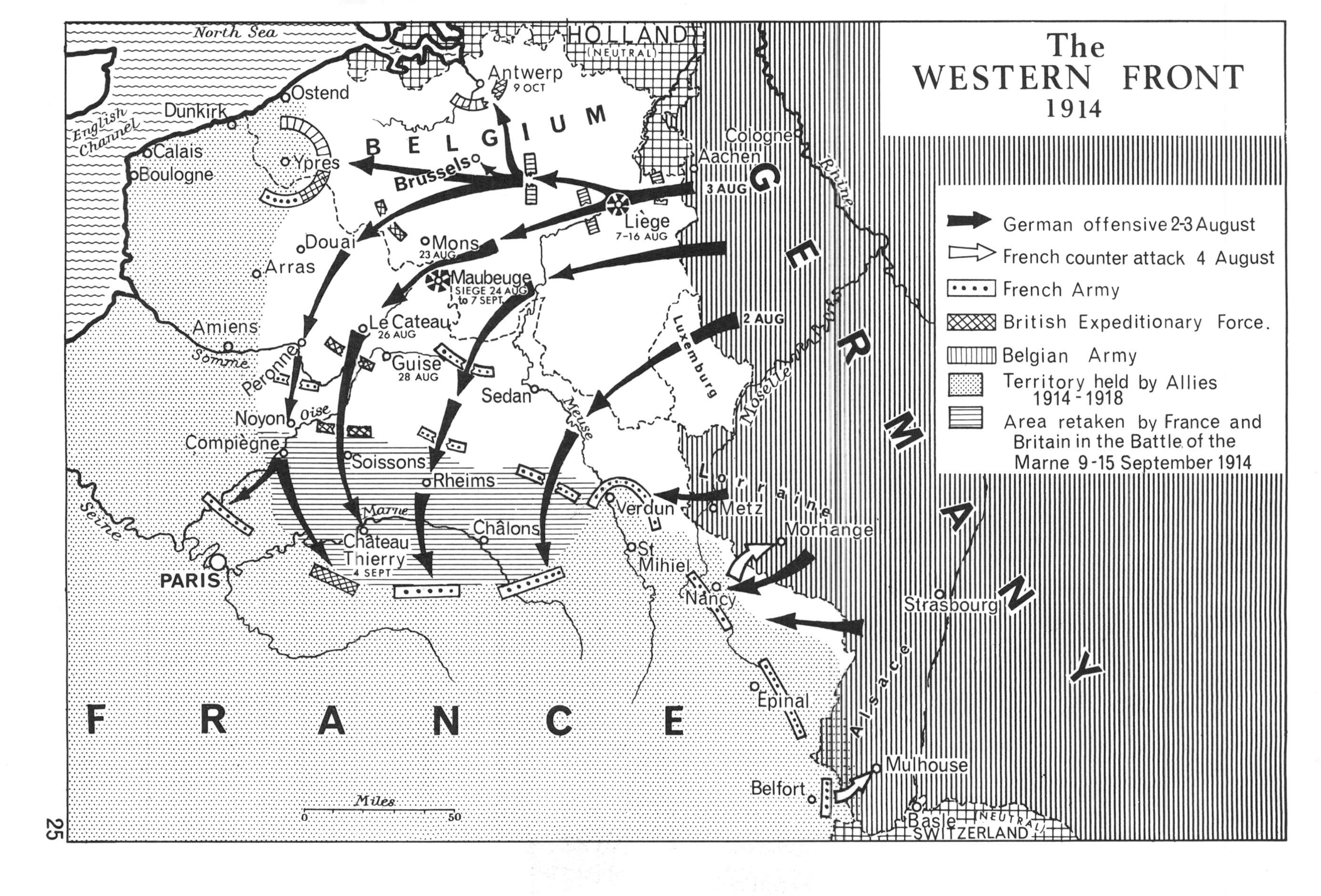
The WESTERN FRONT 1914
German offensive 2-3 August
French counter attack 4 August
French Army
British Expeditionary Force.
Belgian Army
Territory held by Allies 1914 - 1918
Area retaken by France and Britain in the Battle of the Marne 9-15 September 1914
North Sea
English Channel
HOLLAND (NEUTRAL)
BELGIUM
GERMANY
FRANCE
SWITZERLAND (NEUTRAL)
Antwerp 9 OCT
Ostend
Dunkirk
Calais
Boulogne
Ypres
Brussels
Liège 7-16 AUG
Cologne
Aachen
3 AUG
2 AUG
Rhine
Mons 23 AUG
Douai
Arras
Maubeuge SIEGE 24 AUG to 7 SEPT
Le Cateau 26 AUG
Guise 28 AUG
Amiens
Somme
Peronne
Noyon
Oise
Compiègne
Soissons
Rheims
Sedan
Luxemburg
Moselle
Meuse
Lorraine
Verdun
Metz
Morhange
Marne
Châlons
Chateau Thierry 4 SEPT
St Mihiel
Nancy
Strasbourg
Alsace
Epinal
Mulhouse
Belfort
Basle
Seine
PARIS
Miles
0
50

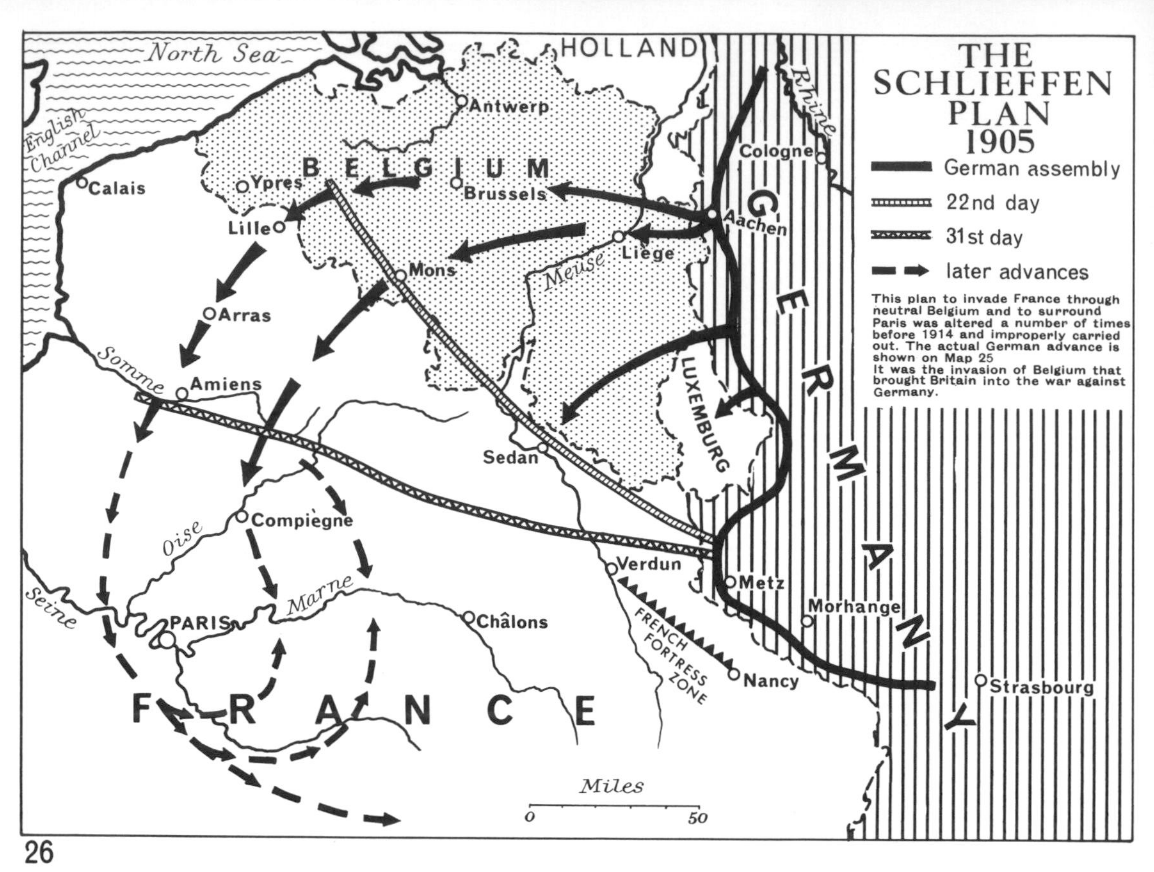

26

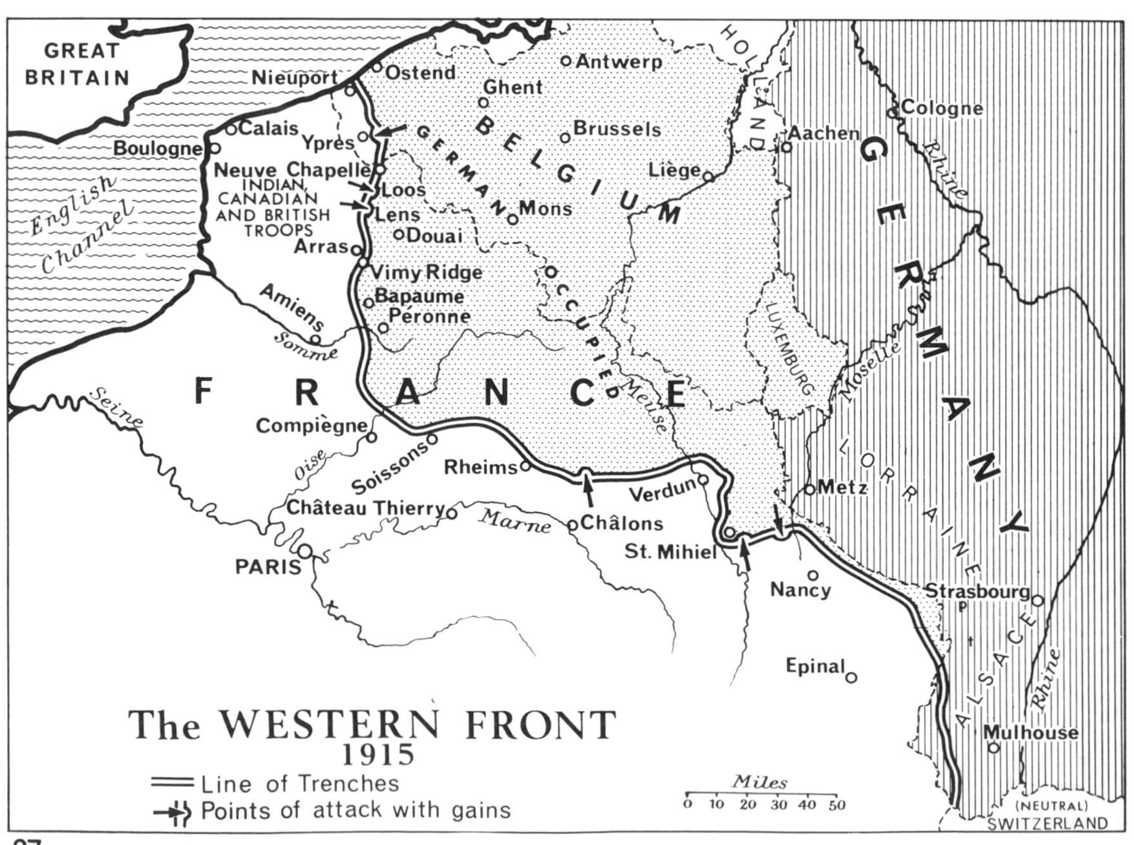

The WESTERN FRONT
1915
Line of Trenches
Points of attack with gains

27

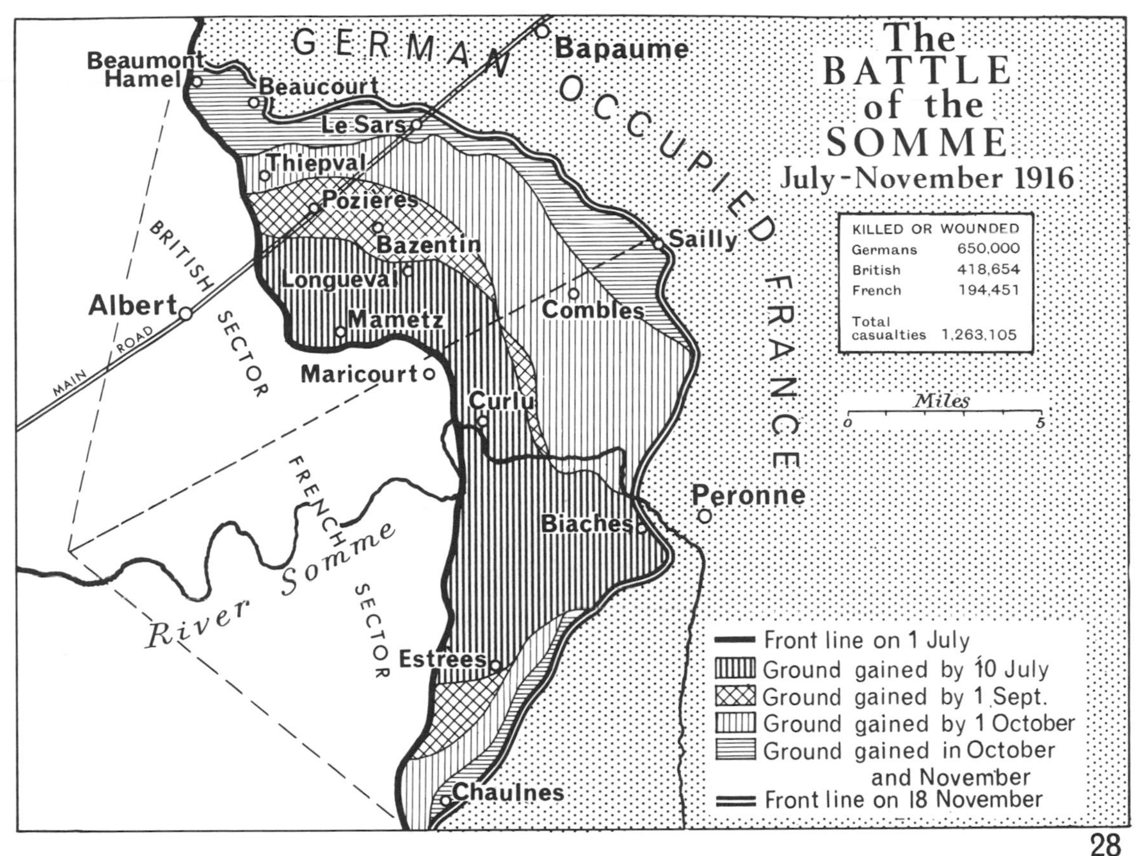

The BATTLE of the SOMME
July-November 1916
KILLED OR WOUNDED
Germans 650,000
British 418,654
French 194,451
Total casualties 1,263,105
Miles
0
5
GERMAN OCCUPIED FRANCE
Bapaume
Beaumont Hamel
Beaucourt
Le Sars
Thiepval
Pozières
Bazentin
Longueval
Mametz
Albert
Maricourt
Combles
Sailly
Curlu
Peronne
Biaches
Estrées
Chaulnes
BRITISH SECTOR
FRENCH SECTOR
MAIN ROAD
River Somme
Front line on 1 July
Ground gained by 10 July
Ground gained by 1 Sept.
Ground gained by 1 October
Ground gained in October and November
Front line on 18 November

28

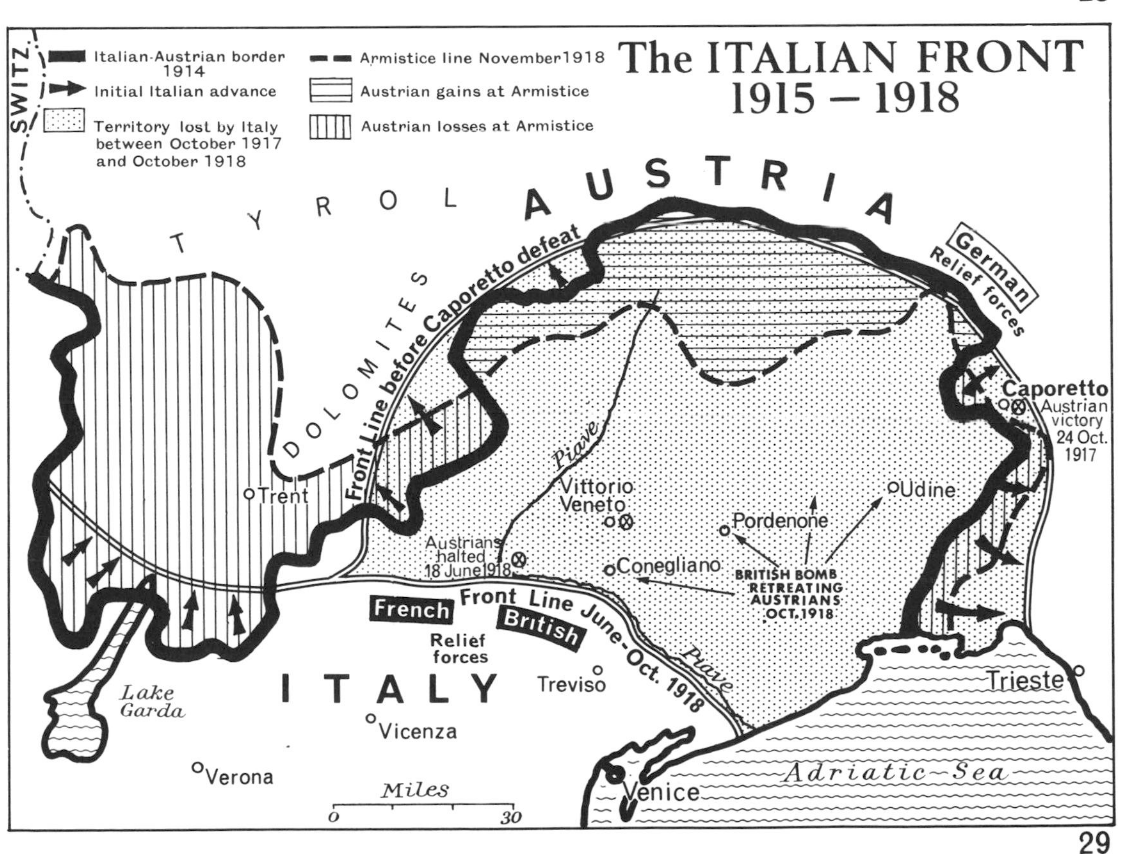

The ITALIAN FRONT 1915 – 1918
Italian-Austrian border 1914
Initial Italian advance
Territory lost by Italy between October 1917 and October 1918
Armistice line November 1918
Austrian gains at Armistice
Austrian losses at Armistice
SWITZ.
TYROL
AUSTRIA
DOLOMITES
Front Line before Caporetto defeat
German Relief forces
Caporetto
Austrian victory 24 Oct. 1917
Trent
Piave
Vittorio Veneto
Udine
Pordenone
Austrians halted 18 June 1918
Conegliano
BRITISH BOMB RETREATING AUSTRIANS OCT. 1918
French
British
Front Line June-Oct. 1918
Relief forces
ITALY
Treviso
Lake Garda
Vicenza
Verona
Trieste
Adriatic Sea
Venice
Miles
0
30

29

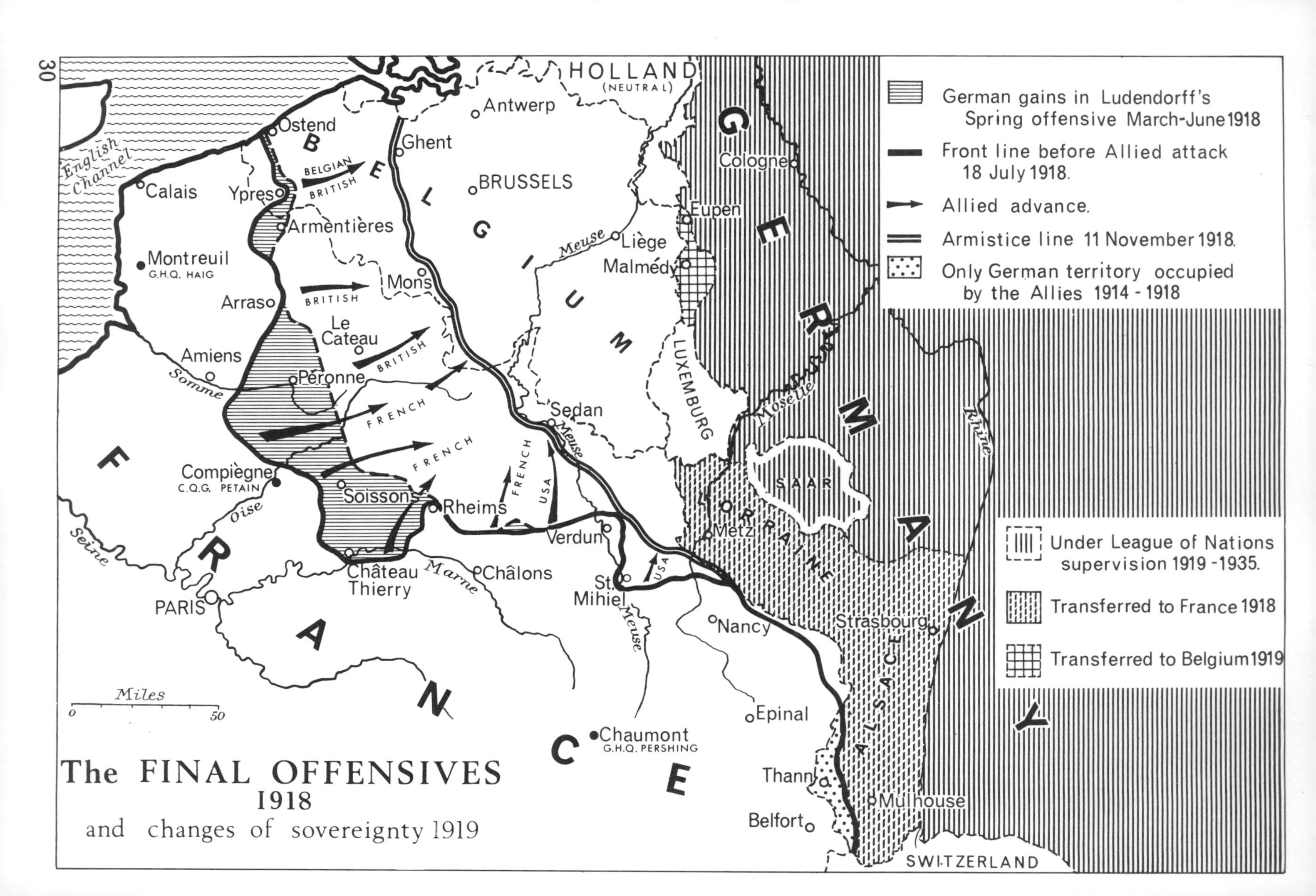

The FINAL OFFENSIVES 1918
and changes of sovereignty 1919

The EASTERN FRONT
August 1914 – January 1915
Baltic Sea
Königsberg
Gumbinnen
(Russian victory 20 Aug)
Danzig
Gerdauen
Elbing
Bischofstein
P R U S S I A
Masurian Lakes
Tannenberg
Russian gains to August 25
German retreat and counterattack
Russian defeat 27 August and attempted line of retreat
German attack 28 September
LODZ: German armies trapped, besieged by Russians, but broke out
Lodz captured 6 December
Vistula
Bug
Pripet
WARSAW
Pinsk
Brest Litovsk
Marshes
Lodz
R U S S I A
Lublin
Krasnik
Komarov
Vistula
San
Rava Russkaya
Tarnow
Cracow
Przemysl
Lemberg
Gorlice
CARPATHIAN MOUNTAINS
A U S T R I A
Stanislau
Dniester
Austrian advance and retreat
Russian advance
Russian losses to Germany 1914
Austrian losses to Russia 1914
Final Winter line 1914-1915.
Miles
0
50
100

The EASTERN FRONT 1915
Area gained by Germany and Austria Jan–July
Area gained by Germany and Austria Aug–Sept
October offensive
Serbian Army – November
Final Serbian withdrawal
French Expeditionary Force
British landings April & August
Miles
0
100
200
SWEDEN (Neutral)
DENMARK (Neutral)
Baltic Sea
Riga
Vilna
Minsk
Königsberg
Danzig
Suvalki
Augustov
Tannenberg
GERMANY
RUSSIA
Front Line in September
Pinsk
Berlin
Warsaw
Lodz
Lublin
POLAND
Front Line in January
Cracow
Tarnow
Lemberg
Przemysl
Gorlice
Czernowitz
AUSTRIA–HUNGARY
Vienna
Budapest
Jassy
Trieste
Austrian forces
German forces
BOSNIA
Belgrade
RUMANIA (Neutral)
Bucharest
Black Sea
Adriatic Sea
SERBIA
Sofia
MONTENEGRO
Skopje
BULGARIA
ALBANIA
Constantinople
Salonika
DARDANELLES
Chanak
GREECE
TURKEY
Corfu
Aegean Sea

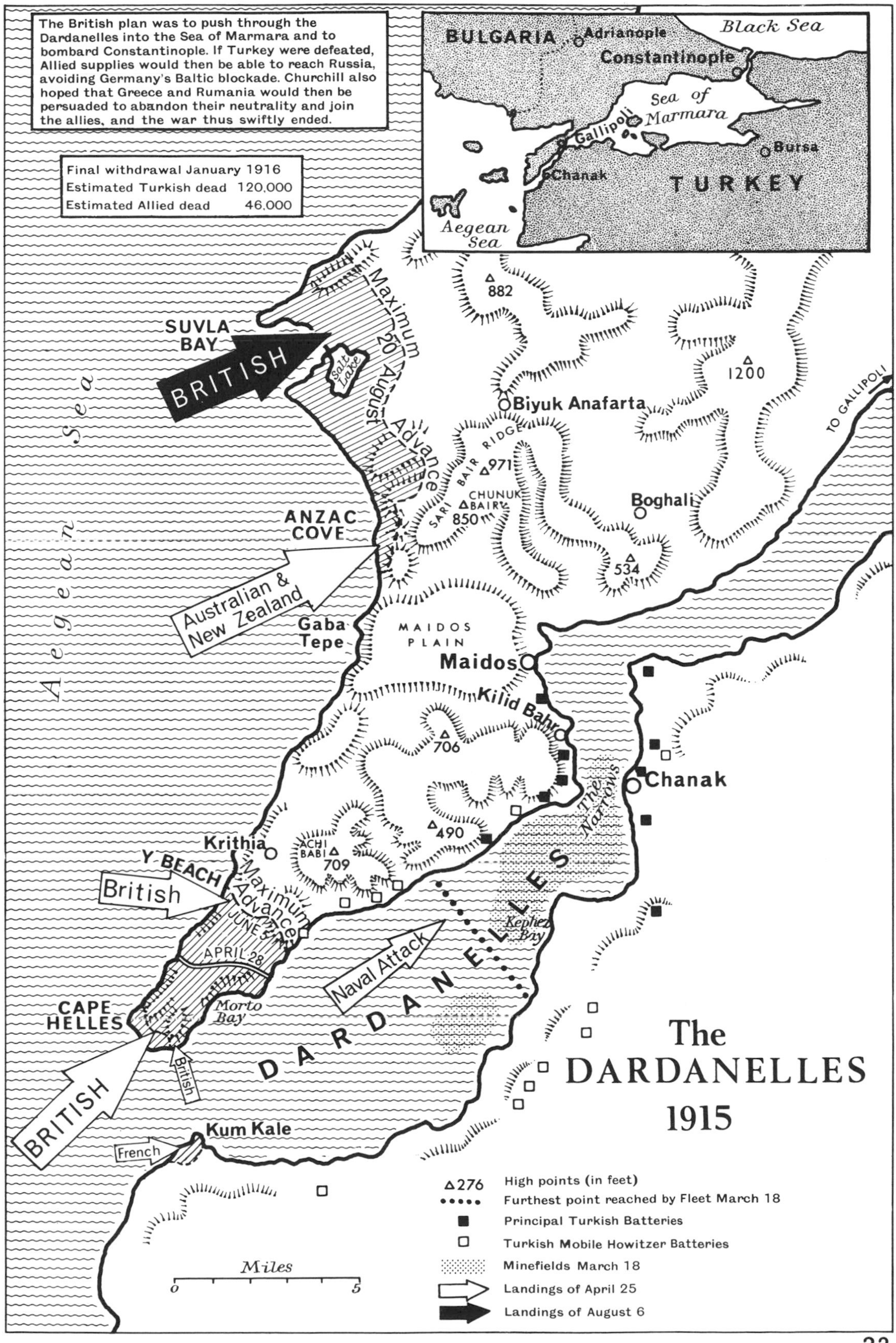
The British plan was to push through the Dardanelles into the Sea of Marmara and to bombard Constantinople. If Turkey were defeated, Allied supplies would then be able to reach Russia, avoiding Germany's Baltic blockade. Churchill also hoped that Greece and Rumania would then be persuaded to abandon their neutrality and join the allies, and the war thus swiftly ended.
Final withdrawal January 1916
Estimated Turkish dead 120,000
Estimated Allied dead 46,000
BULGARIA
Adrianople
Black Sea
Constantinople
Sea of Marmara
Gallipoli
Bursa
Chanak
TURKEY
Aegean Sea
882
SUVLA BAY
BRITISH
Salt Lake
Maximum 20 August Advance
1200
Biyuk Anafarta
TO GALLIPOLI
SARI BAIR RIDGE
971
CHUNUK BAIR
850
Boghali
ANZAC COVE
534
Australian & New Zealand
Gaba Tepe
MAIDOS PLAIN
Maidos
Kilid Bahr
706
Chanak
The Narrows
490
Krithia
ACHI BABI
709
Y BEACH
British
Maximum Advance JUNE 4
APRIL 28
Kephez Bay
Naval Attack
CAPE HELLES
Morto Bay
DARDANELLES
British
BRITISH
Kum Kale
French
The DARDANELLES 1915
276 High points (in feet)
Furthest point reached by Fleet March 18
Principal Turkish Batteries
Turkish Mobile Howitzer Batteries
Minefields March 18
Landings of April 25
Landings of August 6
Miles
0
5

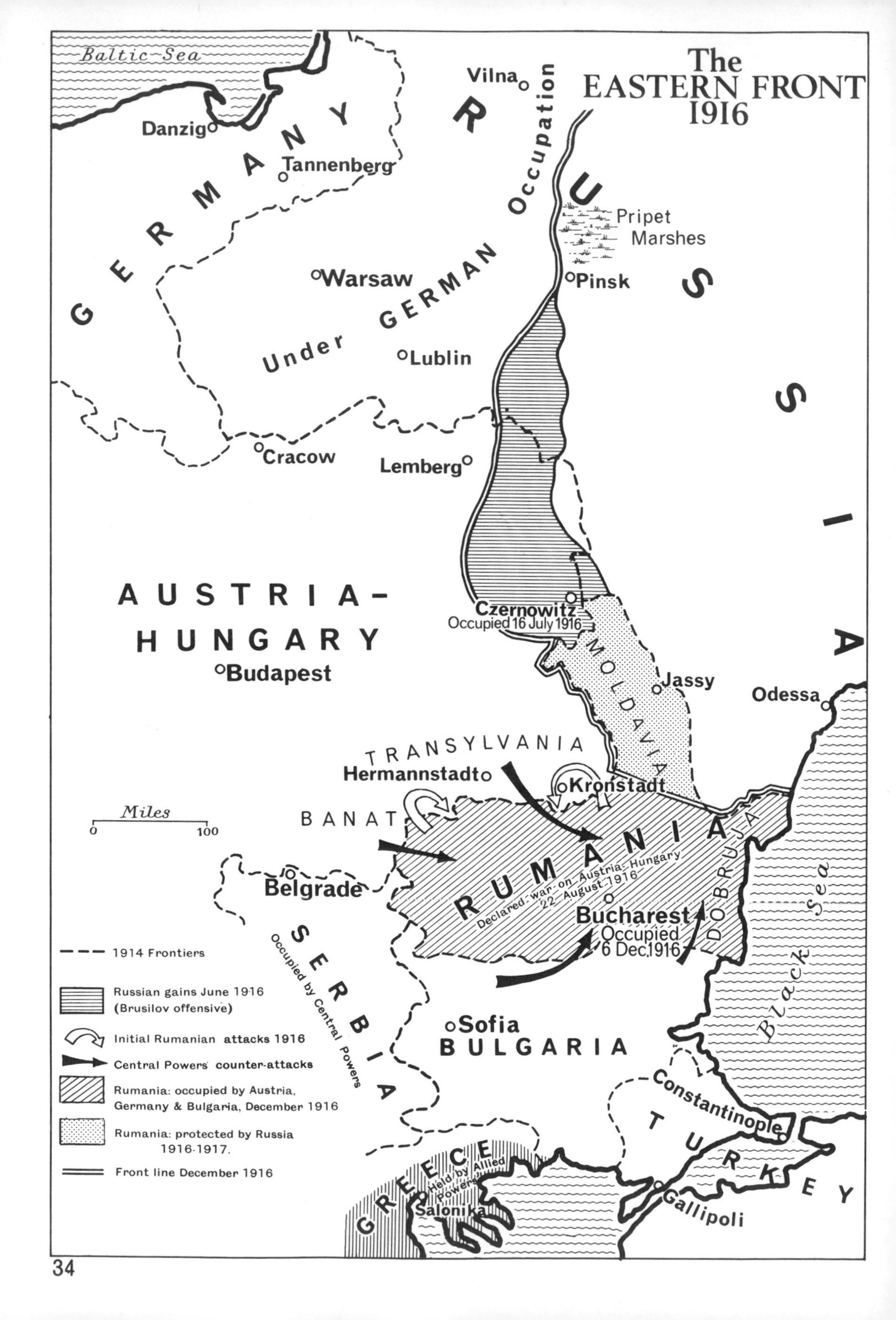
The EASTERN FRONT 1916
Baltic Sea
Danzig
Tannenberg
Vilna
GERMANY
RUSSIA
Under GERMAN Occupation
Pripet Marshes
Warsaw
Pinsk
Lublin
Cracow
Lemberg
AUSTRIA-HUNGARY
Budapest
Czernowitz
Occupied 16 July 1916
MOLDAVIA
Jassy
Odessa
TRANSYLVANIA
Hermannstadt
Kronstadt
BANAT
Miles
0
100
RUMANIA
Declared war on Austria-Hungary 22 August 1916
DOBRUJA
Belgrade
Bucharest
Occupied 6 Dec.1916
SERBIA
Occupied by Central Powers
Black Sea
Sofia
BULGARIA
Constantinople
TURKEY
GREECE
Held by Allied Powers
Salonika
Gallipoli
1914 Frontiers
Russian gains June 1916 (Brusilov offensive)
Initial Rumanian attacks 1916
Central Powers counter-attacks
Rumania: occupied by Austria, Germany & Bulgaria, December 1916
Rumania: protected by Russia 1916-1917.
Front line December 1916

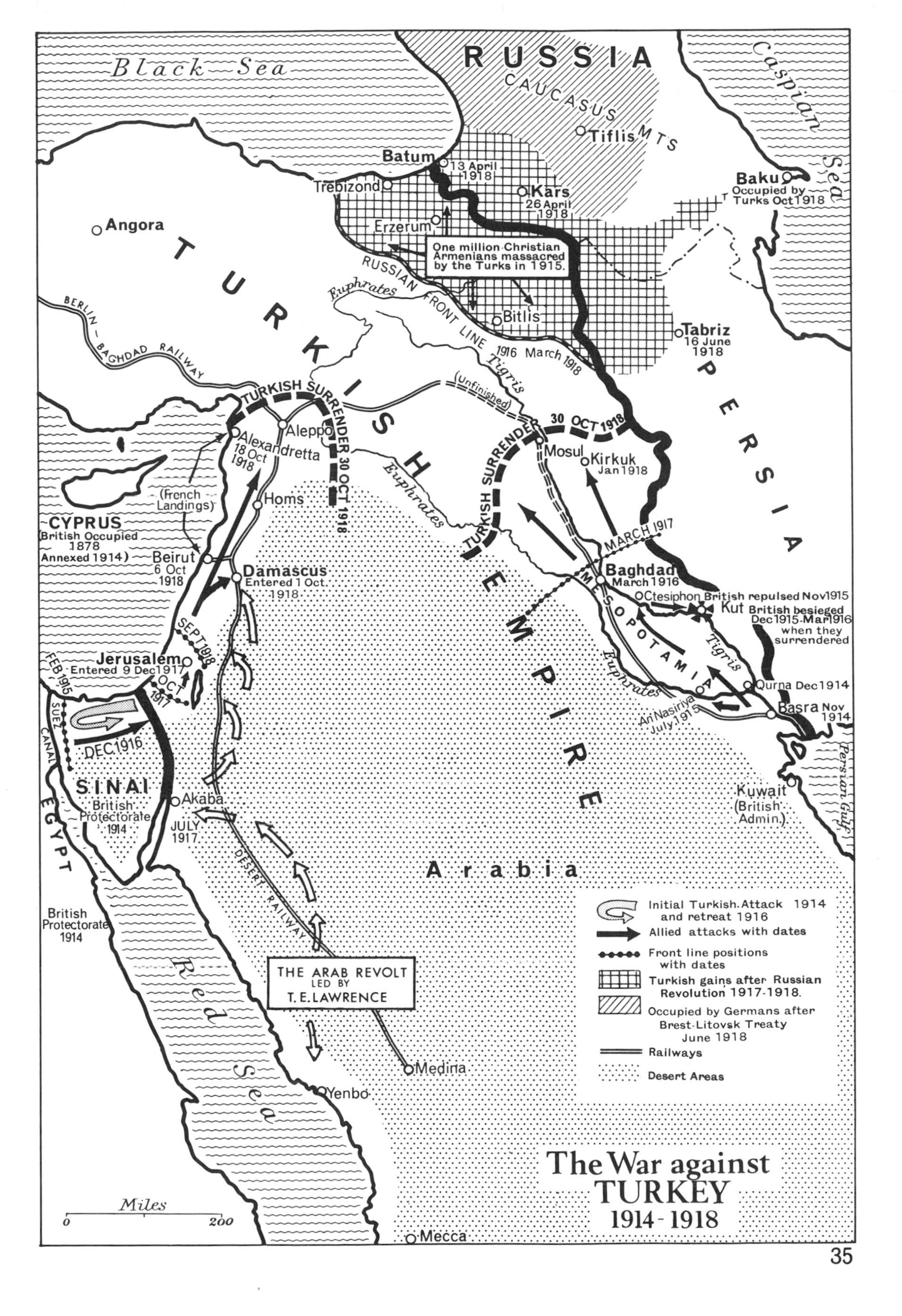
The War against TURKEY 1914-1918
Black Sea
RUSSIA
CAUCASUS MTS
Tiflis
Caspian Sea
Batum
13 April 1918
Trebizond
Kars
26 April 1918
Baku
Occupied by Turks Oct 1918
Angora
Erzerum
One million Christian Armenians massacred by the Turks in 1915.
RUSSIAN FRONT LINE 1916 March 1918
Euphrates
Bitlis
Tabriz
16 June 1918
TURKISH EMPIRE
PERSIA
BERLIN-BAGHDAD RAILWAY
TURKISH SURRENDER 30 OCT 1918
(Unfinished)
Tigris
Aleppo
Alexandretta
18 Oct 1918
Mosul
Kirkuk
Jan 1918
(French Landings)
Homs
CYPRUS
(British Occupied 1878
Annexed 1914)
Beirut
6 Oct 1918
Damascus
Entered 1 Oct. 1918
MARCH 1917
Baghdad
March 1916
MESOPOTAMIA
Ctesiphon British repulsed Nov 1915
Kut British besieged Dec 1915-Mar 1916 when they surrendered
SEPT 1918
Jerusalem
Entered 9 Dec 1917
OCT 1917
FEB 1915
SUEZ CANAL
DEC 1916
Qurna Dec 1914
Basra Nov 1914
An Nasiriya July 1915
SINAI
British Protectorate 1914
Akaba
JULY 1917
EGYPT
Kuwait
(British Admin.)
Persian Gulf
Arabia
DESERT RAILWAY
British Protectorate 1914
Red Sea
THE ARAB REVOLT LED BY T. E. LAWRENCE
Medina
Yenbo
Mecca
Initial Turkish Attack 1914 and retreat 1916
Allied attacks with dates
Front line positions with dates
Turkish gains after Russian Revolution 1917-1918.
Occupied by Germans after Brest-Litovsk Treaty June 1918
Railways
Desert Areas
Miles
0
200

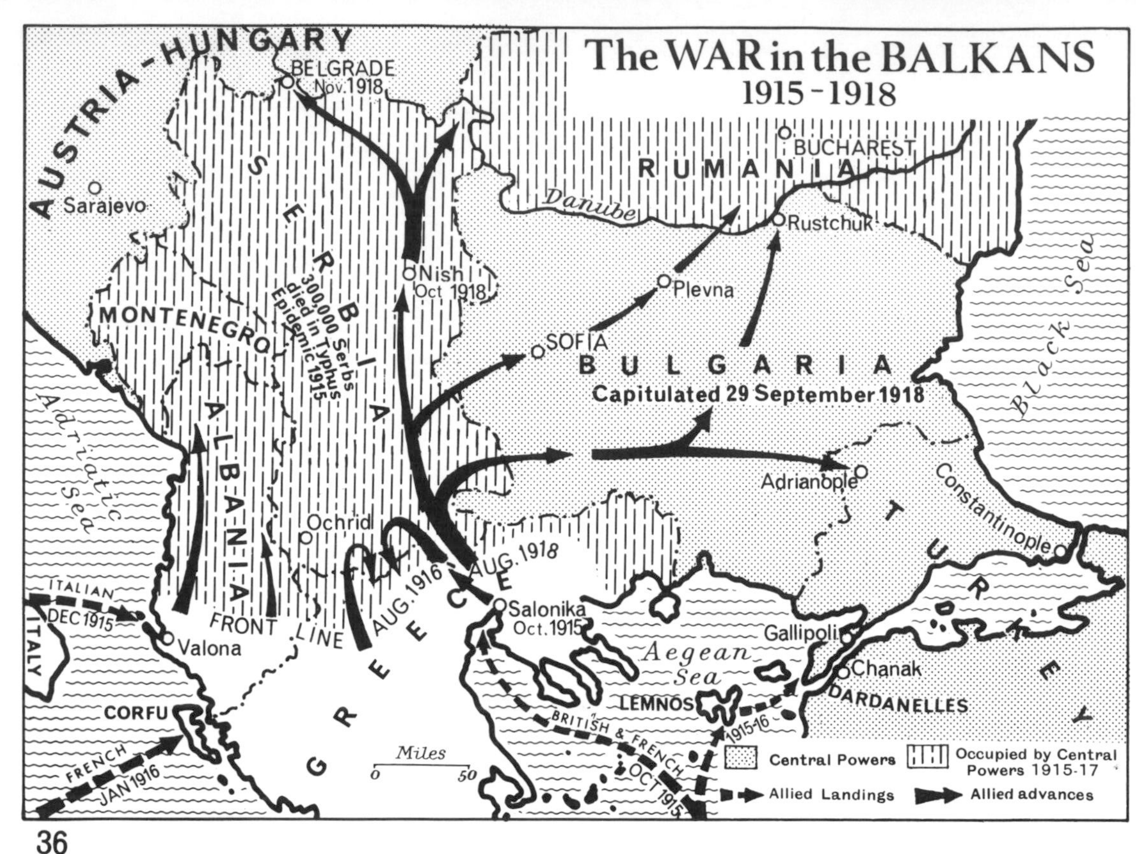
The WAR in the BALKANS
1915-1918
AUSTRIA-HUNGARY
BELGRADE
Nov.1918
Sarajevo
SERBIA
300,000 Serbs died in Typhus Epidemic 1915
MONTENEGRO
ALBANIA
Nish
Oct 1918
RUMANIA
BUCHAREST
Danube
Rustchuk
Plevna
SOFIA
BULGARIA
Capitulated 29 September 1918
Black Sea
Adriatic Sea
Adrianople
Constantinople
TURKEY
Ochrid
AUG.1916
AUG.1918
ITALIAN
DEC 1915
ITALY
Valona
FRONT LINE
GREECE
Salonika
Oct.1915
Aegean Sea
Gallipoli
Chanak
LEMNOS
DARDANELLES
1915-16
CORFU
FRENCH
JAN 1916
BRITISH & FRENCH
OCT 1915
Miles
0
50
Central Powers
Occupied by Central Powers 1915-17
Allied Landings
Allied advances

36

RUSSIAN TERRITORIAL LOSSES 1917-18
The Bolshevik revolution of November 1917 was followed immediately by an appeal to Germany for peace
Petrograd
Tallinn
SWEDEN
Baltic Sea
Riga
Miles
0
200
Moscow
Mohilev
Vilna
Minsk
RUSSIA
Orel
GERMANY
Berlin
Warsaw
Lodz
Brest Litovsk
Don
Kiev
Kharkov
Prague
AUSTRIA-HUNGARY
Vienna
UKRAINE
Dnieper
Dniester
Czernowitz
Rostov
Jassy
Odessa
Sea of Azov
Novorossiisk
RUMANIA
Bucharest
Black Sea
Front line at Armistice 5 December 1917
Ceded by Bolshevik Government to Germany by the Treaty of Brest Litovsk 3 March 1918
Occupied by Germany 1918
Occupied by Austria 1918
Occupied by Rumania 1918

37

BATTLE DEATHS 1914-1918
GT. BRITAIN 900,000
including
CANADA
INDIA
AUSTRALIA &
NEW ZEALAND
SOUTH AFRICA
London
North Sea
English Channel
DENMARK
SWEDEN
Baltic Sea
BATTLE OF JUTLAND 31 MAY 1916
HOLLAND
BELGIUM 13,000
ANTWERP
YPRES
MONS
VIMY RIDGE
SOMME
MARNE
VERDUN
ST MIHIEL
Paris
WESTERN FRONT
FRANCE 1,400,000
SWITZERLAND
SPAIN
GERMANY 1,800,000
Berlin
TANNENBERG
GUMBINNEN
AUGUSTOV
LODZ
Warsaw
KRASNIK
EASTERN FRONT
RUSSIA
War Deaths 1914-1917 1,700,000
Civil War Deaths 1917-1920 1,500,000
Prague
Vienna
AUSTRIA-HUNGARY 1,200,000
Budapest
KRONSTADT
ITALIAN FRONT
CAPORETTO
ITALY 615,000
Rome
Adriatic Sea
Sarajevo
Belgrade
RUMANIA 335,000
Bucharest
BALKAN FRONTS
SERBIA 45,000
NISH
MONTENEGRO 3,000
ALBANIA
VARDAR VALLEY
Salonika
GREECE 5,000
BULGARIA 90,000
TURKEY 325,000
DARDANELLES
Constantinople
Baltic Sea
Aegean Sea
Other Allied Dead
USA 50,000
PORTUGAL 7,000
Total of ALLIED POWERS killed: 5,219,000
Total of CENTRAL POWERS killed: 3,415,000
Central Powers
Allied Powers
Neutral
Major land battles on Central Powers territory
Major land battles on Allied territory
Miles
0
200

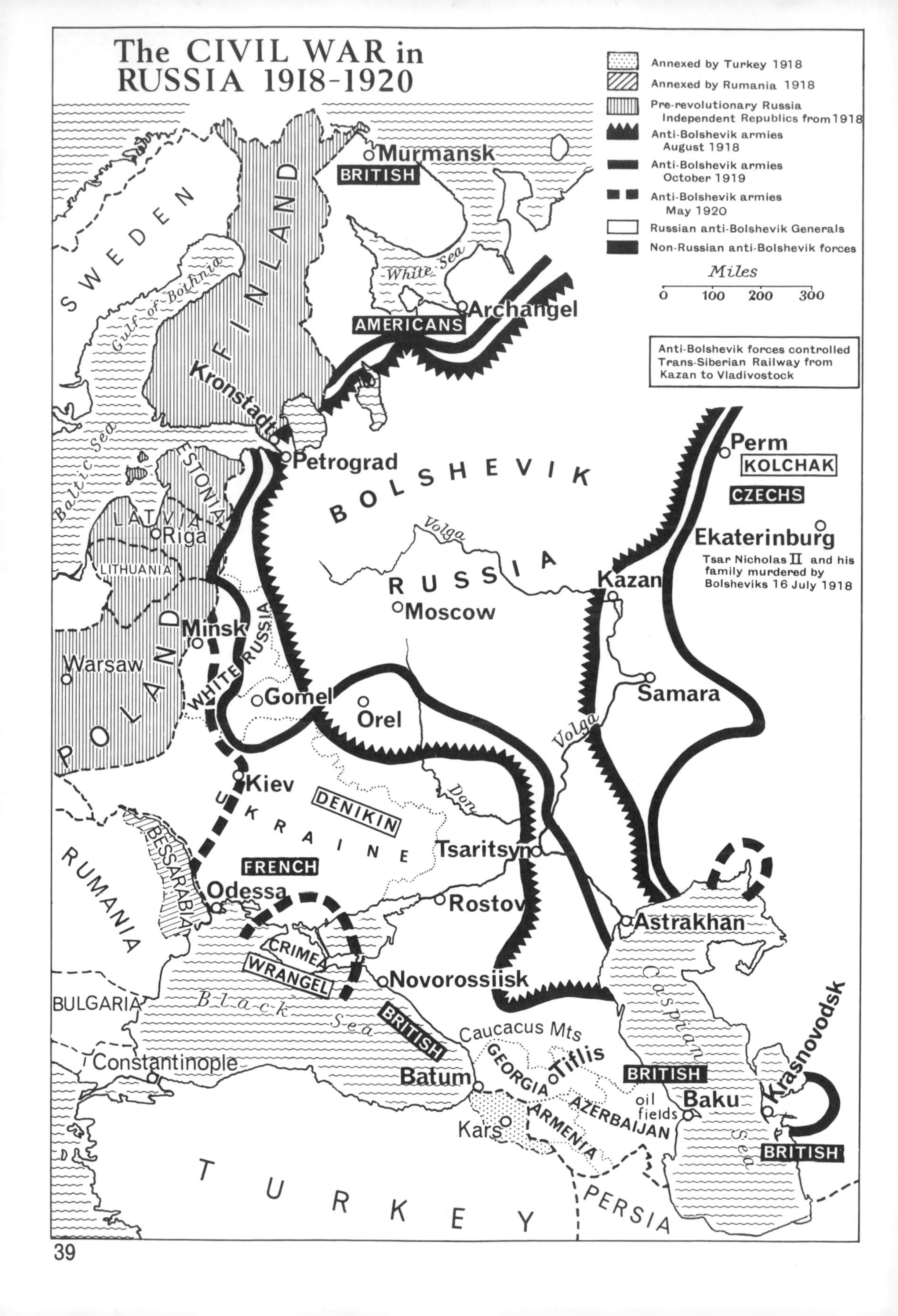

The CIVIL WAR in RUSSIA 1918-1920
Annexed by Turkey 1918
Annexed by Rumania 1918
Pre-revolutionary Russia Independent Republics from 1918
Anti-Bolshevik armies August 1918
Anti-Bolshevik armies October 1919
Anti-Bolshevik armies May 1920
Russian anti-Bolshevik Generals
Non-Russian anti-Bolshevik forces
Miles
0 100 200 300
Anti-Bolshevik forces controlled Trans-Siberian Railway from Kazan to Vladivostock
Murmansk
BRITISH
White Sea
Archangel
AMERICANS
SWEDEN
FINLAND
Gulf of Bothnia
Kronstadt
Petrograd
Baltic Sea
ESTONIA
LATVIA
Riga
LITHUANIA
POLAND
Warsaw
Minsk
WHITE RUSSIA
BOLSHEVIK RUSSIA
Volga
Moscow
Kazan
Perm
KOLCHAK
CZECHS
Ekaterinburg
Tsar Nicholas II and his family murdered by Bolsheviks 16 July 1918
Samara
Gomel
Orel
Kiev
UKRAINE
DENIKIN
Don
Tsaritsyn
FRENCH
Odessa
Rostov
Astrakhan
RUMANIA
BESSARABIA
CRIMEA
WRANGEL
Novorossiisk
BULGARIA
Black Sea
BRITISH
Caspian Sea
Krasnovodsk
Caucacus Mts
GEORGIA
Tiflis
BRITISH
Batum
oil fields
Baku
Constantinople
Kars
ARMENIA
AZERBAIJAN
BRITISH
TURKEY
PERSIA

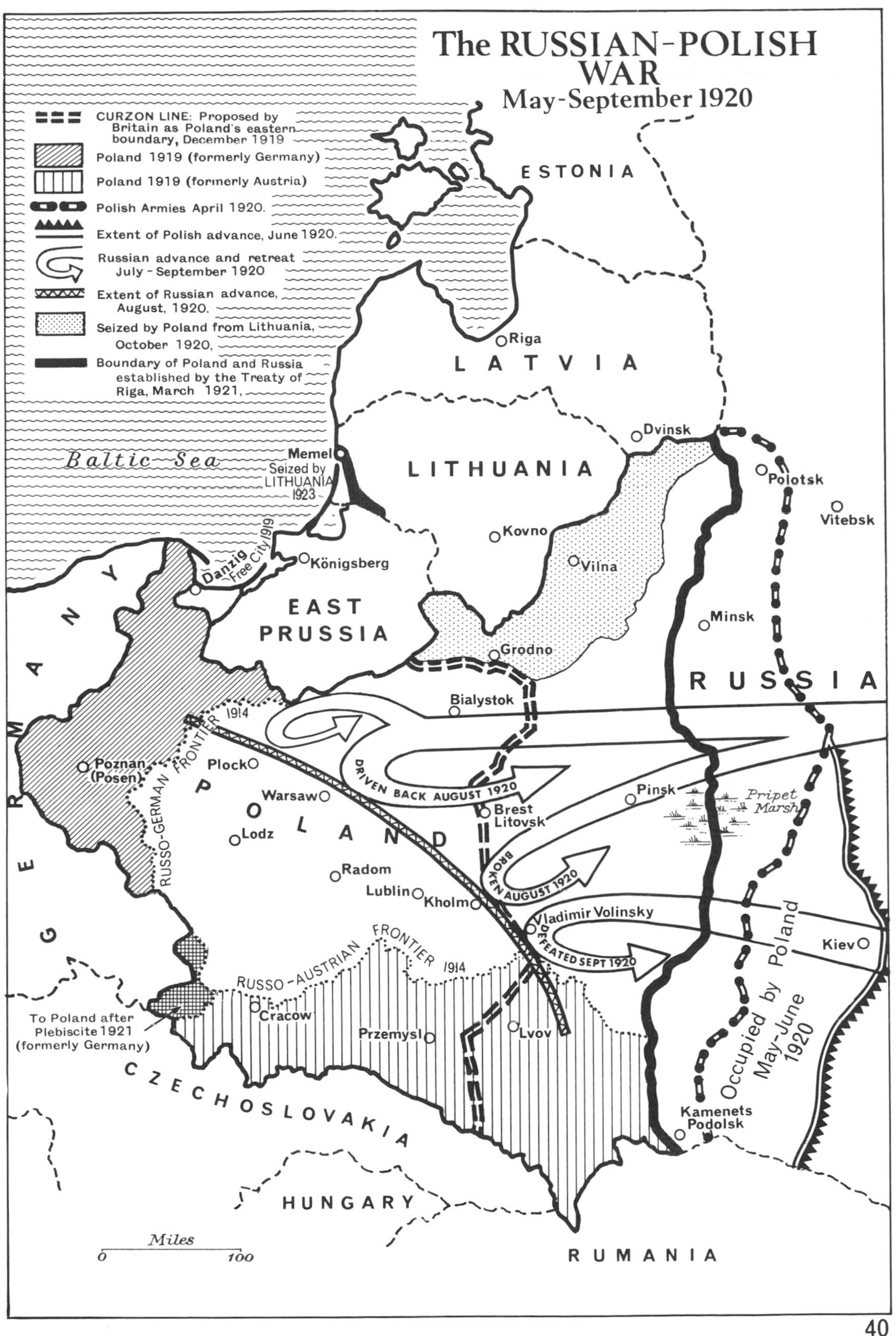
The RUSSIAN-POLISH WAR
May-September 1920
CURZON LINE: Proposed by Britain as Poland's eastern boundary, December 1919
Poland 1919 (formerly Germany)
Poland 1919 (formerly Austria)
Polish Armies April 1920.
Extent of Polish advance, June 1920.
Russian advance and retreat July - September 1920
Extent of Russian advance, August, 1920.
Seized by Poland from Lithuania, October 1920,
Boundary of Poland and Russia established by the Treaty of Riga, March 1921,
ESTONIA
Riga
LATVIA
Dvinsk
Baltic Sea
Memel
Seized by LITHUANIA 1923
LITHUANIA
Polotsk
Vitebsk
Kovno
Vilna
Danzig
Free City 1919
Königsberg
EAST PRUSSIA
Minsk
Grodno
RUSSIA
Bialystok
1914
GERMANY
Poznan (Posen)
RUSSO-GERMAN FRONTIER
Plock
DRIVEN BACK AUGUST 1920
Warsaw
Brest Litovsk
Pinsk
Pripet Marsh
Lodz
POLAND
BROKEN AUGUST 1920
Radom
Lublin
Kholm
Vladimir Volinsky
DEFEATED SEPT 1920
Kiev
RUSSO-AUSTRIAN FRONTIER 1914
Occupied by Poland May-June 1920
To Poland after Plebiscite 1921 (formerly Germany)
Cracow
Przemysl
Lvov
CZECHOSLOVAKIA
Kamenets Podolsk
HUNGARY
Miles
0
100
RUMANIA

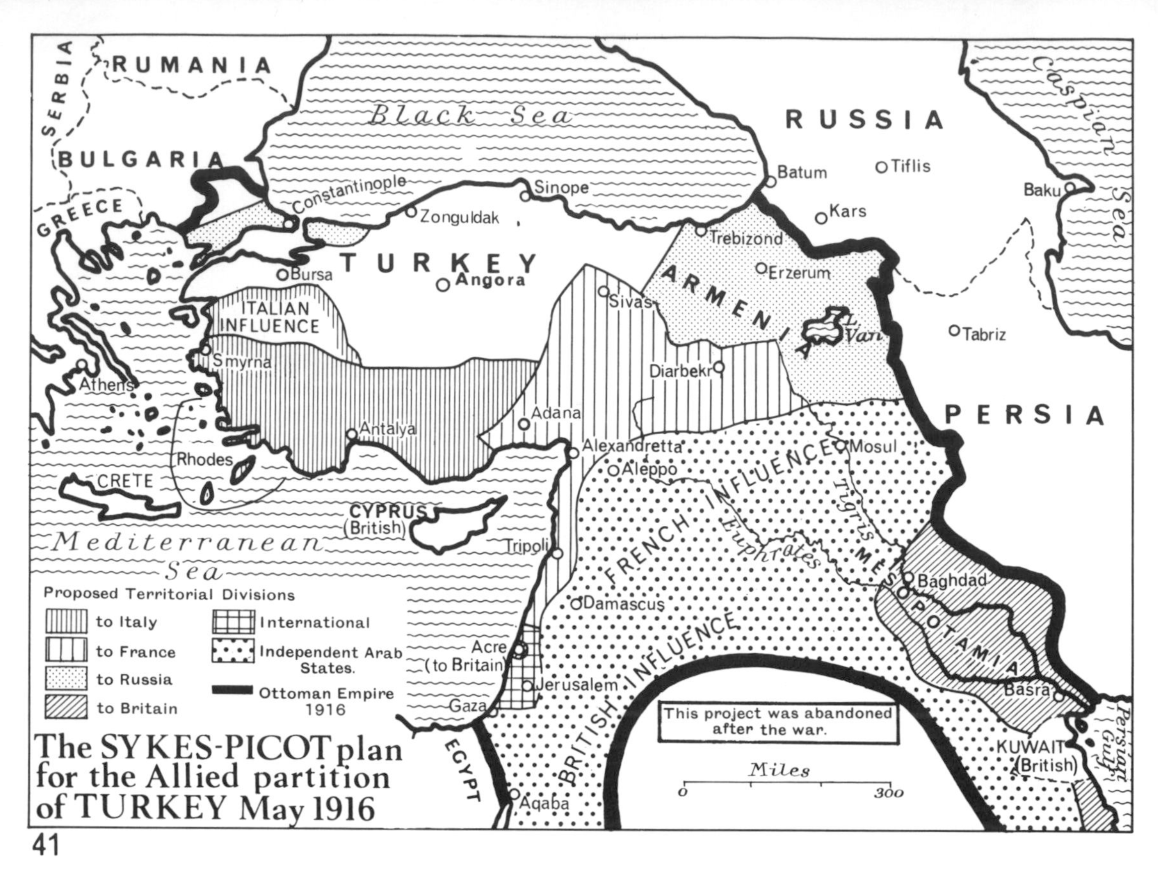
SERBIA
RUMANIA
Black Sea
RUSSIA
Caspian Sea
BULGARIA
GREECE
Constantinople
Sinope
Zonguldak
Batum
Tiflis
Kars
Baku
Trebizond
Bursa
TURKEY
Angora
Erzerum
ARMENIA
Sivas
L. Van
Tabriz
ITALIAN INFLUENCE
Smyrna
Athens
Diarbekr
Adana
PERSIA
Antalya
Alexandretta
Mosul
Rhodes
Aleppo
FRENCH INFLUENCE
CRETE
Tigris
Euphrates
CYPRUS (British)
Mediterranean Sea
Tripoli
MESOPOTAMIA
Baghdad
Damascus
Proposed Territorial Divisions
to Italy
to France
to Russia
to Britain
International
Independent Arab States.
Ottoman Empire 1916
Acre (to Britain)
Jerusalem
Gaza
BRITISH INFLUENCE
Basra
This project was abandoned after the war.
KUWAIT (British)
Persian Gulf
EGYPT
Miles
0
300
Aqaba
The SYKES-PICOT plan for the Allied partition of TURKEY May 1916

41

BULGARIA
YUGOSLAVIA
Greek Minority areas 1918
Awarded to Greece at Treaty of Sevres 1919
British controlled zone of the straits 1920-22.
Turkish advances, 1922.
Transfer of populations after 1922 :-
Greeks 1,377,000
Turks 410,000
Bulgarians.....250,000
Final western frontier of Turkey
BULGARIANS 250,000
GREEKS FROM RUSSIA 12,000
GREEKS FROM CAUCASUS 50,000
Black Sea
GREEKS 50,000
GREEKS FROM TREBIZOND 260,000
GREEKS 310,000
Constantinople
Salonika
Chanak
Mudania
Ankara (Angora)
GREECE
GREEKS 625,000
TURKS 360,000
ANATOLIA
TURKEY
Smyrna
Athens
Miles
0
200
TURKS 25,000
GREEKS 25,000
RHODES
GREEKS FROM SOUTH TURKEY 50,000
DODECANESE (Italian)
CRETE
The War between GREECE & TURKEY 1922

42

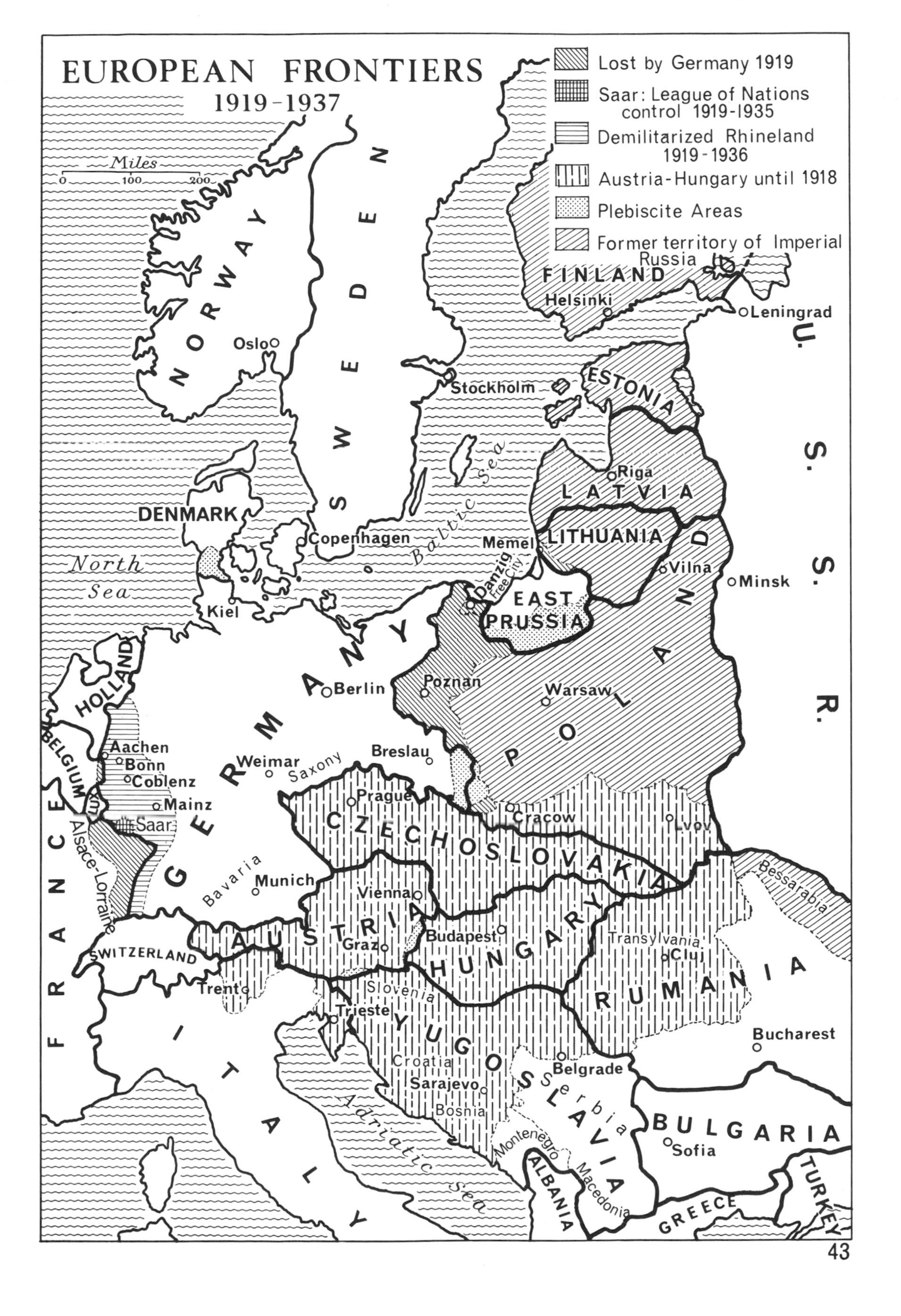
EUROPEAN FRONTIERS
1919-1937
Lost by Germany 1919
Saar: League of Nations control 1919-1935
Demilitarized Rhineland 1919-1936
Austria-Hungary until 1918
Plebiscite Areas
Former territory of Imperial Russia
Miles
0 100 200
NORWAY
SWEDEN
FINLAND
Helsinki
Leningrad
U.S.S.R.
Oslo
Stockholm
ESTONIA
Riga
LATVIA
LITHUANIA
Vilna
Minsk
DENMARK
Copenhagen
Baltic Sea
Memel
Danzig
Free City
EAST PRUSSIA
North Sea
Kiel
HOLLAND
BELGIUM
GERMANY
Berlin
Poznan
Warsaw
POLAND
Aachen
Bonn
Coblenz
Mainz
Weimar
Saxony
Breslau
Lux.
Saar
Alsace-Lorraine
Prague
Cracow
Lvov
CZECHOSLOVAKIA
Bessarabia
Bavaria
Munich
Vienna
FRANCE
SWITZERLAND
AUSTRIA
Graz
Budapest
HUNGARY
Transylvania
Cluj
RUMANIA
Trent
Slovenia
Trieste
YUGOSLAVIA
Croatia
Belgrade
Bucharest
Sarajevo
Bosnia
Serbia
BULGARIA
Sofia
ITALY
Adriatic Sea
Montenegro
ALBANIA
Macedonia
GREECE
TURKEY

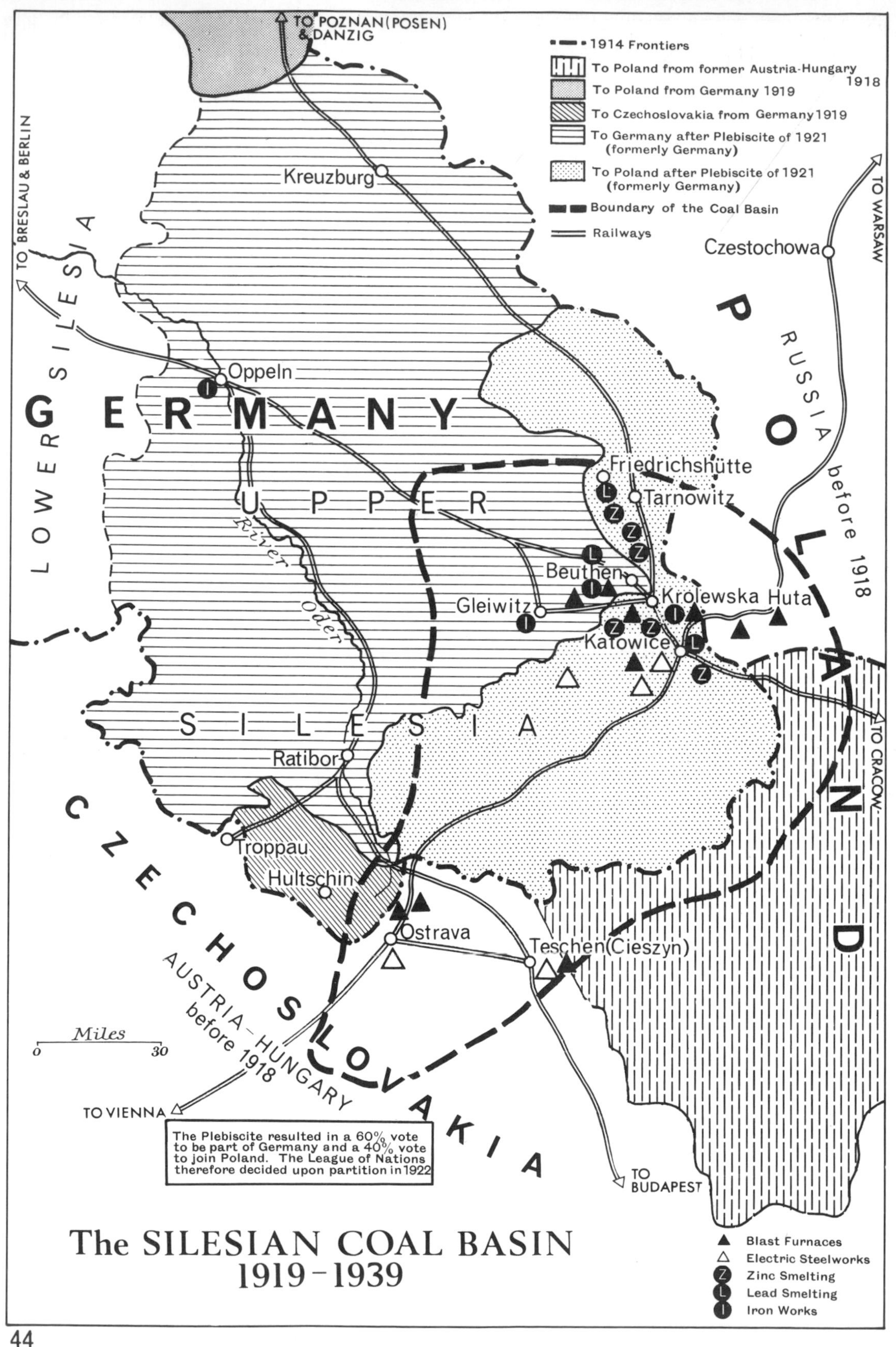

The SILESIAN COAL BASIN 1919-1939

The Disruption of Rail Communications in Central Europe, 1919
Following the break-up of the Habsburg Empire and establishment of customs and tariff barriers.
Boundary of Austria-Hungary 1867-1918
New Boundaries of 1919.
Main railway lines.
Miles
0
100
GERMANY
CZECHOSLOVAKIA
POLAND
AUSTRIA
HUNGARY
RUMANIA
ITALY
YUGOSLAVIA
Adriatic Sea
Prague
Brno
Cracow
Lvov
Munich
Linz
Vienna
Bratislava
Chust
Satmar
Czernowitz
Innsbruck
Budapest
Szeged
Trent
Ljubljana
Zagreb
Trieste
Fiume
Kikinda
Timisoara
Belgrade
Sarajevo

45

HUNGARY since 1867
Boundary of Hungary, 1867-1918.
Territory lost in 1919
Hungary as laid down by the Treaty of Trianon 1920.
Territory regained from 1938 and lost in 1945
Miles
0
50
100
CZECHOSLOVAKIA
RUSSIA
AUSTRIA
RUMANIA
YUGOSLAVIA
HUNGARY
1920-1938 and since 1945
FROM CZECHOSLOVAKIA 1938-1945
FROM CZECHOSLOVAKIA 1940-1944
FROM RUMANIA 1941-1945
FROM YUGOSLAVIA 1941-1945
Vienna
Bratislava
Sopron
Gyor
Miskolc
Chust
Debrecen
Budapest
Kolozsvar
(Cluj)
Szeged
Arad
Pecs
Subotica
Temisoara
Zagreb
(Agram)
Brasov
Fiume
Belgrade

46

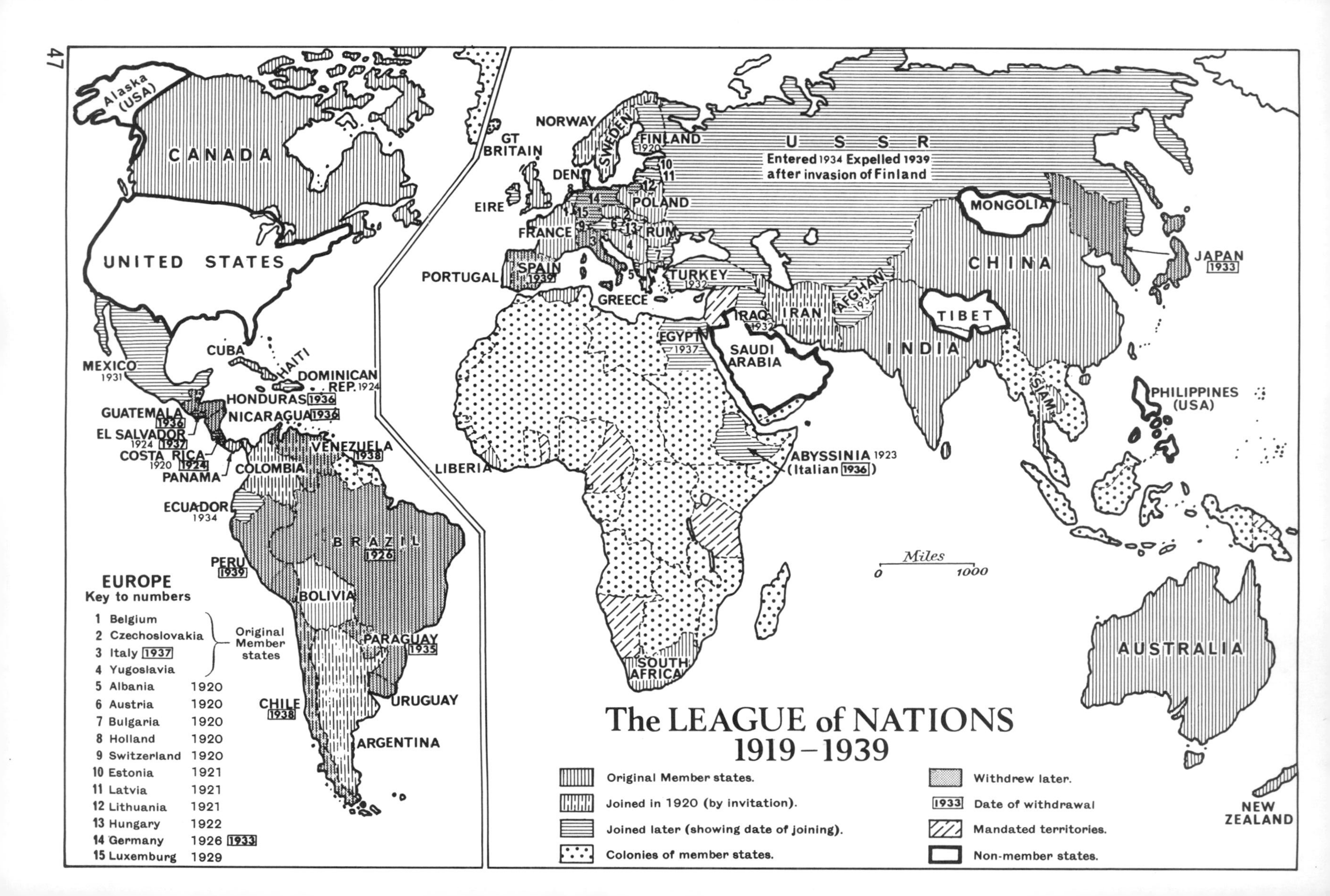

The LEAGUE of NATIONS
1919–1939
Original Member states.
Joined in 1920 (by invitation).
Joined later (showing date of joining).
Colonies of member states.
Withdrew later.
1933 Date of withdrawal
Mandated territories.
Non-member states.
Miles
0 1000
EUROPE
Key to numbers
1 Belgium
2 Czechoslovakia
3 Italy 1937
4 Yugoslavia
Original Member states
5 Albania 1920
6 Austria 1920
7 Bulgaria 1920
8 Holland 1920
9 Switzerland 1920
10 Estonia 1921
11 Latvia 1921
12 Lithuania 1921
13 Hungary 1922
14 Germany 1926 1933
15 Luxemburg 1929
Alaska (USA)
CANADA
UNITED STATES
MEXICO 1931
CUBA
HAITI
DOMINICAN REP. 1924
HONDURAS 1936
NICARAGUA 1936
GUATEMALA 1936
EL SALVADOR 1924 1937
COSTA RICA 1920 1924
PANAMA
COLOMBIA
VENEZUELA 1938
ECUADOR 1934
PERU 1939
BRAZIL 1926
BOLIVIA
PARAGUAY 1935
CHILE 1938
URUGUAY
ARGENTINA
NORWAY
GT BRITAIN
EIRE
DEN
SWEDEN
FINLAND 1920
POLAND
FRANCE
RUM
PORTUGAL
SPAIN 1939
GREECE
TURKEY 1932
U S S R
Entered 1934 Expelled 1939
after invasion of Finland
MONGOLIA
CHINA
JAPAN 1933
TIBET
IRAQ 1932
IRAN
AFGHAN 1934
INDIA
SIAM
EGYPT 1937
SAUDI ARABIA
LIBERIA
ABYSSINIA 1923
(Italian 1936)
SOUTH AFRICA
PHILIPPINES (USA)
AUSTRALIA
NEW ZEALAND

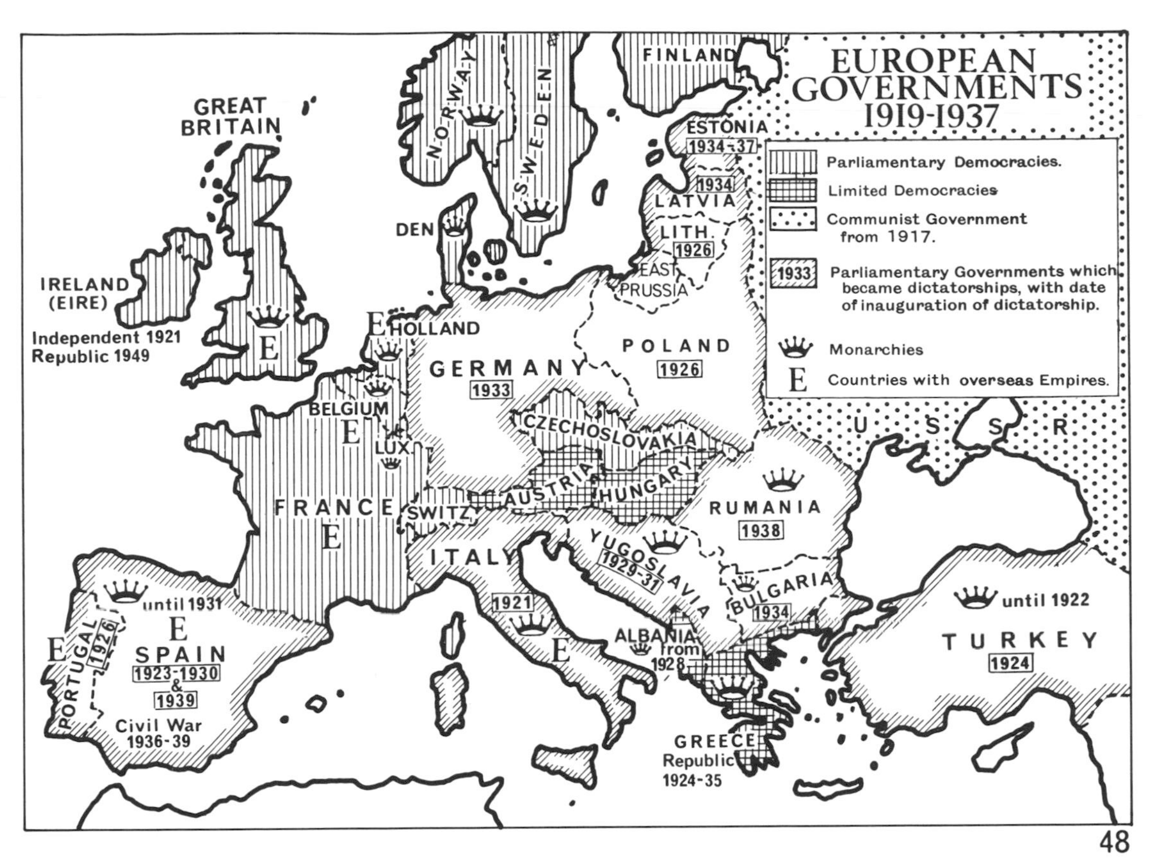
EUROPEAN GOVERNMENTS 1919-1937
Parliamentary Democracies.
Limited Democracies
Communist Government from 1917.
1933 Parliamentary Governments which became dictatorships, with date of inauguration of dictatorship.
Monarchies
E Countries with overseas Empires.
FINLAND
NORWAY
SWEDEN
GREAT BRITAIN
ESTONIA 1934-37
LATVIA 1934
LITH. 1926
DEN
EAST PRUSSIA
IRELAND (EIRE)
Independent 1921
Republic 1949
HOLLAND
GERMANY 1933
POLAND 1926
BELGIUM
LUX.
CZECHOSLOVAKIA
U S S R
AUSTRIA
HUNGARY
FRANCE
SWITZ
RUMANIA 1938
ITALY
YUGOSLAVIA 1929-31
BULGARIA 1934
until 1931
PORTUGAL 1926
SPAIN 1923-1930 & 1939
Civil War 1936-39
1921
ALBANIA from 1928
until 1922
TURKEY 1924
GREECE
Republic 1924-35

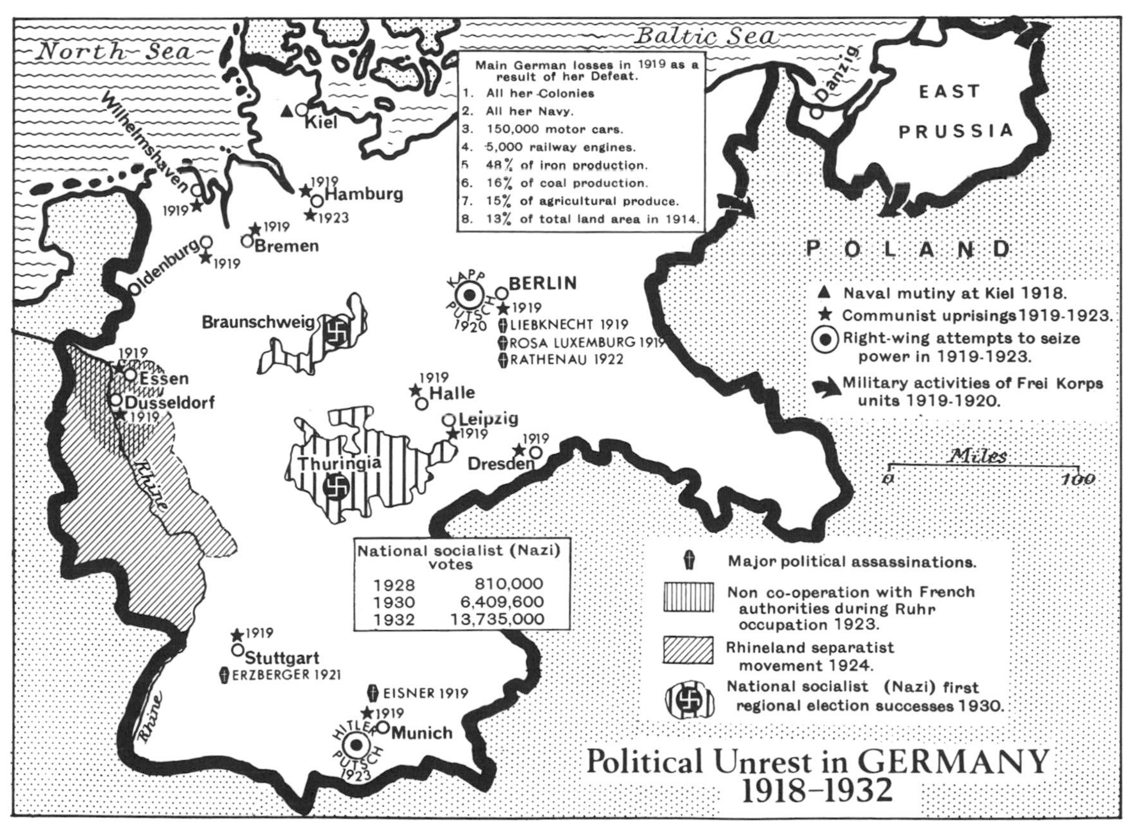
North Sea
Baltic Sea
Main German losses in 1919 as a result of her Defeat.
1. All her Colonies
2. All her Navy.
3. 150,000 motor cars.
4. 5,000 railway engines.
5. 48% of iron production.
6. 16% of coal production.
7. 15% of agricultural produce.
8. 13% of total land area in 1914.
Danzig
EAST PRUSSIA
Kiel
Wilhelmshaven
1919
Hamburg
1923
Bremen
Oldenburg
POLAND
KAPP PUTSCH 1920
BERLIN
LIEBKNECHT 1919
ROSA LUXEMBURG 1919
RATHENAU 1922
Braunschweig
Naval mutiny at Kiel 1918.
Communist uprisings 1919-1923.
Right-wing attempts to seize power in 1919-1923.
Military activities of Frei Korps units 1919-1920.
Essen
Dusseldorf
Halle
Leipzig
Dresden
Thuringia
Rhine
Miles
0
100
National socialist (Nazi) votes
1928 810,000
1930 6,409,600
1932 13,735,000
Major political assassinations.
Non co-operation with French authorities during Ruhr occupation 1923.
Rhineland separatist movement 1924.
National socialist (Nazi) first regional election successes 1930.
Stuttgart
ERZBERGER 1921
EISNER 1919
Munich
HITLER PUTSCH 1923
Political Unrest in GERMANY 1918-1932

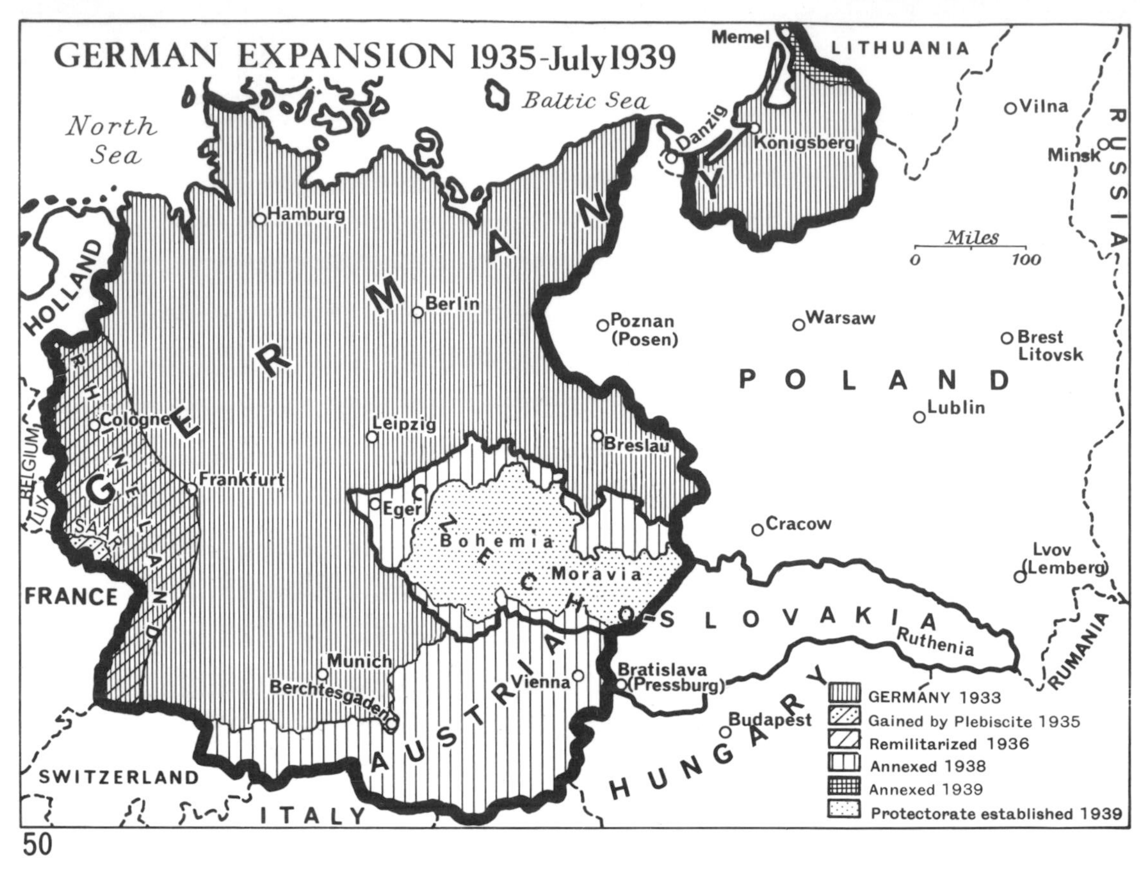
GERMAN EXPANSION 1935-July 1939
North Sea
Baltic Sea
Memel
LITHUANIA
Vilna
Minsk
RUSSIA
Danzig
Königsberg
Hamburg
Berlin
Miles
0
100
HOLLAND
Poznan (Posen)
Warsaw
Brest Litovsk
POLAND
Lublin
Cologne
Leipzig
Breslau
BELGIUM
LUX
Frankfurt
SAAR
RHINELAND
GERMANY
Eger
Bohemia
Moravia
CZECHOSLOVAKIA
Cracow
Lvov (Lemberg)
FRANCE
Ruthenia
RUMANIA
Munich
Berchtesgaden
Vienna
AUSTRIA
Bratislava (Pressburg)
Budapest
HUNGARY
SWITZERLAND
ITALY
GERMANY 1933
Gained by Plebiscite 1935
Remilitarized 1936
Annexed 1938
Annexed 1939
Protectorate established 1939

50

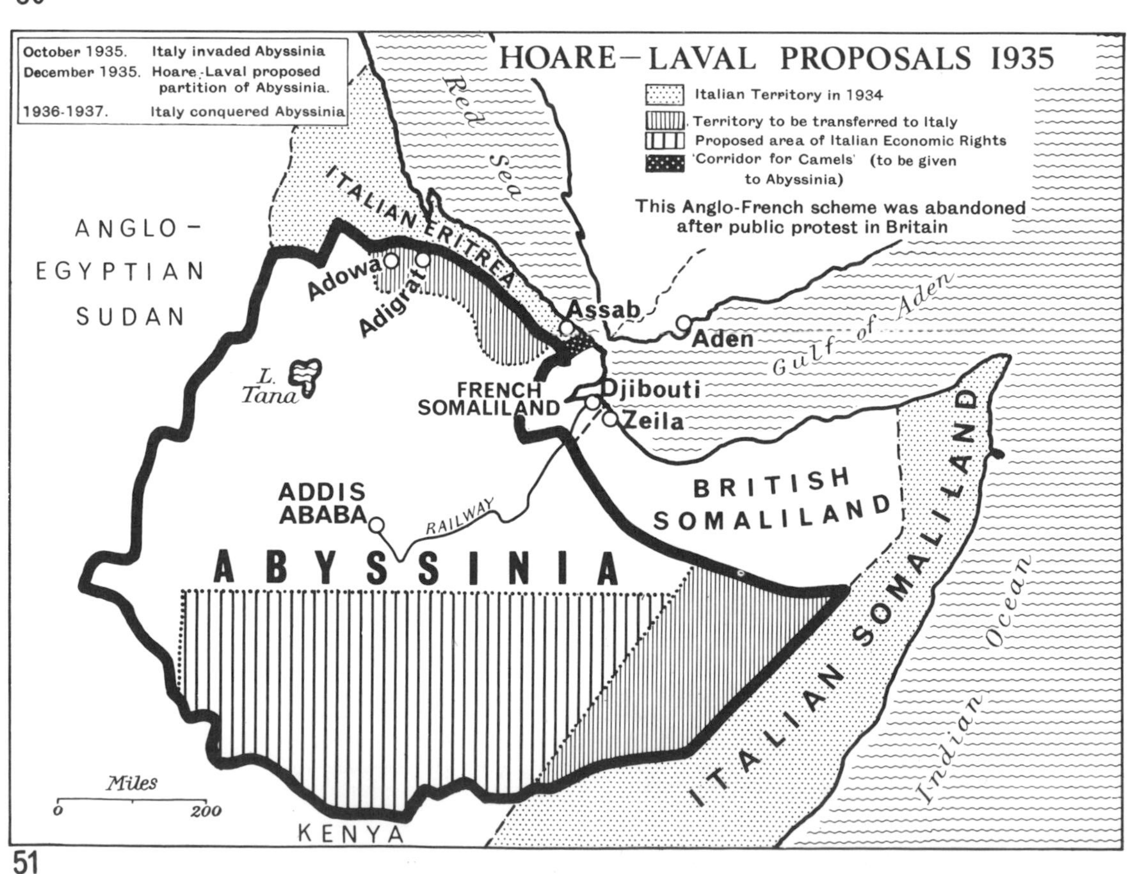
October 1935. Italy invaded Abyssinia
December 1935. Hoare-Laval proposed partition of Abyssinia.
1936-1937. Italy conquered Abyssinia
HOARE–LAVAL PROPOSALS 1935
Italian Territory in 1934
Territory to be transferred to Italy
Proposed area of Italian Economic Rights
'Corridor for Camels' (to be given to Abyssinia)
This Anglo-French scheme was abandoned after public protest in Britain
Red Sea
ITALIAN ERITREA
ANGLO-EGYPTIAN SUDAN
Adowa
Adigrat
Assab
Aden
Gulf of Aden
L. Tana
FRENCH SOMALILAND
Djibouti
Zeila
BRITISH SOMALILAND
ADDIS ABABA
RAILWAY
ABYSSINIA
ITALIAN SOMALILAND
Indian Ocean
Miles
0
200
KENYA

51

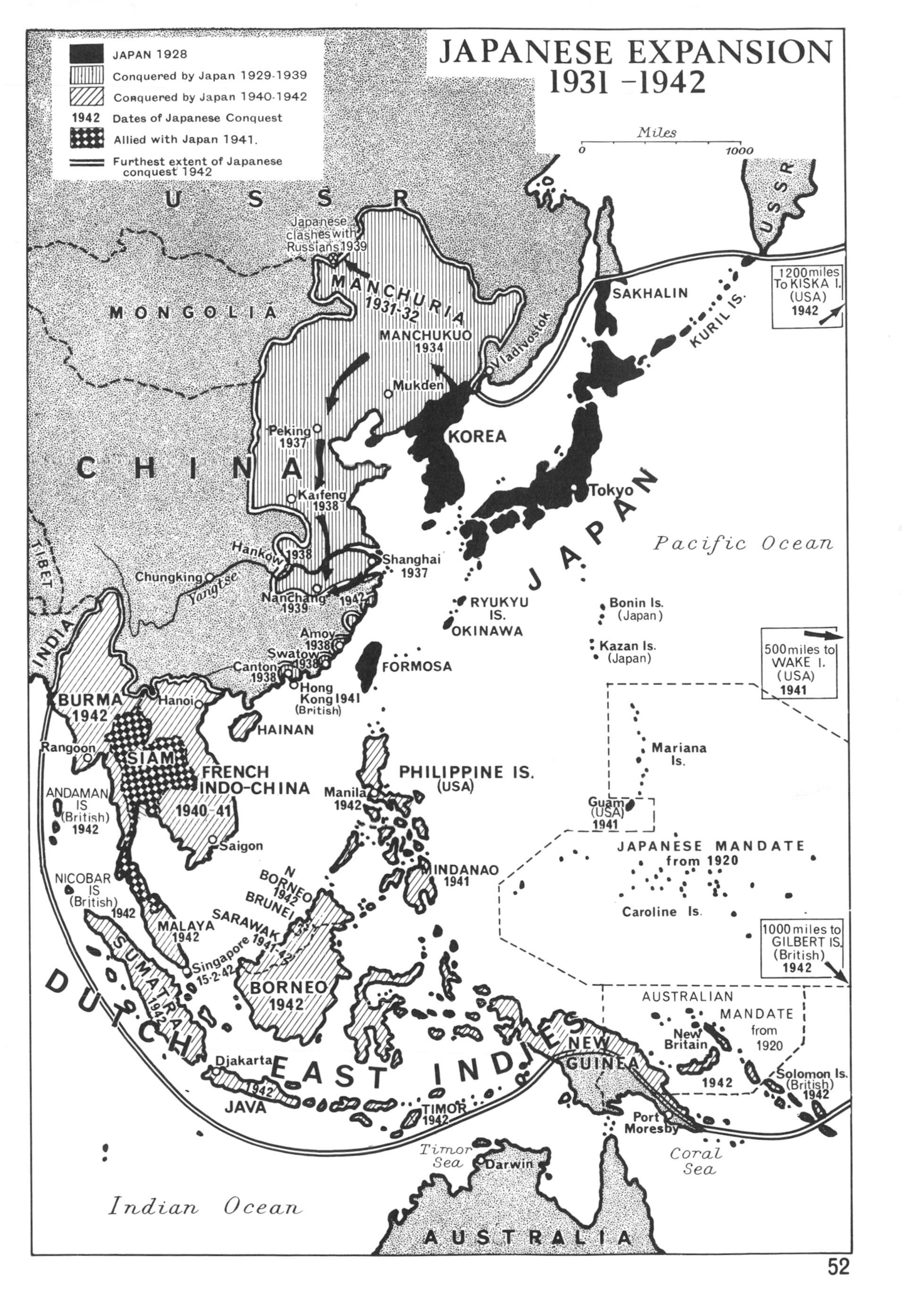
JAPANESE EXPANSION 1931 -1942
JAPAN 1928
Conquered by Japan 1929-1939
Conquered by Japan 1940-1942
1942 Dates of Japanese Conquest
Allied with Japan 1941.
Furthest extent of Japanese conquest 1942
Miles
0
1000
U S S R
USSR
Japanese clashes with Russians 1939
MANCHURIA 1931-32
MANCHUKUO 1934
MONGOLIA
Vladivostok
Mukden
SAKHALIN
KURIL IS.
1200 miles To KISKA I. (USA) 1942
KOREA
Peking 1937
CHINA
Kaifeng 1938
Tokyo
JAPAN
Pacific Ocean
TIBET
Hankow 1938
Shanghai 1937
Chungking
Yangtse
Nanchang 1939
1942
RYUKYU IS.
OKINAWA
Bonin Is. (Japan)
Kazan Is. (Japan)
500 miles to WAKE I. (USA) 1941
INDIA
Amoy 1938
Swatow 1938
Canton 1938
Hong Kong 1941 (British)
FORMOSA
BURMA 1942
Hanoi
HAINAN
Mariana Is.
Rangoon
SIAM
FRENCH INDO-CHINA
1940-41
PHILIPPINE IS. (USA)
Manila 1942
Guam (USA) 1941
ANDAMAN IS (British) 1942
Saigon
JAPANESE MANDATE from 1920
N BORNEO 1942
BRUNEI
SARAWAK
MINDANAO 1941
NICOBAR IS (British)
1942
Caroline Is.
MALAYA 1942
Singapore 15-2-42
1941-42
1000 miles to GILBERT IS. (British) 1942
SUMATRA 1942
BORNEO 1942
AUSTRALIAN MANDATE from 1920
New Britain
1942
DUTCH EAST INDIES
NEW GUINEA
Solomon Is. (British) 1942
Djakarta
1942
JAVA
TIMOR 1942
Port Moresby
Timor Sea
Darwin
Coral Sea
Indian Ocean
AUSTRALIA

The Partitioning of CZECHOSLOVAKIA 1938
GERMANY
Silesia
POLAND
SUDETENLAND
Asch
Eger
Prague
Bohemia
Cracow
Teschen
Miles
0
100
Bavaria
Moravia
Brno
Slovakia
Ruthenia (Carpatho-Ukraine)
Danube
Vienna
Bratislava
Occupied by Hungary on 14 March 1939
Budapest
Austria
HUNGARY
RUMANIA
Czech territory ceded to Germany at Munich, 30 September 1938
Czech territory given to Hungary by Germany and Italy at Vienna, 2 October 1938
Czech territory siezed by Poland in September 1938 and formally annexed on 1 November 1938

53

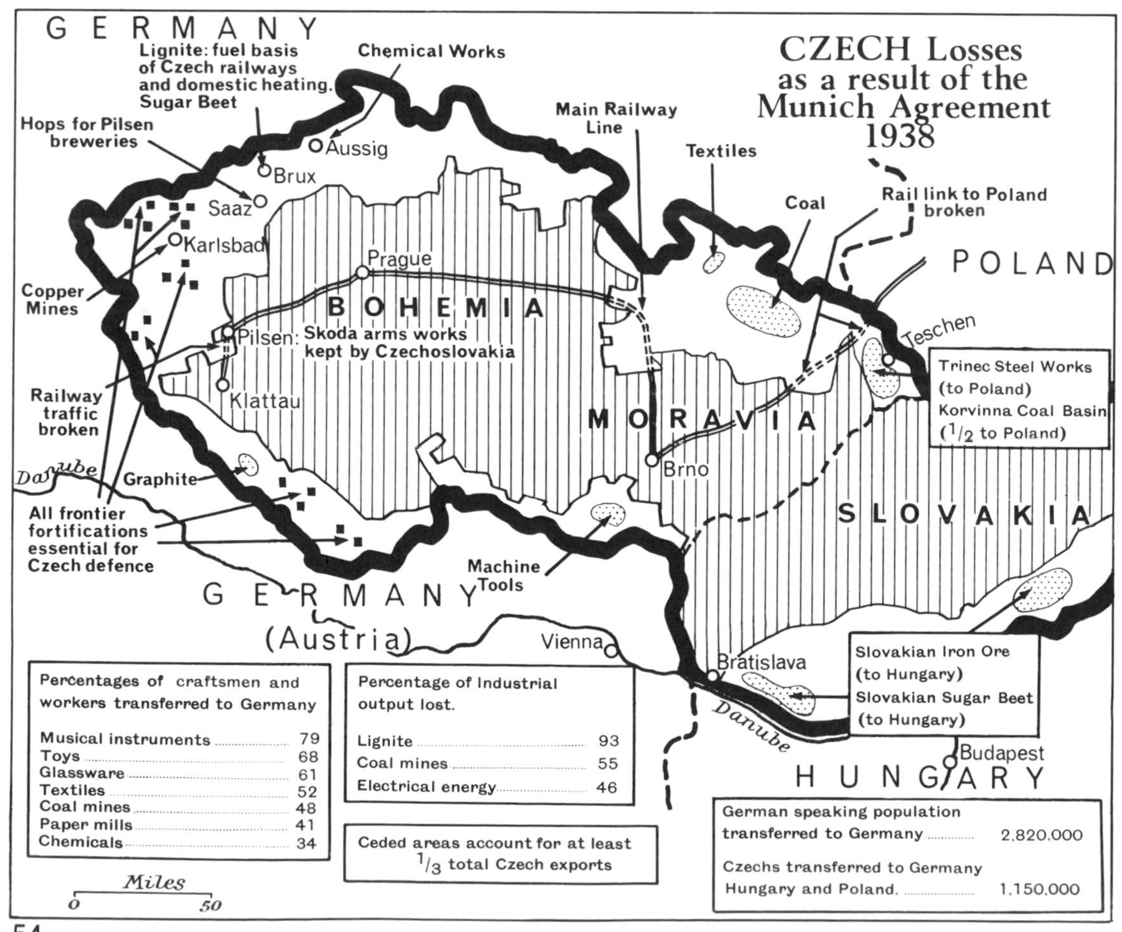
GERMANY
Lignite: fuel basis of Czech railways and domestic heating. Sugar Beet
Chemical Works
CZECH Losses as a result of the Munich Agreement 1938
Hops for Pilsen breweries
Aussig
Brux
Main Railway Line
Textiles
Coal
Rail link to Poland broken
Saaz
Karlsbad
Prague
POLAND
Copper Mines
BOHEMIA
Pilsen: Skoda arms works kept by Czechoslovakia
Teschen
Trinec Steel Works (to Poland)
Korvinna Coal Basin (1/2 to Poland)
Railway traffic broken
Klattau
MORAVIA
Danube
Graphite
Brno
All frontier fortifications essential for Czech defence
SLOVAKIA
Machine Tools
GERMANY (Austria)
Vienna
Bratislava
Slovakian Iron Ore (to Hungary)
Slovakian Sugar Beet (to Hungary)
Danube
Budapest
HUNGARY
Percentages of craftsmen and workers transferred to Germany
Musical instruments 79
Toys 68
Glassware 61
Textiles 52
Coal mines 48
Paper mills 41
Chemicals 34
Percentage of Industrial output lost.
Lignite 93
Coal mines 55
Electrical energy 46
Ceded areas account for at least 1/3 total Czech exports
German speaking population transferred to Germany 2,820,000
Czechs transferred to Germany Hungary and Poland. 1,150,000
Miles
0
50

54

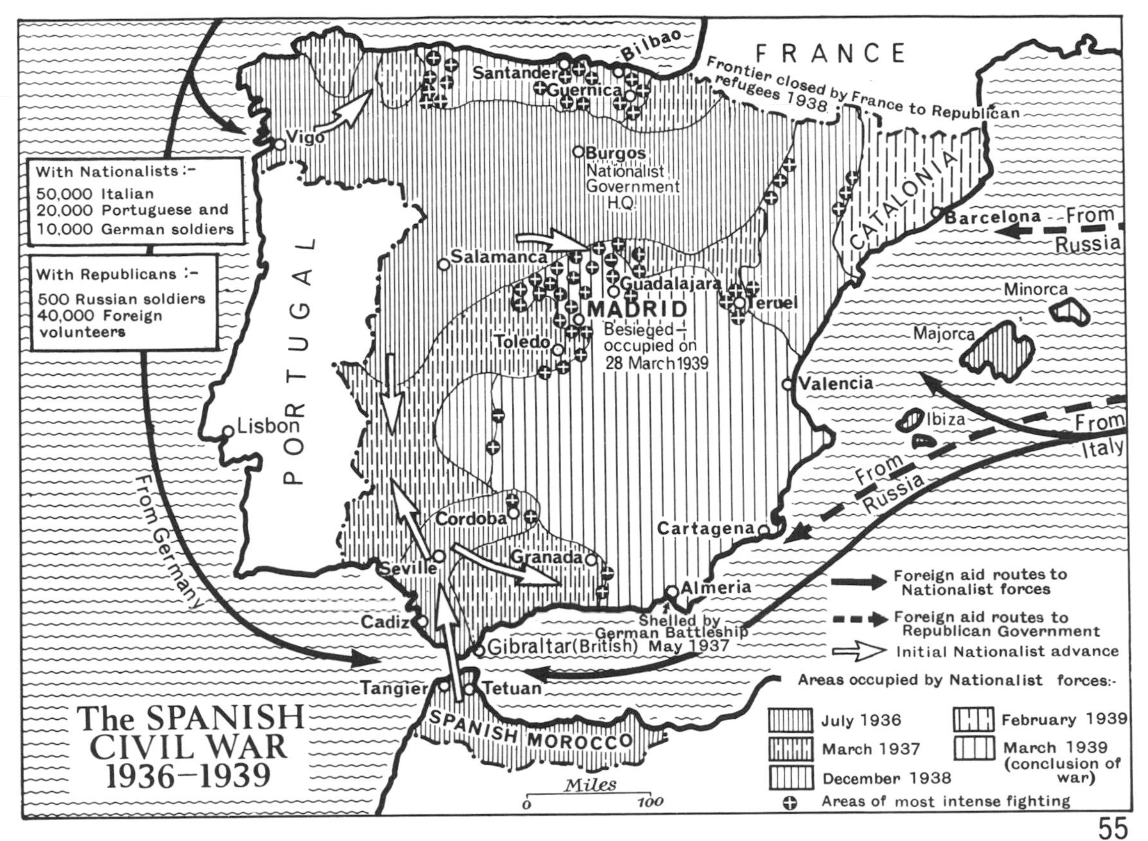
The SPANISH CIVIL WAR 1936–1939
FRANCE
Bilbao
Santander
Guernica
Frontier closed by France to Republican refugees 1938
Vigo
Burgos
Nationalist Government H.Q.
CATALONIA
Barcelona
From Russia
With Nationalists :-
50,000 Italian
20,000 Portuguese and
10,000 German soldiers
With Republicans :-
500 Russian soldiers
40,000 Foreign volunteers
PORTUGAL
Salamanca
Guadalajara
Teruel
MADRID
Besieged – occupied on 28 March 1939
Toledo
Minorca
Majorca
Valencia
Ibiza
From Italy
From Russia
Lisbon
From Germany
Cordoba
Granada
Seville
Cartagena
Almeria
Cadiz
Shelled by German Battleship May 1937
Gibraltar(British)
Tangier
Tetuan
SPANISH MOROCCO
Foreign aid routes to Nationalist forces
Foreign aid routes to Republican Government
Initial Nationalist advance
Areas occupied by Nationalist forces:-
July 1936
March 1937
December 1938
February 1939
March 1939 (conclusion of war)
Areas of most intense fighting
Miles
0
100

ITALIAN EXPANSION 1939 – 1943
SWITZERLAND
AUSTRIA 1938
BRENNER PASS
Budapest
HUNGARY
Miles
0
100
FRANCE 1942
Milan
Turin
Venice
Trieste
1941
SLOVENIA
Zagreb
Occupied by Hungary
1941
YUGOSLAVIA
CROATIA
Belgrade
RUMANIA
ITALY
Nice (From France)
Adriatic Sea
DALMATIA
BOSNIA
1941
SERBIA
BULGARIA
Sofia
CORSICA (From France)
ROME
Cattaro (Kotor)
ALBANIA
MACEDONIA 1941
Occupied by Bulgaria
1941
Durazzo
Naples
Valona
SARDINIA
Tyrrhenian Sea
Aegean Sea
GREECE 1941
Ionian Sea
Palermo
SICILY
Athens
ITALY January 1939.
Occupied by Italy April 1939.
Occupied by Italy 1940-1943.
Occupied by Germany
Joint German-Italian occupation, 1941-1943

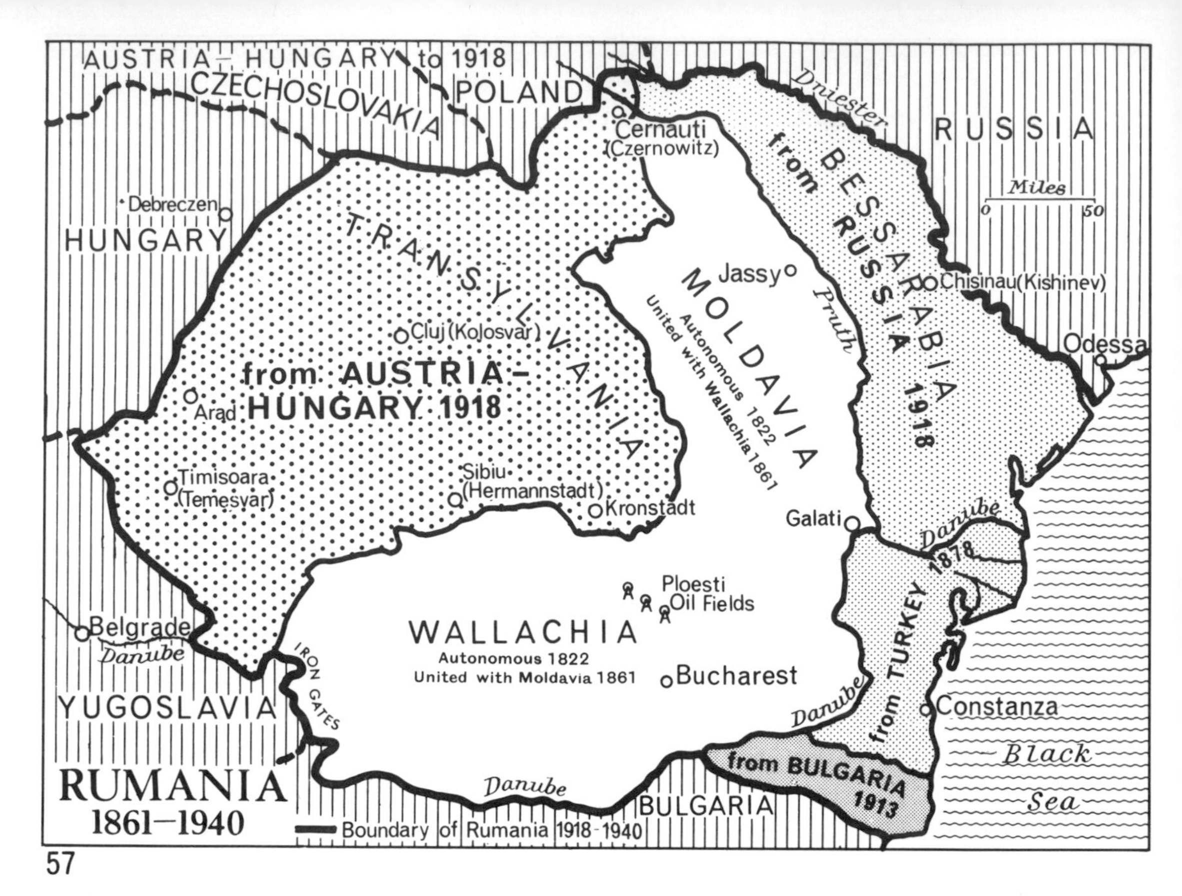

AUSTRIA-HUNGARY to 1918
CZECHOSLOVAKIA
POLAND
Dniester
Cernauti
(Czernowitz)
RUSSIA
from RUSSIA
BESSARABIA
1918
Miles
0
50
Debreczen
HUNGARY
TRANSYLVANIA
MOLDAVIA
Autonomous 1822
United with Wallachia 1861
Jassy
Pruth
Chisinau(Kishinev)
Cluj (Kolosvar)
from AUSTRIA-HUNGARY 1918
Arad
Odessa
Timisoara
(Temesvar)
Sibiu
(Hermannstadt)
Kronstadt
Galati
Danube
1878
Ploesti
Oil Fields
Belgrade
Danube
WALLACHIA
Autonomous 1822
United with Moldavia 1861
IRON GATES
from TURKEY
Bucharest
YUGOSLAVIA
Danube
Constanza
Black
Sea
from BULGARIA 1913
RUMANIA
1861–1940
Danube
BULGARIA
Boundary of Rumania 1918-1940

57

POLAND
RUSSIA since 1945
Cernauti(Czernowitz)
Dniester
RUSSIA
to RUSSIA 1940-1
and since 1945
BESSARABIA
Miles
0
50
Debreczen
HUNGARY
to HUNGARY
1940 – 1944
TRANSYLVANIA
Jassy
Pruth
Chisinau(Kishinev)
Oradea
Odessa
Cluj(Kolsovar)
Arad
Timisoara
(Temesvar)
Sibiu(Hermannstadt)
Brasov
(Kronstadt)
Galati
Danube
Ploesti Oil
Fields
Belgrade
Danube
IRON GATES
Craiova
Bucharest
YUGOSLAVIA
Danube
Constanza
Black
Sea
to BULGARIA
1940
RUMANIA
since 1940
Danube
BULGARIA
Boundary of Rumania since 1944

58

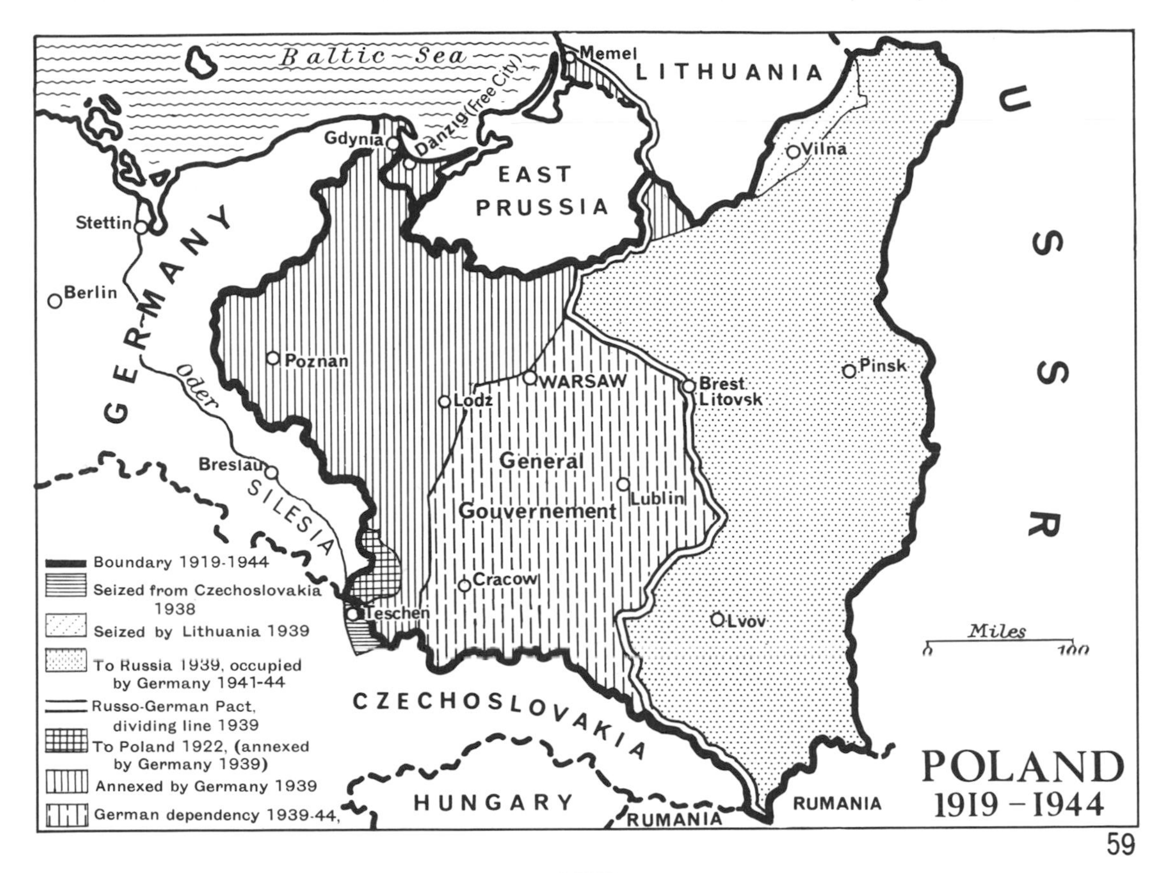
Baltic Sea
Memel
LITHUANIA
Danzig (free City)
Gdynia
EAST PRUSSIA
Vilna
Stettin
GERMANY
Berlin
U S S R
Poznan
WARSAW
Brest Litovsk
Pinsk
Lodz
Oder
General Gouvernement
Breslau
Lublin
SILESIA
Cracow
Teschen
Lvov
Miles
0
100
CZECHOSLOVAKIA
HUNGARY
RUMANIA
RUMANIA
Boundary 1919-1944
Seized from Czechoslovakia 1938
Seized by Lithuania 1939
To Russia 1939, occupied by Germany 1941-44
Russo-German Pact, dividing line 1939
To Poland 1922, (annexed by Germany 1939)
Annexed by Germany 1939
German dependency 1939-44,
POLAND
1919 – 1944

59

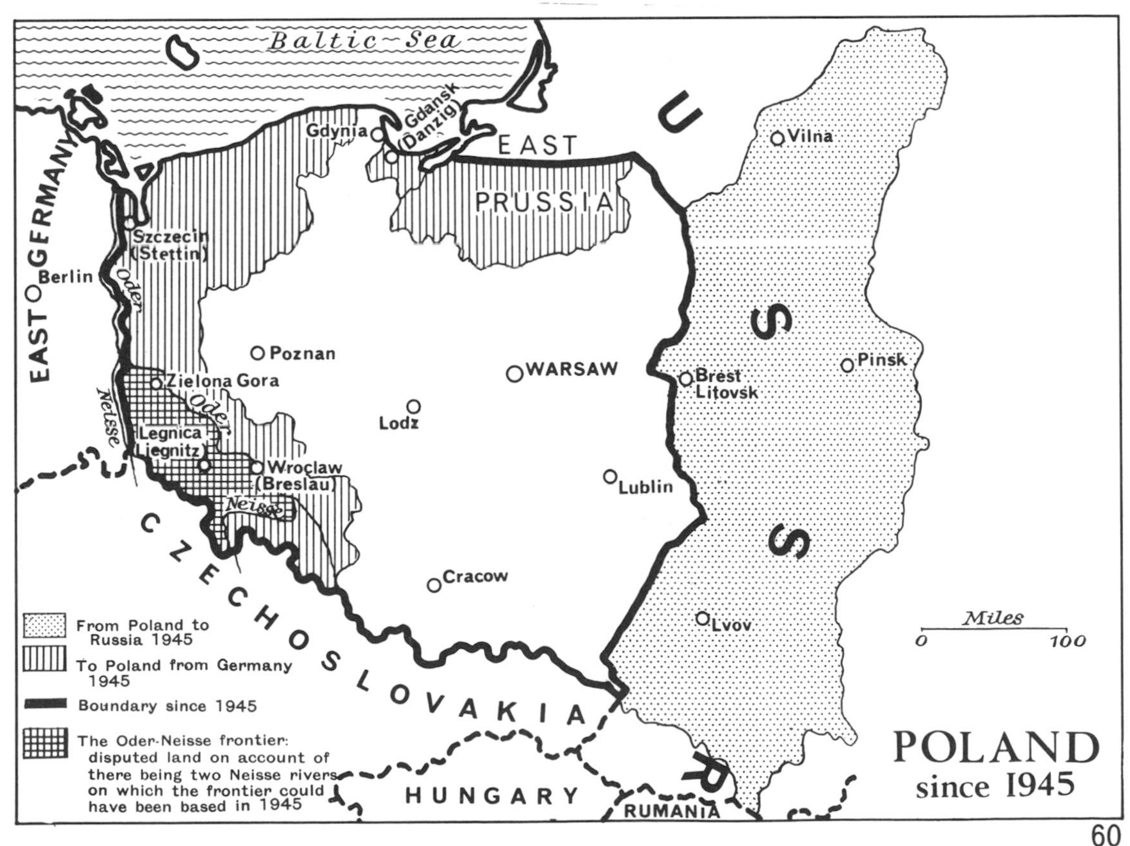
Baltic Sea
Gdynia
Gdansk (Danzig)
EAST
PRUSSIA
U S S R
Vilna
EAST GERMANY
Szczecin (Stettin)
Berlin
Oder
Poznan
WARSAW
Brest Litovsk
Pinsk
Zielona Gora
Oder
Lodz
Neisse
Legnica Liegnitz
Wroclaw (Breslau)
Lublin
Neisse
Cracow
CZECHOSLOVAKIA
Lvov
Miles
0
100
HUNGARY
RUMANIA
From Poland to Russia 1945
To Poland from Germany 1945
Boundary since 1945
The Oder-Neisse frontier: disputed land on account of there being two Neisse rivers on which the frontier could have been based in 1945
POLAND
since 1945

The PEOPLES of POLAND 1920-1939
Baltic Sea
LITHUANIA
Danzig (Free City)
Königsberg
EAST PRUSSIA
GERMANY
Vilna
White Russia
Minsk
U S S R
Poznan
Warsaw
Lodz
Lublin
Breslau
Cracow
Brest Litovsk
Pinsk
Lvov (Lemberg)
Ukraine
CZECHOSLOVAKIA
HUNGARY
RUMANIA
Miles 0 100
Poles 18¾ million
Isolated Polish communities
Curzon Line (British proposals for Polish frontier 1919)
MINORITIES
Ukrainians 3¾ million
Dispersed: Jews 3 million
White Russians 1 million
Germans 1 million
Lithuanians 700,000

61

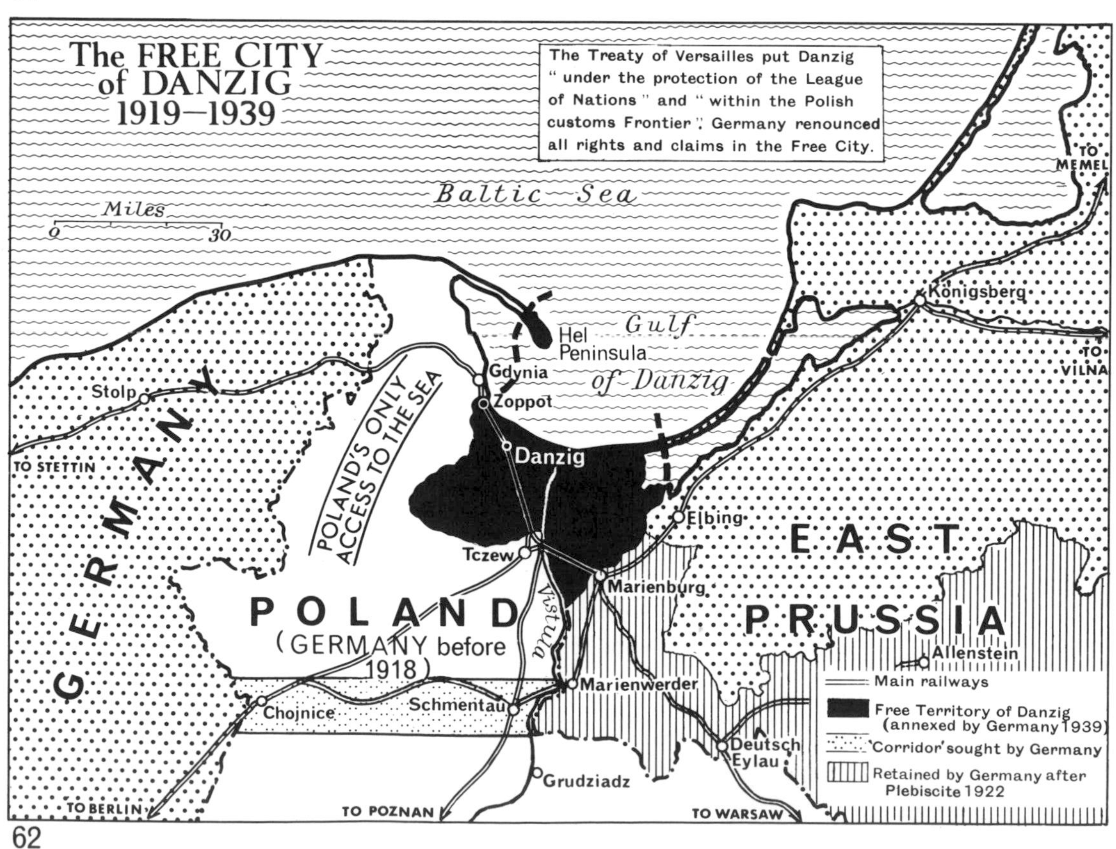
The FREE CITY of DANZIG 1919–1939
The Treaty of Versailles put Danzig "under the protection of the League of Nations" and "within the Polish customs Frontier". Germany renounced all rights and claims in the Free City.
Baltic Sea
Miles 0 30
TO MEMEL
Königsberg
TO VILNA
Hel Peninsula
Gulf of Danzig
Gdynia
Zoppot
Danzig
Stolp
TO STETTIN
GERMANY
POLAND'S ONLY ACCESS TO THE SEA
Elbing
EAST PRUSSIA
Tczew
Marienburg
Vistula
POLAND (GERMANY before 1918)
Allenstein
Marienwerder
Chojnice
Schmentau
Deutsch Eylau
Grudziadz
TO BERLIN
TO POZNAN
TO WARSAW
Main railways
Free Territory of Danzig (annexed by Germany 1939)
'Corridor' sought by Germany
Retained by Germany after Plebiscite 1922

62

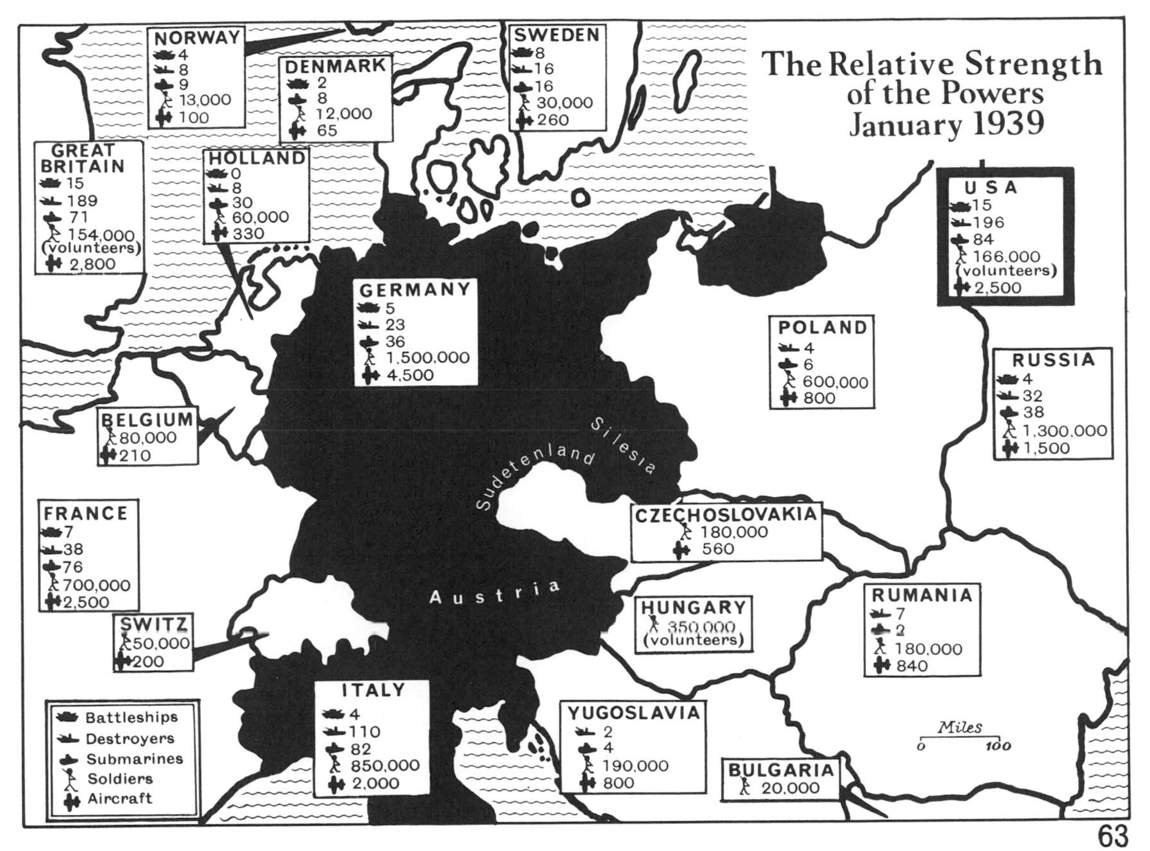
The Relative Strength of the Powers January 1939
NORWAY
4
8
9
13,000
100
SWEDEN
8
16
16
30,000
260
DENMARK
2
8
12,000
65
GREAT BRITAIN
15
189
71
154,000 (volunteers)
2,800
HOLLAND
0
8
30
60,000
330
USA
15
196
84
166,000 (volunteers)
2,500
GERMANY
5
23
36
1,500,000
4,500
POLAND
4
6
600,000
800
RUSSIA
4
32
38
1,300,000
1,500
BELGIUM
80,000
210
Silesia
Sudetenland
FRANCE
7
38
76
700,000
2,500
CZECHOSLOVAKIA
180,000
560
Austria
HUNGARY
350,000 (volunteers)
RUMANIA
7
2
180,000
840
SWITZ
50,000
200
ITALY
4
110
82
850,000
2,000
YUGOSLAVIA
2
4
190,000
800
BULGARIA
20,000
Battleships
Destroyers
Submarines
Soldiers
Aircraft
Miles
0
100

63

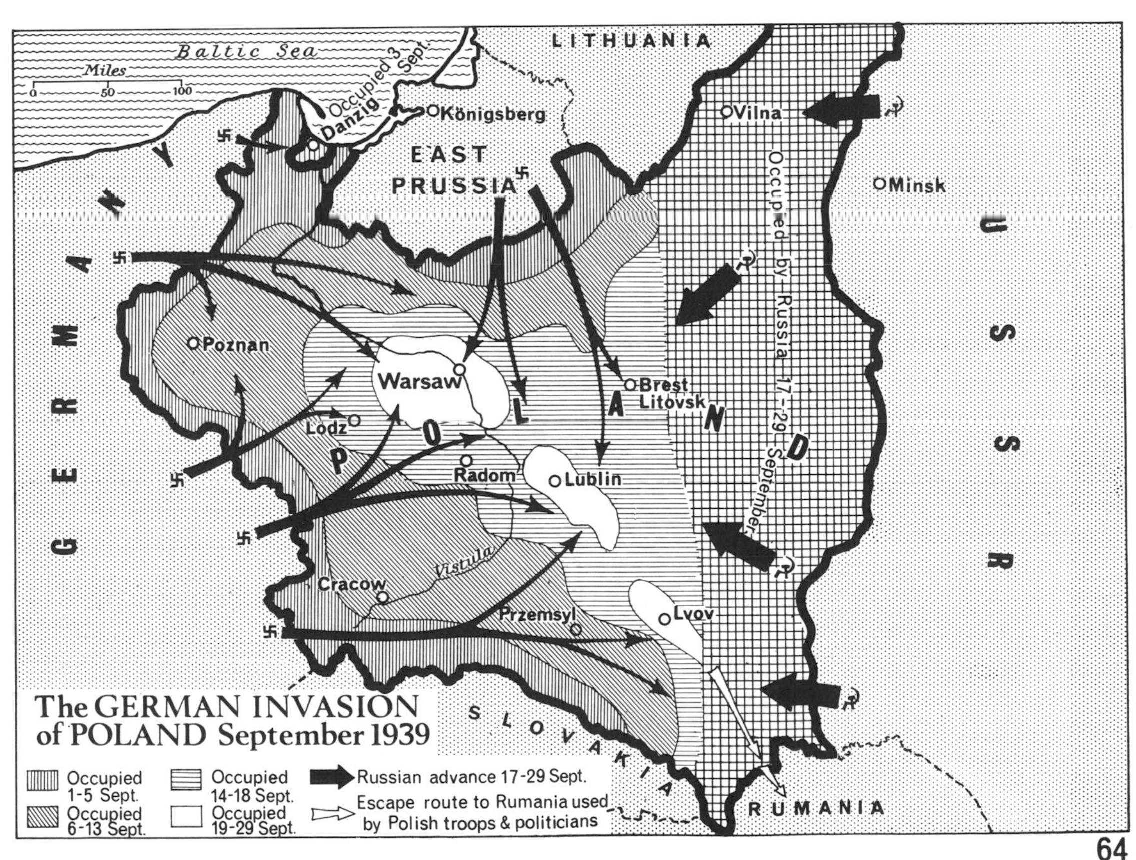
LITHUANIA
Baltic Sea
Miles
0
50
100
Occupied 3 Sept.
Danzig
Königsberg
EAST PRUSSIA
Vilna
Minsk
Occupied by Russia 17-29 September
GERMANY
USSR
POLAND
Poznan
Warsaw
Brest Litovsk
Lodz
Radom
Lublin
Vistula
Cracow
Przemsyl
Lvov
SLOVAKIA
RUMANIA
The GERMAN INVASION of POLAND September 1939
Occupied 1-5 Sept.
Occupied 6-13 Sept.
Occupied 14-18 Sept.
Occupied 19-29 Sept.
Russian advance 17-29 Sept.
Escape route to Rumania used by Polish troops & politicians

64

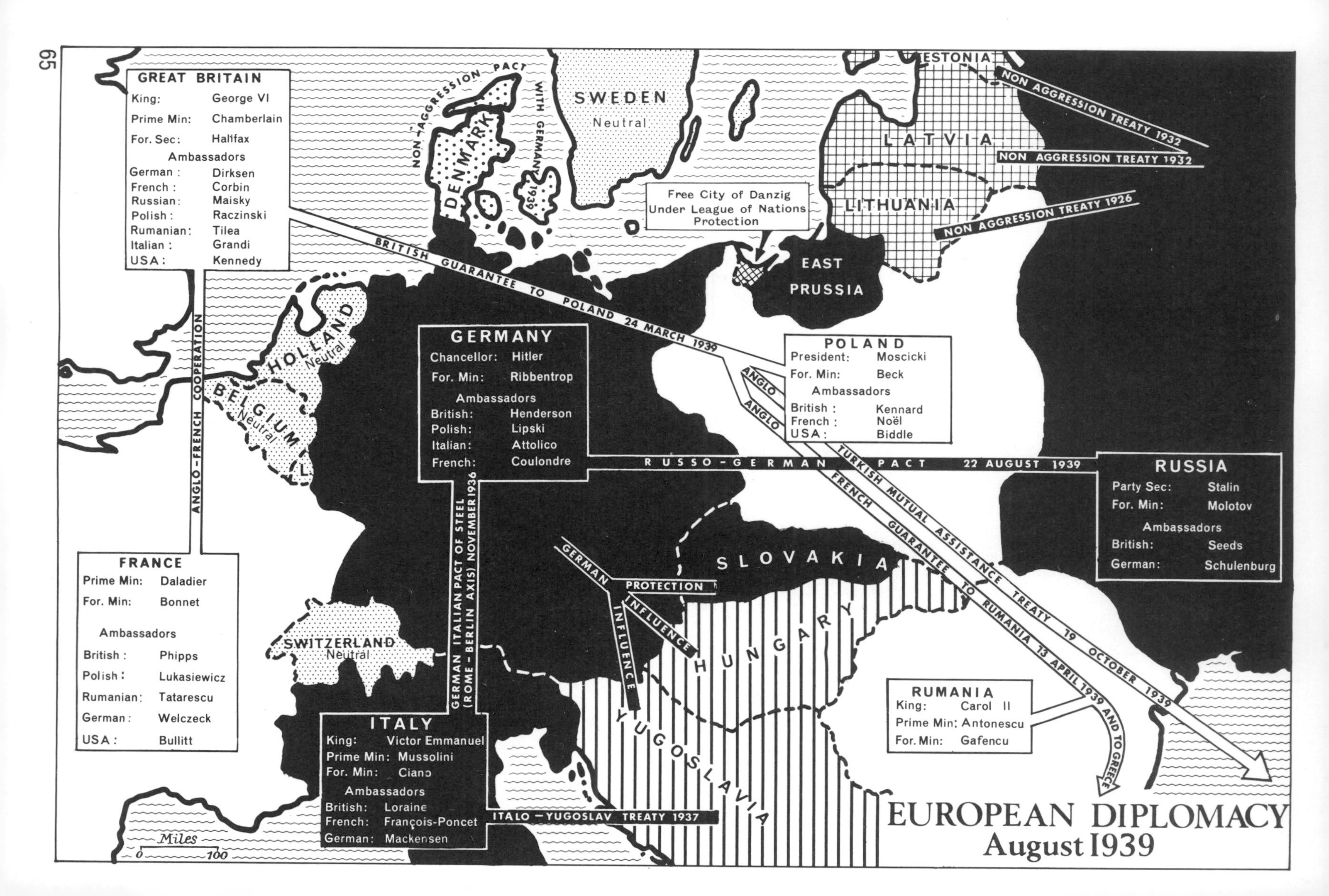
EUROPEAN DIPLOMACY
August 1939
GREAT BRITAIN
King: George VI
Prime Min: Chamberlain
For. Sec: Halifax
Ambassadors
German: Dirksen
French: Corbin
Russian: Maisky
Polish: Raczinski
Rumanian: Tilea
Italian: Grandi
USA: Kennedy
FRANCE
Prime Min: Daladier
For. Min: Bonnet
Ambassadors
British: Phipps
Polish: Lukasiewicz
Rumanian: Tatarescu
German: Welczeck
USA: Bullitt
GERMANY
Chancellor: Hitler
For. Min: Ribbentrop
Ambassadors
British: Henderson
Polish: Lipski
Italian: Attolico
French: Coulondre
POLAND
President: Moscicki
For. Min: Beck
Ambassadors
British: Kennard
French: Noël
USA: Biddle
RUSSIA
Party Sec: Stalin
For. Min: Molotov
Ambassadors
British: Seeds
German: Schulenburg
ITALY
King: Victor Emmanuel
Prime Min: Mussolini
For. Min: Ciano
Ambassadors
British: Loraine
French: François-Poncet
German: Mackensen
RUMANIA
King: Carol II
Prime Min: Antonescu
For. Min: Gafencu
Free City of Danzig
Under League of Nations
Protection
SWEDEN
Neutral
DENMARK
NON AGGRESSION PACT WITH GERMANY 1939
ESTONIA
LATVIA
LITHUANIA
EAST PRUSSIA
NON AGGRESSION TREATY 1932
NON AGGRESSION TREATY 1932
NON AGGRESSION TREATY 1926
HOLLAND
Neutral
BELGIUM
Neutral
SWITZERLAND
Neutral
SLOVAKIA
HUNGARY
YUGOSLAVIA
ANGLO-FRENCH COOPERATION
BRITISH GUARANTEE TO POLAND 24 MARCH 1939
RUSSO-GERMAN PACT 22 AUGUST 1939
ANGLO TURKISH MUTUAL ASSISTANCE TREATY 19 OCTOBER 1939
ANGLO FRENCH GUARANTEE TO RUMANIA 13 APRIL 1939 AND TO GREECE
GERMAN ITALIAN PACT OF STEEL
(ROME - BERLIN AXIS) NOVEMBER 1936
ITALO-YUGOSLAV TREATY 1937
GERMAN
PROTECTION
INFLUENCE
INFLUENCE
Miles
0
100

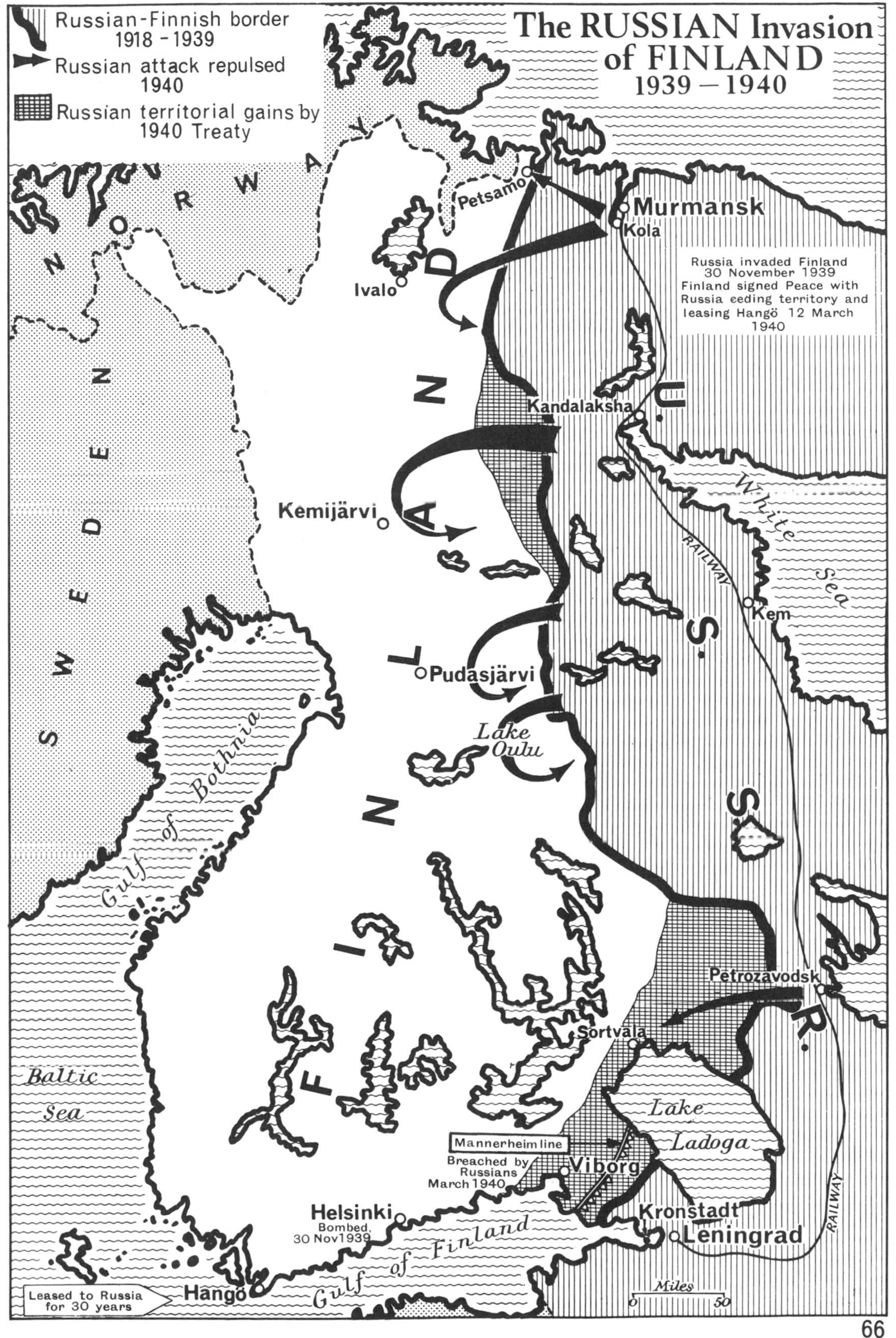

The RUSSIAN Invasion of FINLAND
1939 – 1940
Russian-Finnish border 1918 - 1939
Russian attack repulsed 1940
Russian territorial gains by 1940 Treaty
Russia invaded Finland 30 November 1939
Finland signed Peace with Russia ceding territory and leasing Hangö 12 March 1940
NORWAY
SWEDEN
FINLAND
U.S.S.R.
Petsamo
Murmansk
Kola
Ivalo
Kandalaksha
Kemijärvi
White Sea
RAILWAY
Kem
Pudasjärvi
Lake Oulu
Gulf of Bothnia
Petrozavodsk
Sortvala
Baltic Sea
Lake Ladoga
Mannerheim line
Breached by Russians March 1940
Viborg
Helsinki
Bombed 30 Nov 1939
Kronstadt
Leningrad
Gulf of Finland
Hangö
Leased to Russia for 30 years
Miles
0
50

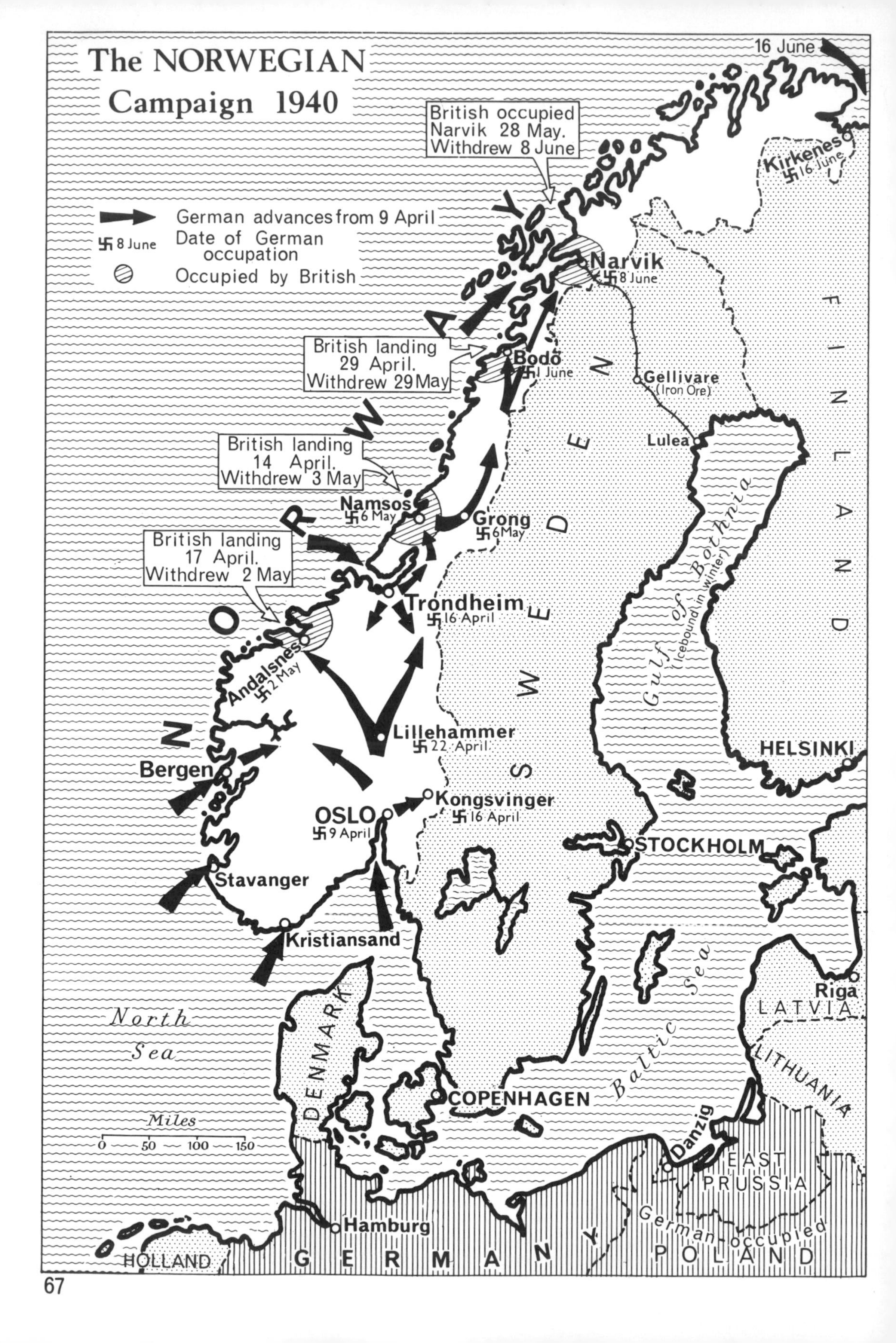

The NORWEGIAN Campaign 1940
German advances from 9 April
8 June
Date of German occupation
Occupied by British
British occupied Narvik 28 May. Withdrew 8 June
16 June
Kirkenes
16 June
Narvik
8 June
British landing 29 April. Withdrew 29 May
Bodö
1 June
Gellivare
(Iron Ore)
Lulea
British landing 14 April. Withdrew 3 May
Namsos
6 May
Grong
6 May
British landing 17 April. Withdrew 2 May
Trondheim
16 April
Andalsnes
2 May
Lillehammer
22 April
Bergen
OSLO
9 April
Kongsvinger
16 April
Stavanger
Kristiansand
NORWAY
SWEDEN
FINLAND
Gulf of Bothnia
(Icebound in winter)
HELSINKI
STOCKHOLM
Riga
LATVIA
LITHUANIA
North Sea
Baltic Sea
DENMARK
COPENHAGEN
Miles
0 50 100 150
Danzig
EAST PRUSSIA
German occupied POLAND
Hamburg
HOLLAND
GERMANY

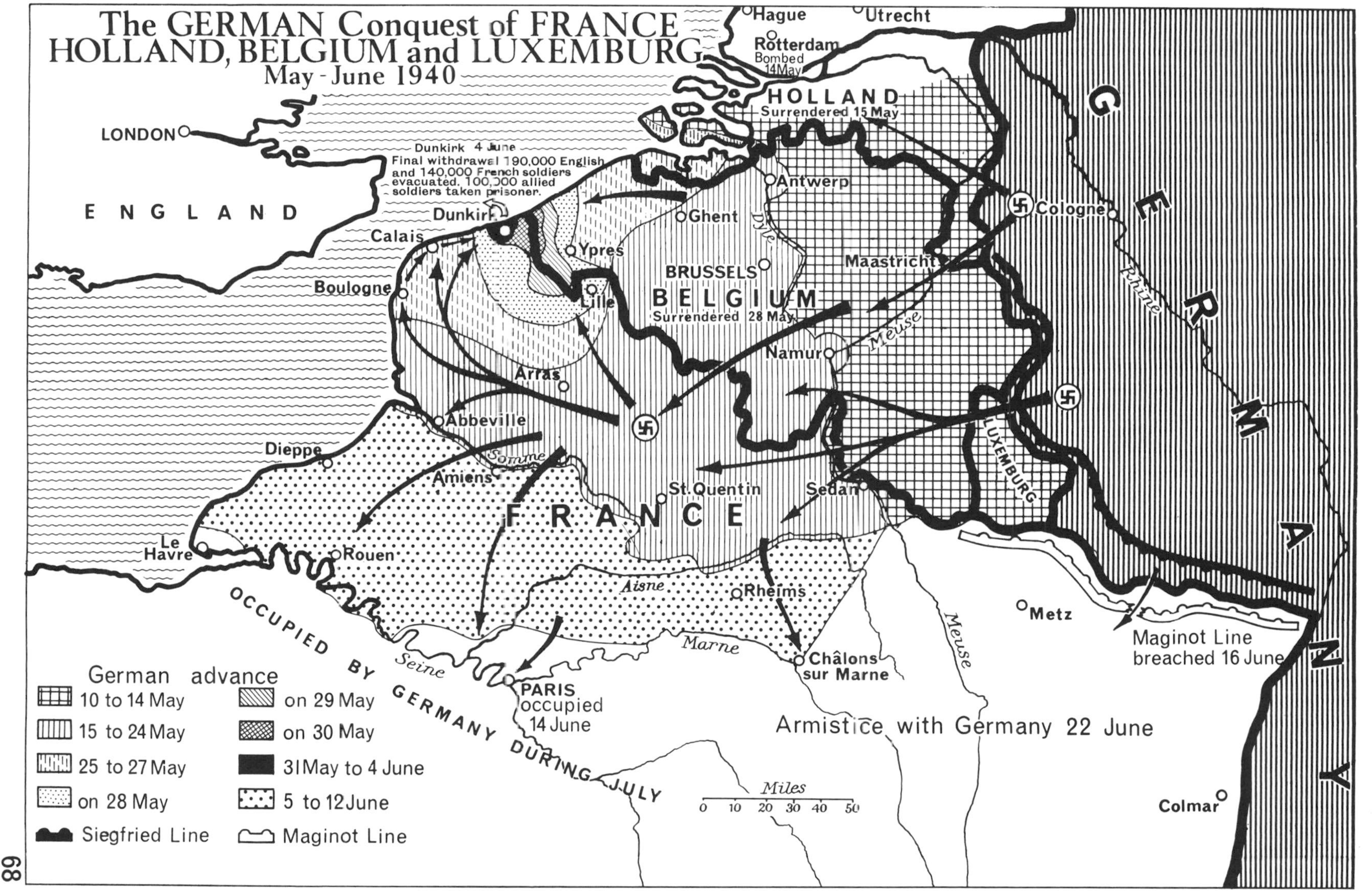
The GERMAN Conquest of FRANCE
HOLLAND, BELGIUM and LUXEMBURG
May - June 1940
LONDON
ENGLAND
Dunkirk 4 June
Final withdrawal 190,000 English and 140,000 French soldiers evacuated. 100,000 allied soldiers taken prisoner.
Dunkirk
Calais
Boulogne
Hague
Utrecht
Rotterdam
Bombed 14May
HOLLAND
Surrendered 15 May
Antwerp
Ghent
Dyle
Ypres
BRUSSELS
BELGIUM
Surrendered 28 May
Lille
Maastricht
Cologne
Rhine
Meuse
Namur
Arras
Abbeville
Dieppe
Somme
Amiens
St.Quentin
Sedan
LUXEMBURG
FRANCE
Le Havre
Rouen
Aisne
Rheims
Metz
Maginot Line breached 16 June
GERMANY
Marne
Châlons sur Marne
Meuse
Seine
PARIS
occupied 14 June
OCCUPIED BY GERMANY DURING JULY
Armistice with Germany 22 June
Miles
0 10 20 30 40 50
Colmar
German advance
10 to 14 May
15 to 24 May
25 to 27 May
on 28 May
on 29 May
on 30 May
31 May to 4 June
5 to 12 June
Siegfried Line
Maginot Line

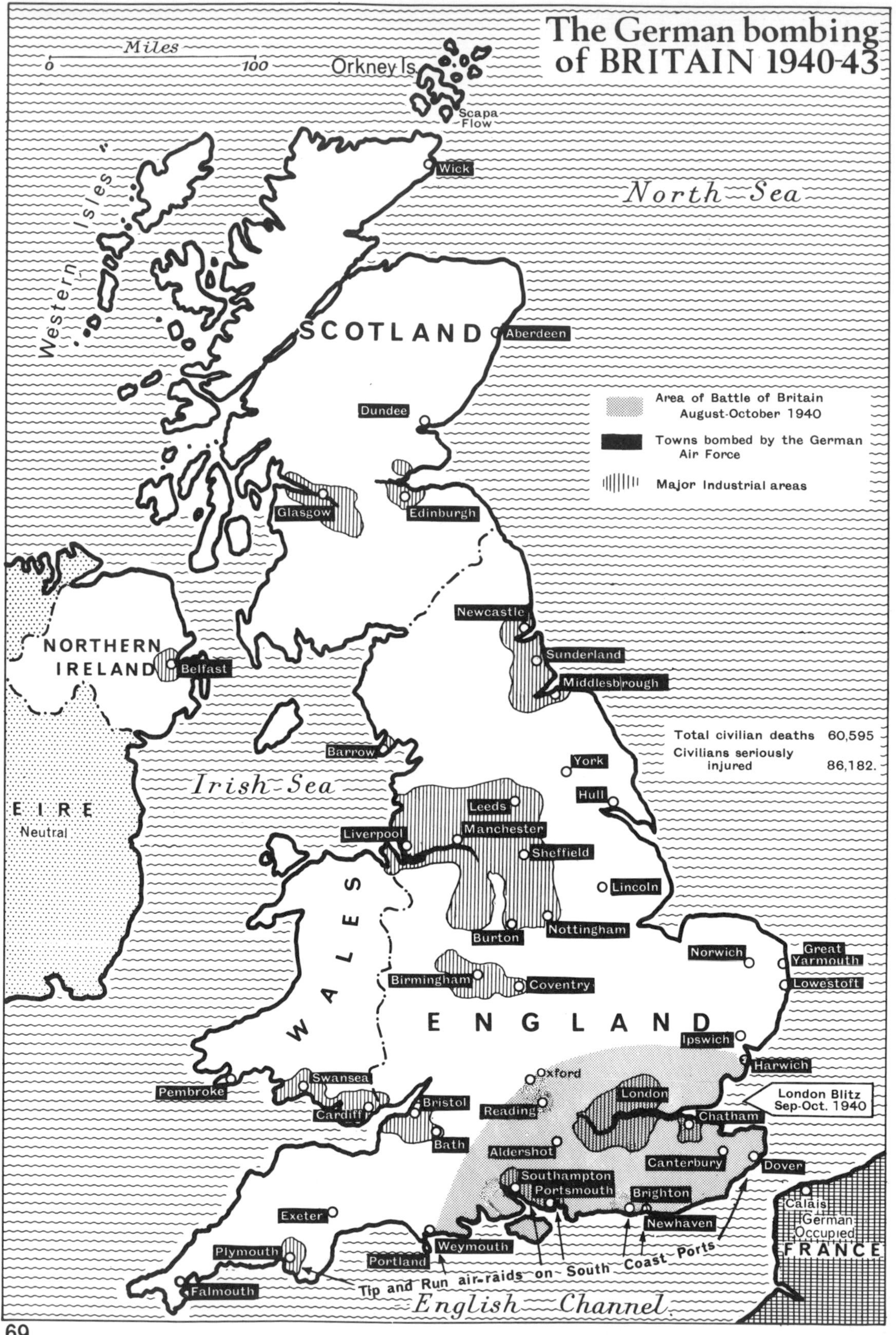
The German bombing of BRITAIN 1940-43
Miles
0
100
Orkney Is.
Scapa Flow
Wick
North Sea
Western Isles
SCOTLAND
Aberdeen
Dundee
Area of Battle of Britain August-October 1940
Towns bombed by the German Air Force
Major Industrial areas
Glasgow
Edinburgh
Newcastle
NORTHERN IRELAND
Belfast
Sunderland
Middlesbrough
Total civilian deaths 60,595
Civilians seriously injured 86,182.
Barrow
York
Irish Sea
Hull
EIRE
Neutral
Leeds
Liverpool
Manchester
Sheffield
Lincoln
WALES
Burton
Nottingham
Norwich
Great Yarmouth
Birmingham
Coventry
Lowestoft
ENGLAND
Ipswich
Harwich
Oxford
Swansea
London
London Blitz Sep-Oct. 1940
Pembroke
Bristol
Reading
Chatham
Cardiff
Bath
Aldershot
Canterbury
Dover
Southampton
Portsmouth
Brighton
Calais
German Occupied
Exeter
Newhaven
FRANCE
Weymouth
Plymouth
Portland
Tip and Run air-raids on South Coast Ports
Falmouth
English Channel

The GERMAN CONQUEST of YUGOSLAVIA and GREECE
6-30 April 1941

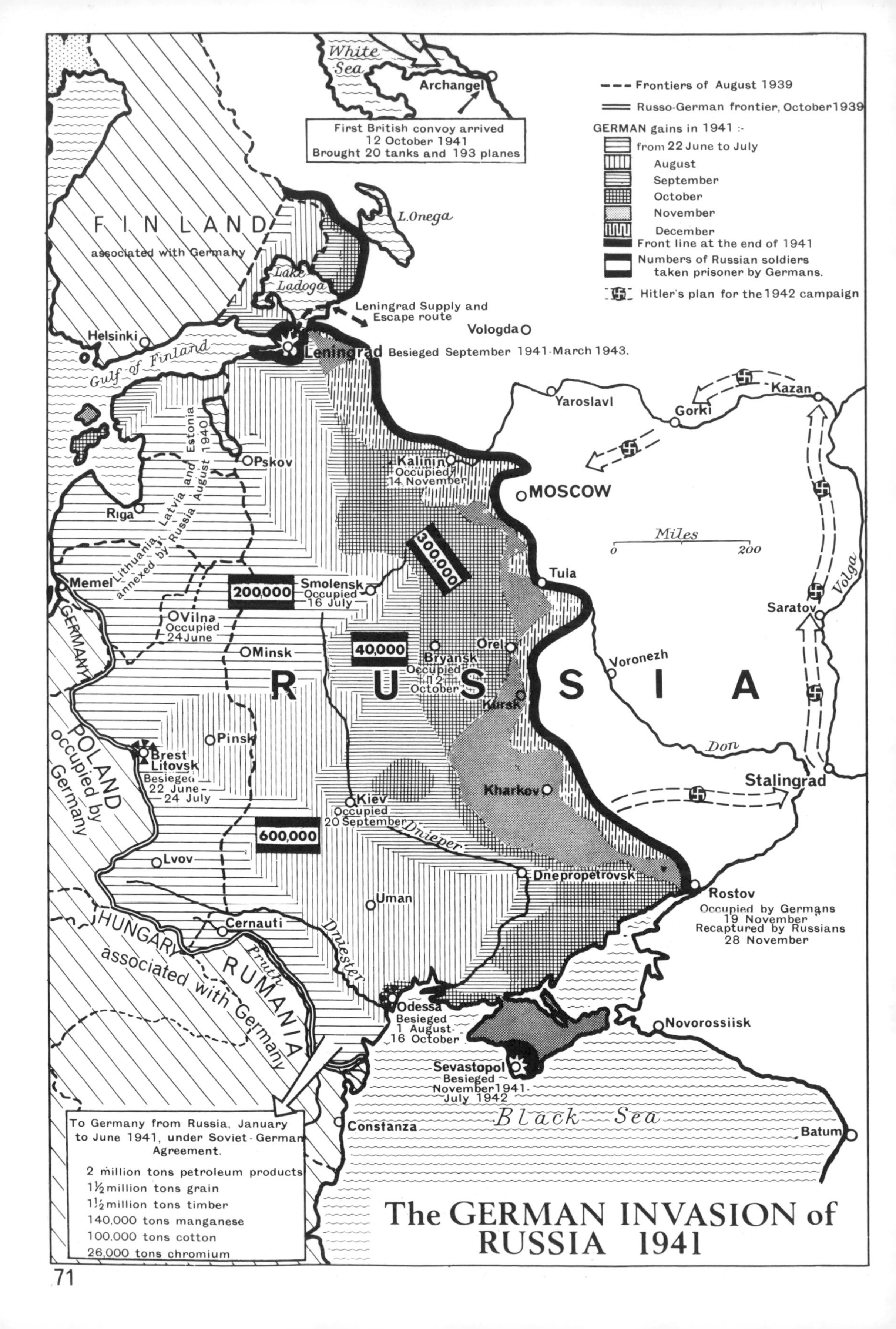
The GERMAN INVASION of RUSSIA 1941
Frontiers of August 1939
Russo-German frontier, October 1939
GERMAN gains in 1941 :-
from 22 June to July
August
September
October
November
December
Front line at the end of 1941
Numbers of Russian soldiers taken prisoner by Germans.
Hitler's plan for the 1942 campaign
White Sea
Archangel
First British convoy arrived 12 October 1941 Brought 20 tanks and 193 planes
FINLAND associated with Germany
L.Onega
Lake Ladoga
Leningrad Supply and Escape route
Vologda
Helsinki
Gulf of Finland
Leningrad Besieged September 1941-March 1943.
Yaroslavl
Gorki
Kazan
Lithuania, Latvia and Estonia annexed by Russia August 1940
Pskov
Kalinin Occupied 14 November
MOSCOW
Riga
Miles
0
200
300,000
Tula
Memel
200,000
Smolensk Occupied 16 July
Volga
Saratov
GERMANY
Vilna Occupied 24 June
Minsk
40,000
Orel
Bryansk Occupied 12 October
Voronezh
RUSSIA
Kursk
POLAND occupied by Germany
Pinsk
Brest Litovsk Besieged 22 June-24 July
Don
Stalingrad
Kharkov
Kiev Occupied 20 September
Dnieper
600,000
Lvov
Dnepropetrovsk
Rostov
Occupied by Germans 19 November
Recaptured by Russians 28 November
Uman
Cernauti
HUNGARY associated with Germany
Pruth
RUMANIA
Dniester
Odessa Besieged 1 August-16 October
Novorossiisk
Sevastopol Besieged November 1941-July 1942
Black Sea
Constanza
Batum
To Germany from Russia, January to June 1941, under Soviet-German Agreement.
2 million tons petroleum products
1½ million tons grain
1½ million tons timber
140,000 tons manganese
100,000 tons cotton
26,000 tons chromium

The GERMAN MASTERY
of EUROPE
1942
GREAT BRITAIN
EIRE
London
North Sea
NORWAY
Oslo
SWEDEN
Stockholm
FINLAND
Leningrad
ESTONIA
LATVIA
Riga
LITHUANIA
DENMARK
Copenhagen
Baltic Sea
Danzig
HOLLAND
BELGIUM
LUXEMBURG
Channel Islands Occupied 1940-45 by Germany
Paris
FRANCE
Vichy
SWITZERLAND
GERMANY
Berlin
Prague
Vienna
POLAND
Warsaw
Brest Litovsk
Lvov
Minsk
Kiev
Dnieper
Moscow
RUSSIA
Stalingrad
Rostov
SLOVAKIA
Budapest
HUNGARY
RUMANIA
Bucharest
YUGOSLAVIA
Belgrade
BULGARIA
Sofia
ALBANIA
GREECE
TURKEY
Black Sea
SPAIN
Corsica
Sardinia
Rome
ITALY
Sicily
Mediterranean Sea
ALGERIA
Axis Powers in 1939
Powers co-operating with Axis
Territory occupied by Axis
France - Vichy Governed
Neutrals
Unconquered
Miles
0
300

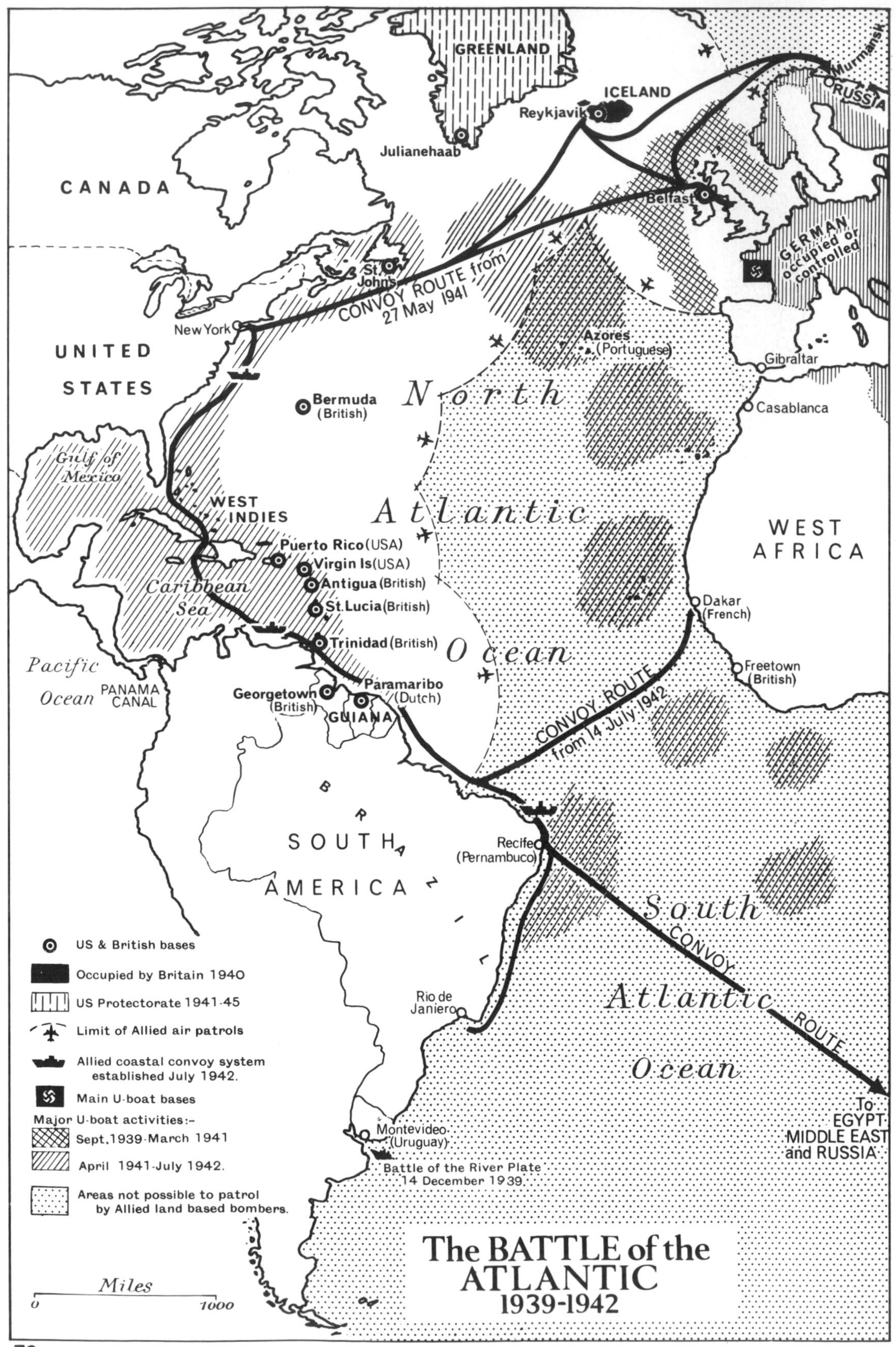

GREENLAND
ICELAND
Reykjavik
Julianehaab
Murmansk
RUSSIA
CANADA
Belfast
GERMAN occupied or controlled
St. John's
CONVOY ROUTE from 27 May 1941
New York
UNITED STATES
Azores (Portuguese)
Gibraltar
Casablanca
Bermuda (British)
North Atlantic Ocean
Gulf of Mexico
WEST INDIES
WEST AFRICA
Puerto Rico (USA)
Virgin Is (USA)
Antigua (British)
St. Lucia (British)
Caribbean Sea
Dakar (French)
Trinidad (British)
Freetown (British)
Pacific Ocean
PANAMA CANAL
Georgetown (British)
Paramaribo (Dutch)
GUIANA
CONVOY ROUTE from 14 July 1942
BRAZIL
SOUTH AMERICA
Recife (Pernambuco)
South Atlantic Ocean
CONVOY ROUTE
Rio de Janiero
To EGYPT MIDDLE EAST and RUSSIA
Montevideo (Uruguay)
Battle of the River Plate 14 December 1939
US & British bases
Occupied by Britain 1940
US Protectorate 1941-45
Limit of Allied air patrols
Allied coastal convoy system established July 1942.
Main U-boat bases
Major U-boat activities:-
Sept. 1939-March 1941
April 1941-July 1942.
Areas not possible to patrol by Allied land based bombers.
Miles
0
1000
The BATTLE of the ATLANTIC 1939-1942

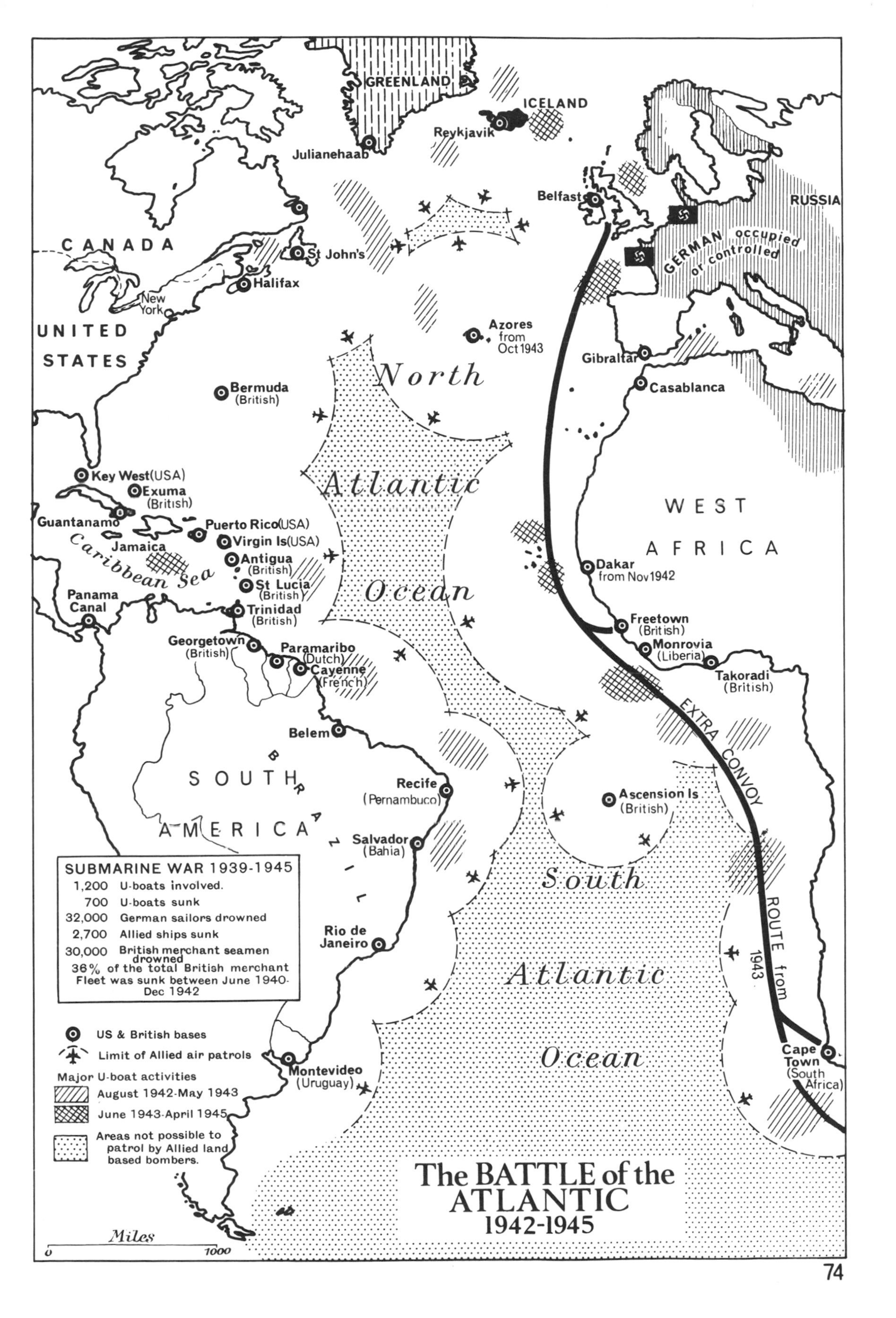
The BATTLE of the ATLANTIC 1942-1945
SUBMARINE WAR 1939-1945
1,200 U-boats involved.
700 U-boats sunk
32,000 German sailors drowned
2,700 Allied ships sunk
30,000 British merchant seamen drowned
36% of the total British merchant Fleet was sunk between June 1940-Dec 1942
US & British bases
Limit of Allied air patrols
Major U-boat activities
August 1942-May 1943
June 1943-April 1945
Areas not possible to patrol by Allied land based bombers.
Miles
0
1000
GREENLAND
ICELAND
Reykjavik
Julianehaab
CANADA
UNITED STATES
St John's
Halifax
New York
Belfast
RUSSIA
GERMAN occupied or controlled
Azores from Oct 1943
Gibraltar
Casablanca
North Atlantic Ocean
Bermuda (British)
Key West (USA)
Exuma (British)
Guantanamo
Jamaica
Puerto Rico (USA)
Virgin Is (USA)
Antigua (British)
St Lucia (British)
Caribbean Sea
Panama Canal
Trinidad (British)
Georgetown (British)
Paramaribo (Dutch)
Cayenne (French)
WEST AFRICA
Dakar from Nov 1942
Freetown (British)
Monrovia (Liberia)
Takoradi (British)
EXTRA CONVOY ROUTE from 1943
Belem
SOUTH AMERICA
BRAZIL
Recife (Pernambuco)
Salvador (Bahia)
Ascension Is (British)
South Atlantic Ocean
Rio de Janeiro
Montevideo (Uruguay)
Cape Town (South Africa)

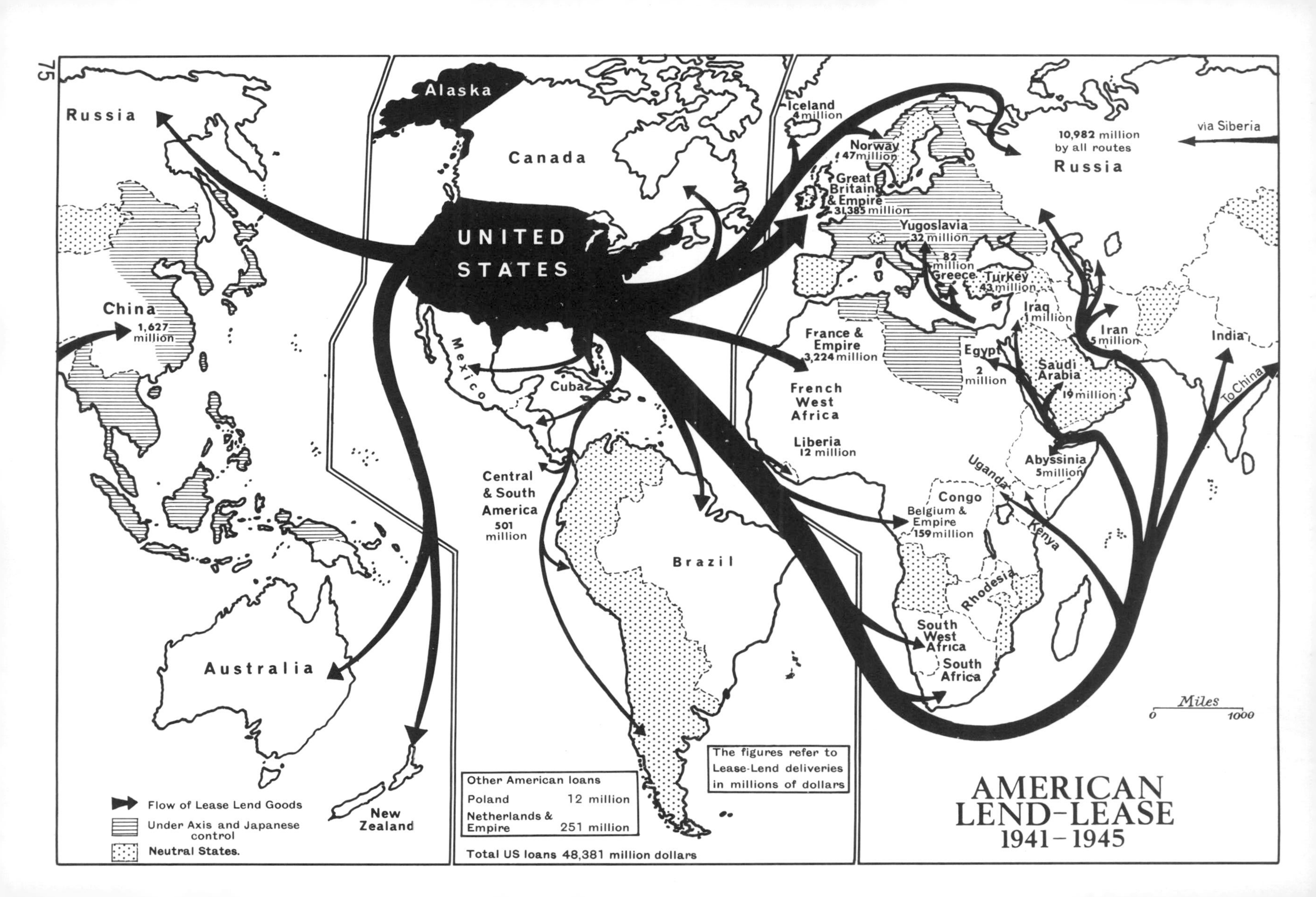
AMERICAN
LEND-LEASE
1941–1945
Russia
China
1,627 million
Australia
New Zealand
Alaska
Canada
UNITED STATES
Mexico
Cuba
Central & South America
501 million
Brazil
Iceland
4 million
Norway
47 million
Great Britain & Empire
31,385 million
Yugoslavia
32 million
82 million
Greece
Turkey
43 million
10,982 million
by all routes
Russia
via Siberia
Iraq
1 million
Iran
5 million
India
To China
Egypt
2 million
Saudi Arabia
19 million
France & Empire
3,224 million
French West Africa
Liberia
12 million
Abyssinia
5 million
Uganda
Kenya
Congo
Belgium & Empire
159 million
Rhodesia
South West Africa
South Africa
Miles
0
1000
Flow of Lease Lend Goods
Under Axis and Japanese control
Neutral States.
Other American loans
Poland 12 million
Netherlands & Empire 251 million
Total US loans 48,381 million dollars
The figures refer to Lease-Lend deliveries in millions of dollars

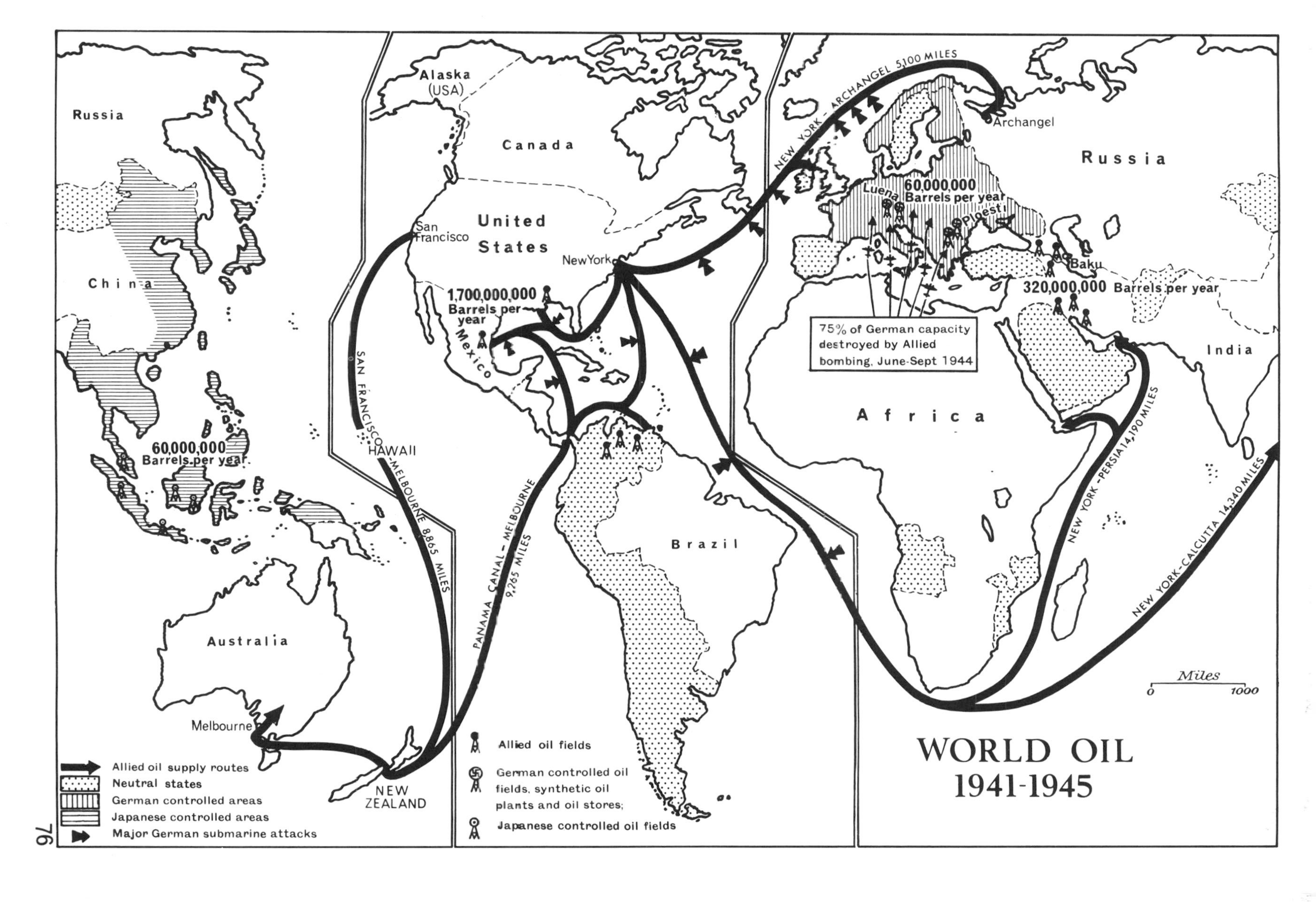
WORLD OIL
1941-1945
Russia
China
60,000,000
Barrels per year
Australia
Melbourne
NEW
ZEALAND
Alaska
(USA)
Canada
United
States
San
Francisco
NewYork
1,700,000,000
Barrels per
year
Mexico
Brazil
SAN FRANCISCO-HAWAII-MELBOURNE 8,865 MILES
PANAMA CANAL - MELBOURNE
9,265 MILES
NEW YORK - ARCHANGEL 5,100 MILES
Archangel
Russia
Luena
60,000,000
Barrels per year
Ploesti
Baku
320,000,000 Barrels per year
75% of German capacity
destroyed by Allied
bombing, June-Sept 1944
India
Africa
NEW YORK - PERSIA 14,190 MILES
NEW YORK-CALCUTTA 14,340 MILES
Miles
0
1000
Allied oil supply routes
Neutral states
German controlled areas
Japanese controlled areas
Major German submarine attacks
Allied oil fields
German controlled oil fields, synthetic oil plants and oil stores;
Japanese controlled oil fields

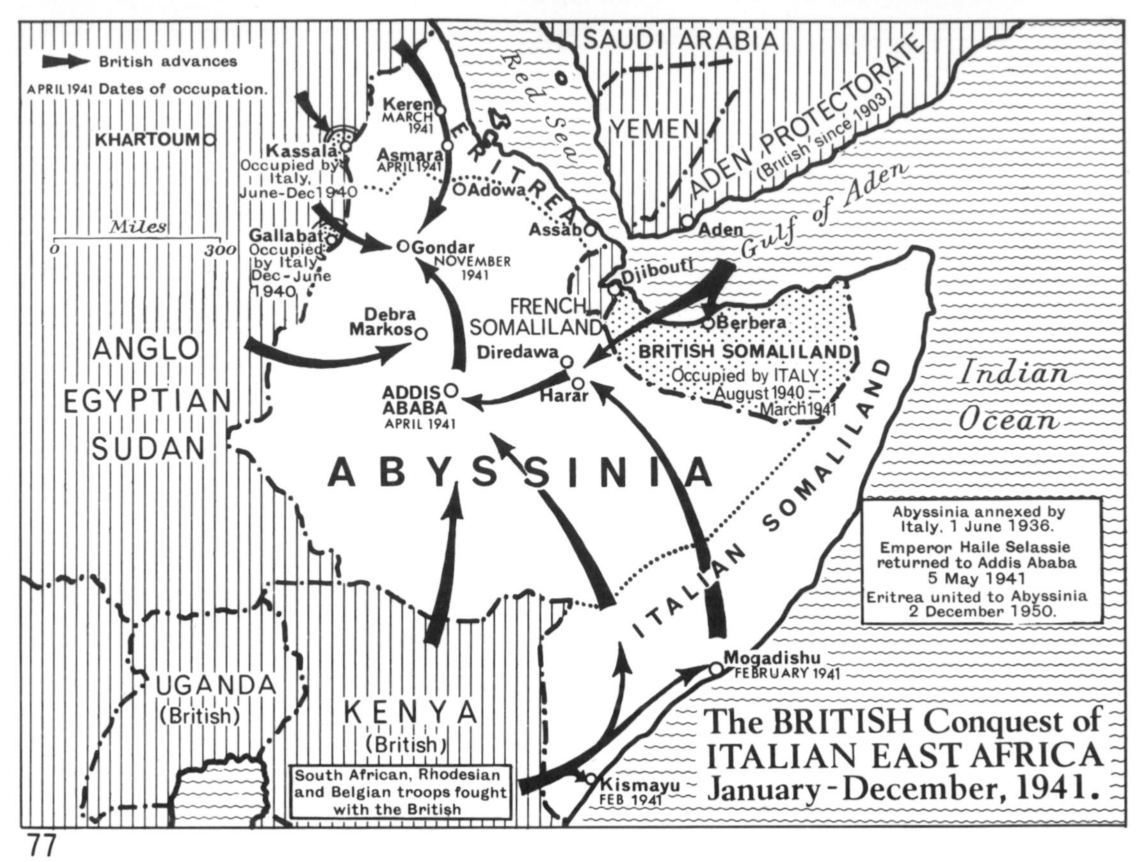

The BRITISH Conquest of ITALIAN EAST AFRICA January - December, 1941.

77

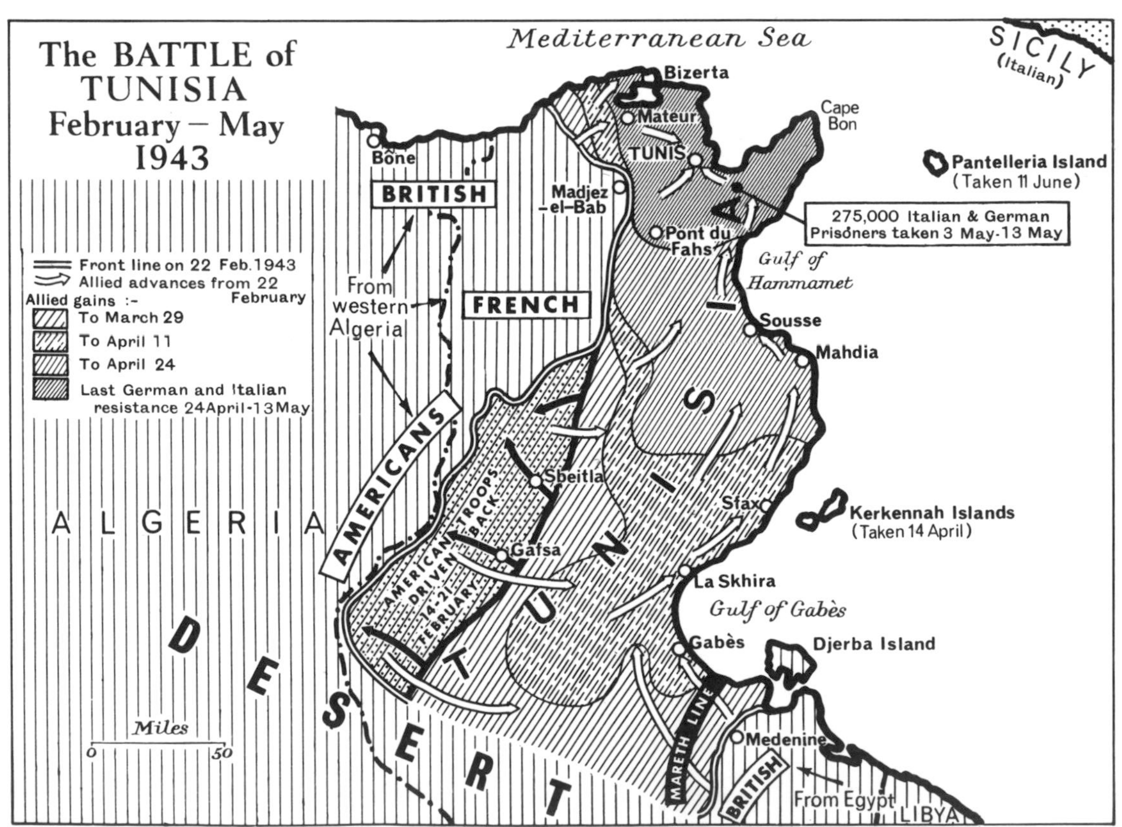

The BATTLE of TUNISIA February – May 1943

78

The ALLIED INVASION of ITALY 1943 – 1945
GERMANY
SWITZERLAND
Brenner Pass
Mussolini executed by Italian partisans 28 April 1945
Vipiteno
US troops met 4 May
Dongo
L. Como
New Zealand troops entered 2 May 1945
Trieste
Salo
L. Garda
Milan 26 April
Verona
Venice 29 April
YUGOSLAVIA
Turin
Allied Advances 20-30 April 1945
Bologna
Genoa
Ravenna
US Advance 20-30 April 1945
WINTER LINE JAN-APRIL 1945
Zara
Florence
Adriatic Sea
Liberated by Free French forces September 1943
by 4 August
Elba Occupied 18 June
CORSICA
Revolt of Resistance Movement, summer 1943
Termoli
ROME Entered 4 June
by 9 June
WINTER LINE 1943-44
Monte Cassino 18 May
Anzio Beachhead 22 Jan 22 May 1944
by 8 October
Bari
Naples
Brindisi
Salerno
by 14 Sept
Taranto
by 25 September
Occupied by Anglo-American troops, autumn 1943
Tyrrhenian Sea
SARDINIA
9 Sept 1943
9 Sept 1943
by 14 Sept.
Mussolini overthrown 25 July 1943
Italy surrendered 3 September 1943
Germans occupied Italy September 1943
Italy declared war on Germany 13 Oct 1943
Germans in Italy surrendered 29 April 1945
Entered 17 Aug.
Messina
Palermo
3 Sept
Miles
0
100
by 17 August
by 23 July
Catania
Licata
by 15 July
Syracuse
AMERICANS
ANGLO-AMERICAN occupation
Tunis
See Map 78
10 July 1943
Landings from NORTH AFRICA
BRITISH

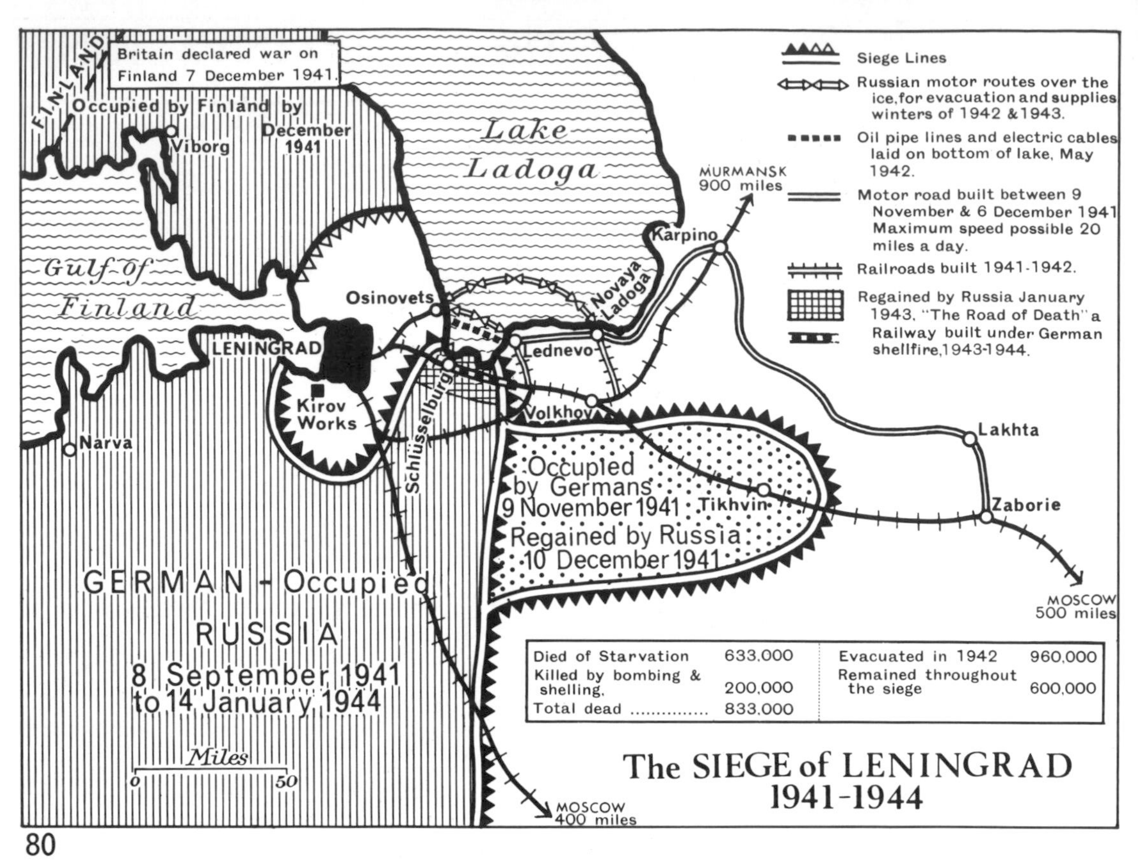

Died of Starvation	633,000	Evacuated in 1942	960,000
Killed by bombing & shelling.	200,000	Remained throughout the siege	600,000
Total dead	833,000		

The SIEGE of LENINGRAD 1941-1944

80

The RUSSIAN ADVANCE 1942-1944

81

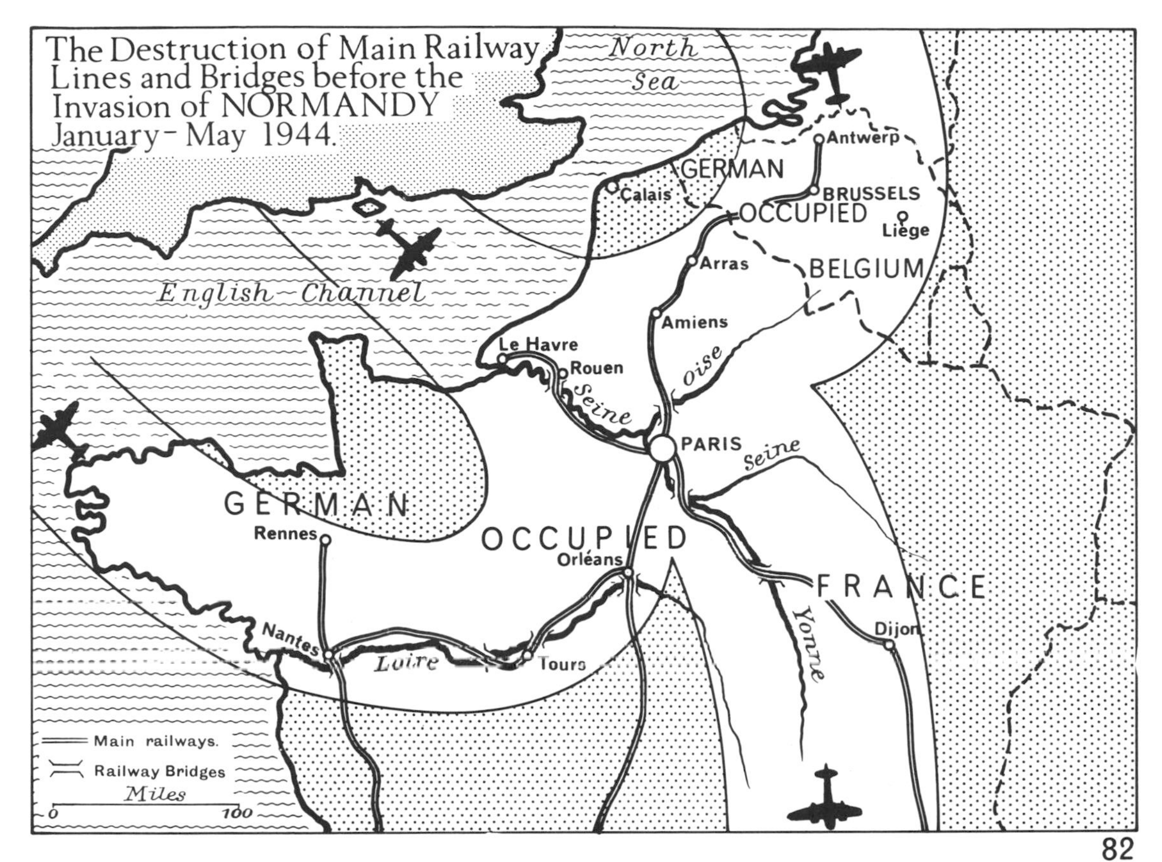
The Destruction of Main Railway Lines and Bridges before the Invasion of NORMANDY January - May 1944.
North Sea
Antwerp
GERMAN
Calais
BRUSSELS
OCCUPIED
Liège
Arras
BELGIUM
English Channel
Amiens
Le Havre
Rouen
Oise
Seine
PARIS
Seine
GERMAN
OCCUPIED
Rennes
Orléans
FRANCE
Yonne
Nantes
Dijon
Loire
Tours
Main railways.
Railway Bridges
Miles
0
100

82

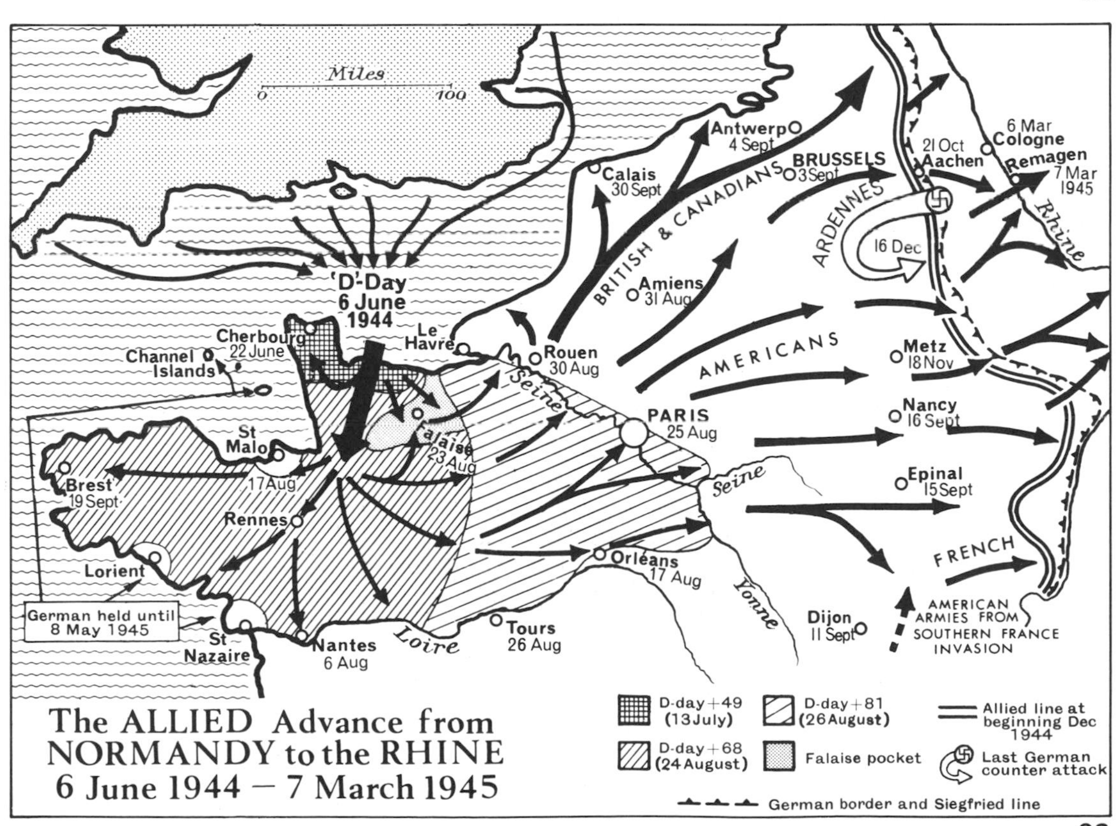
Miles
0
100
Antwerp
4 Sept
6 Mar
Cologne
21 Oct
Aachen
Remagen
7 Mar 1945
Calais
30 Sept
BRUSSELS
3 Sept
BRITISH & CANADIANS
ARDENNES
Rhine
16 Dec
'D'-Day
6 June
1944
Amiens
31 Aug
Cherbourg
22 June
Channel Islands
Le Havre
Rouen
30 Aug
AMERICANS
Metz
18 Nov
Seine
St Malo
Falaise
23 Aug
PARIS
25 Aug
Nancy
16 Sept
Brest
19 Sept
17 Aug
Seine
Epinal
15 Sept
Rennes
Lorient
Orléans
17 Aug
FRENCH
German held until
8 May 1945
Yonne
St Nazaire
Nantes
6 Aug
Loire
Tours
26 Aug
Dijon
11 Sept
AMERICAN ARMIES FROM SOUTHERN FRANCE INVASION
The ALLIED Advance from NORMANDY to the RHINE 6 June 1944 – 7 March 1945
D-day+49 (13 July)
D-day+81 (26 August)
Allied line at beginning Dec 1944
D-day+68 (24 August)
Falaise pocket
Last German counter attack
German border and Siegfried line

83

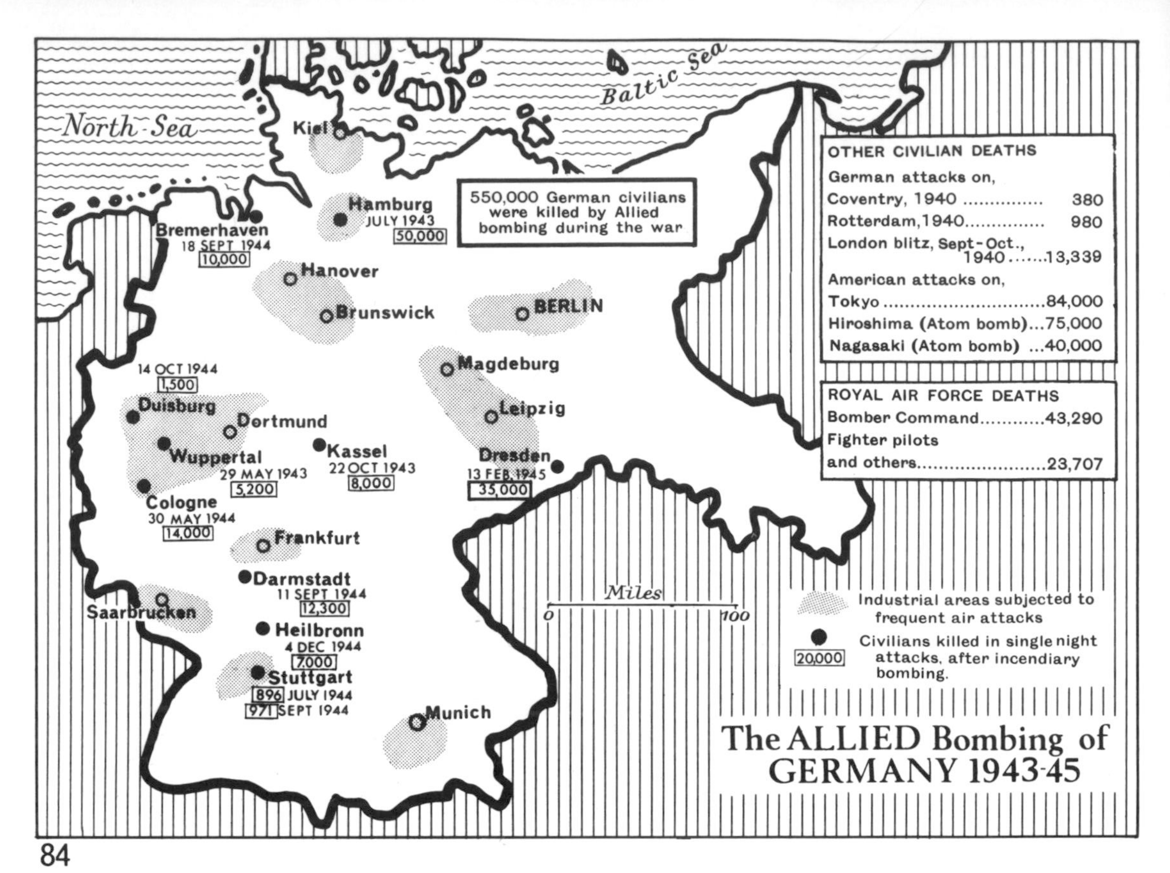

The ALLIED Bombing of GERMANY 1943-45
North Sea
Baltic Sea
Kiel
Hamburg
JULY 1943
50,000
550,000 German civilians were killed by Allied bombing during the war
Bremerhaven
18 SEPT 1944
10,000
Hanover
Brunswick
BERLIN
Magdeburg
Leipzig
Dresden
13 FEB 1945
35,000
14 OCT 1944
1,500
Duisburg
Dortmund
Wuppertal
29 MAY 1943
5,200
Kassel
22 OCT 1943
8,000
Cologne
30 MAY 1944
14,000
Frankfurt
Darmstadt
11 SEPT 1944
12,300
Saarbrucken
Heilbronn
4 DEC 1944
7,000
Stuttgart
896 JULY 1944
971 SEPT 1944
Munich
Miles
0
100
OTHER CIVILIAN DEATHS
German attacks on,
Coventry, 1940 380
Rotterdam, 1940............... 980
London blitz, Sept-Oct., 1940.......13,339
American attacks on,
Tokyo 84,000
Hiroshima (Atom bomb)...75,000
Nagasaki (Atom bomb) ...40,000
ROYAL AIR FORCE DEATHS
Bomber Command............43,290
Fighter pilots and others.......................23,707
Industrial areas subjected to frequent air attacks
20,000
Civilians killed in single night attacks, after incendiary bombing.

84

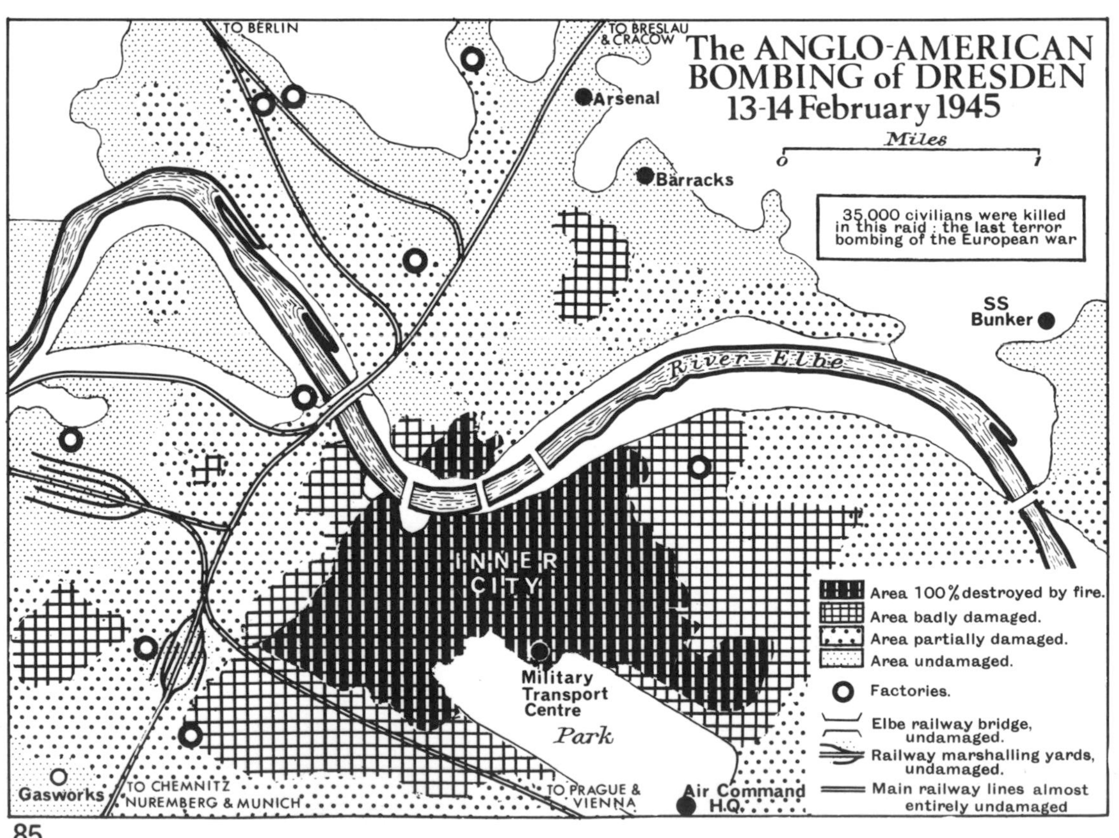

The ANGLO-AMERICAN BOMBING of DRESDEN 13-14 February 1945
TO BERLIN
TO BRESLAU & CRACOW
Arsenal
Barracks
Miles
0
1
35,000 civilians were killed in this raid : the last terror bombing of the European war
SS Bunker
River Elbe
INNER CITY
Military Transport Centre
Park
Gasworks
TO CHEMNITZ NUREMBERG & MUNICH
TO PRAGUE & VIENNA
Air Command H.Q.
Area 100% destroyed by fire.
Area badly damaged.
Area partially damaged.
Area undamaged.
Factories.
Elbe railway bridge, undamaged.
Railway marshalling yards, undamaged.
Main railway lines almost entirely undamaged

85

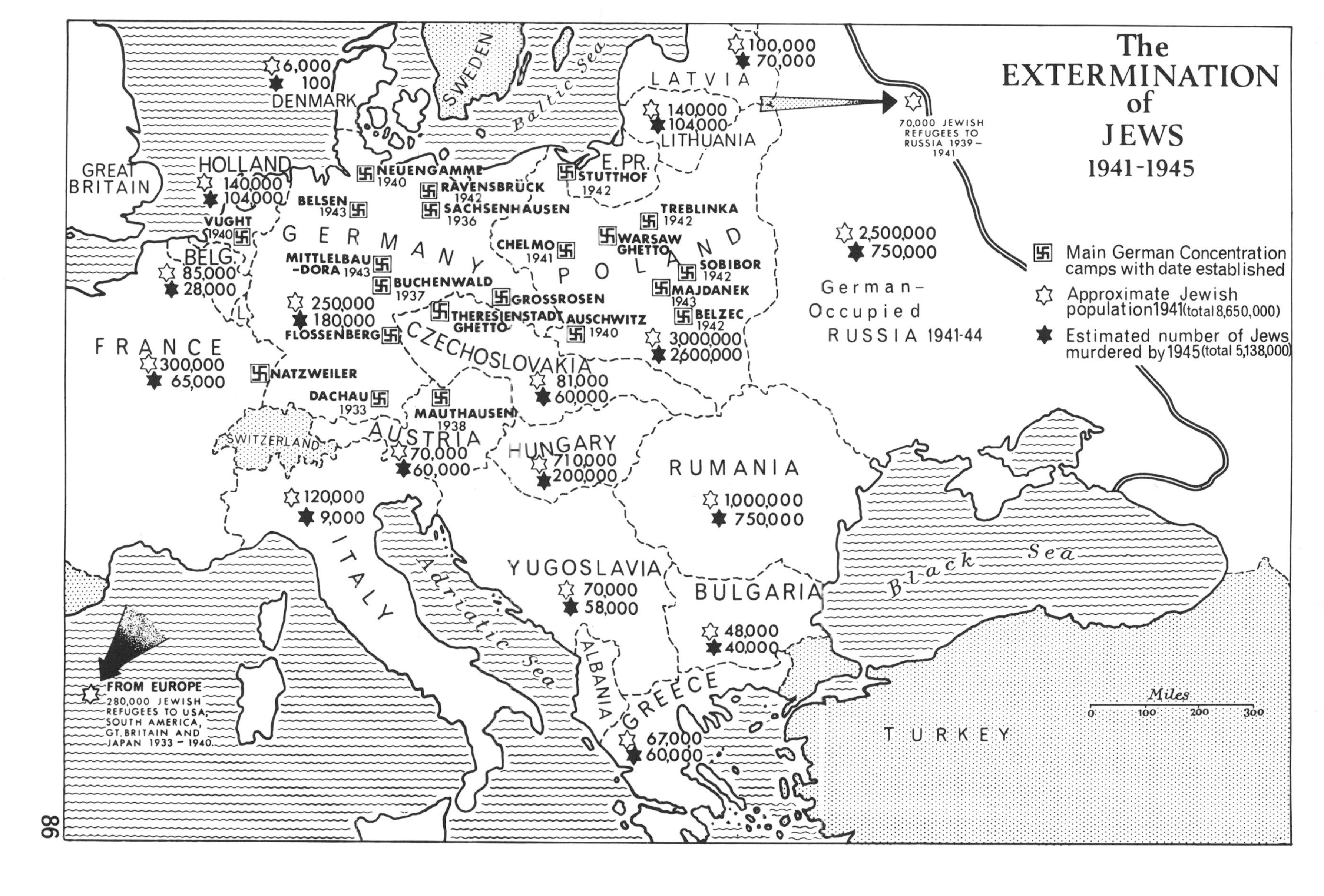
The EXTERMINATION of JEWS 1941-1945
Main German Concentration camps with date established
Approximate Jewish population 1941 (total 8,650,000)
Estimated number of Jews murdered by 1945 (total 5,138,000)
GREAT BRITAIN
HOLLAND 140,000 104,000
VUGHT 1940
BELG. 85,000 28,000
FRANCE 300,000 65,000
DENMARK 6,000 100
SWEDEN
Baltic Sea
GERMANY
BELSEN 1943
NEUENGAMME 1940
RAVENSBRÜCK 1942
SACHSENHAUSEN 1936
MITTELBAU -DORA 1943
BUCHENWALD 1937
250,000 180,000
FLOSSENBERG
NATZWEILER
DACHAU 1933
SWITZERLAND
THERESIENSTADT GHETTO
GROSSROSEN
CZECHOSLOVAKIA 81,000 60,000
AUSTRIA 70,000 60,000
MAUTHAUSEN 1938
HUNGARY 710,000 200,000
ITALY 120,000 9,000
Adriatic Sea
YUGOSLAVIA 70,000 58,000
ALBANIA
GREECE 67,000 60,000
BULGARIA 48,000 40,000
RUMANIA 1,000,000 750,000
TURKEY
Black Sea
POLAND
STUTTHOF 1942
E. PR.
CHELMO 1941
TREBLINKA 1942
WARSAW GHETTO
SOBIBOR 1942
MAJDANEK 1943
BELZEC 1942
AUSCHWITZ 1940
3,000,000 2,600,000
LITHUANIA 140,000 104,000
LATVIA 100,000 70,000
German-Occupied RUSSIA 1941-44
2,500,000 750,000
70,000 JEWISH REFUGEES TO RUSSIA 1939-1941
FROM EUROPE 280,000 JEWISH REFUGEES TO USA, SOUTH AMERICA, GT. BRITAIN AND JAPAN 1933 - 1940
Miles
0 100 200 300

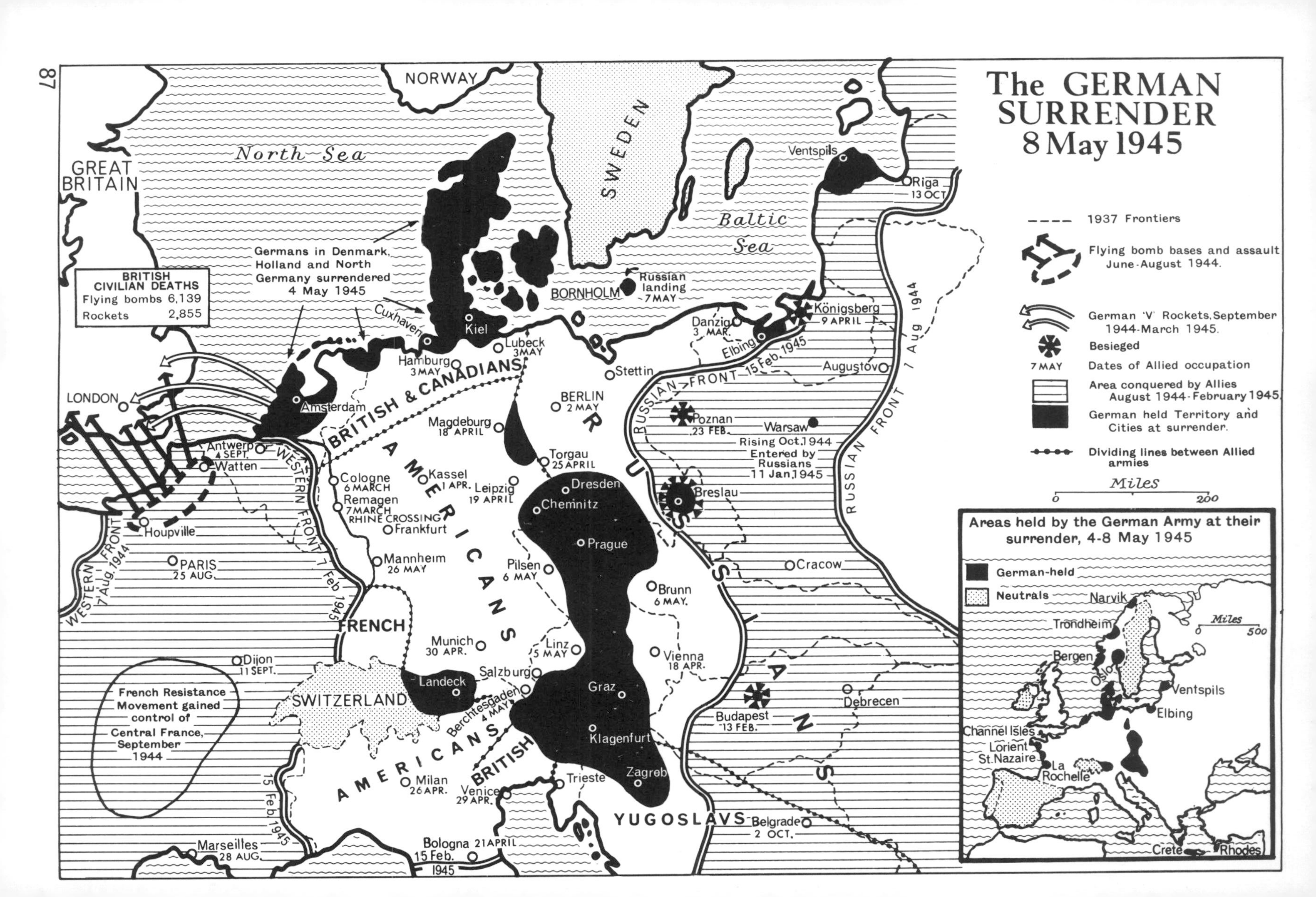

The GERMAN SURRENDER 8 May 1945
1937 Frontiers
Flying bomb bases and assault June-August 1944.
German 'V' Rockets, September 1944-March 1945.
Besieged
7 MAY
Dates of Allied occupation
Area conquered by Allies August 1944-February 1945
German held Territory and Cities at surrender.
Dividing lines between Allied armies
Miles
0
200
Areas held by the German Army at their surrender, 4-8 May 1945
German-held
Neutrals
Narvik
Trondheim
Bergen
Oslo
Ventspils
Elbing
Channel Isles
Lorient
St. Nazaire
La Rochelle
Crete
Rhodes
Miles
500
GREAT BRITAIN
NORWAY
SWEDEN
North Sea
Baltic Sea
BRITISH CIVILIAN DEATHS
Flying bombs 6,139
Rockets 2,855
Germans in Denmark, Holland and North Germany surrendered 4 May 1945
Cuxhaven
Kiel
BORNHOLM
Russian landing 7 MAY
Ventspils
Riga 13 OCT
Königsberg 9 APRIL
Danzig 3 MAR.
Elbing
RUSSIAN FRONT 15 Feb. 1945
RUSSIAN FRONT 7 Aug 1944
Augustov
Stettin
LONDON
Amsterdam
Lubeck 3 MAY
Hamburg 3 MAY
BRITISH & CANADIANS
BERLIN 2 MAY
Magdeburg 18 APRIL
Poznan 23 FEB.
Warsaw
Rising Oct. 1944
Entered by Russians 11 Jan. 1945
Antwerp 4 SEPT.
Watten
WESTERN FRONT 7 Feb 1945
Torgau 25 APRIL
Cologne 6 MARCH
Kassel 1 APR.
Leipzig 19 APRIL
Dresden
Breslau
Remagen 7 MARCH
RHINE CROSSING
Frankfurt
Chemnitz
Houpville
Prague
WESTERN FRONT 7 Aug. 1944
PARIS 25 AUG.
Mannheim 26 MAY
Pilsen 6 MAY
Cracow
Brunn 6 MAY.
FRENCH
AMERICANS
RUSSIANS
Munich 30 APR.
Linz 5 MAY
Vienna 18 APR.
Dijon 11 SEPT.
Salzburg
Landeck
Berchtesgaden 4 MAY
Graz
Debrecen
SWITZERLAND
Budapest 13 FEB.
French Resistance Movement gained control of Central France, September 1944
Klagenfurt
BRITISH
Milan 26 APR.
Venice 29 APR.
Trieste
Zagreb
15 Feb. 1945
YUGOSLAVS
Belgrade 2 OCT.
Marseilles 28 AUG.
Bologna 21 APRIL
15 Feb. 1945

The RETURN of GERMANS to GERMANY During the War 1939-1944
North Sea
DENMARK
SWEDEN
Baltic Sea
ESTONIA
LATVIA
LITHUANIA
78,000
57,000
Miles
0
200
RUSSIA
Berlin
GERMANY
350,000
33,000
30,000
POLAND
Protectorate
SLOVAKIA
4000
SWITZ
Austria
96,000
HUNGARY
80,000
118000
36,000
RUMANIA
ITALY
Adriatic Sea
YUGOSLAVIA
Black Sea
1939 Boundaries
Boundary of the German Reich 1940
Returning Germans (total 882,000)
Major resettlement area 1940-44

The EXPULSION of GERMANS from CENTRAL EUROPE 1945-1947
North Sea
DENMARK
SWEDEN
Baltic Sea
RUSSIA
400,000
2,000,000
175,000
Berlin
WEST GERMANY
2,500,000
POLAND
3,500,000
CZECHOSLOVAKIA
400,000
SWITZ
AUSTRIA
50,000
200,000
HUNGARY
ITALIANS
40,000
TRIESTE
RUMANIA
ITALY
250,000
Adriatic Sea
YUGOSLAVIA
Black Sea
Miles
0
200
1945 Boundaries
The Eastern boundary of Germany 1940
The Boundary of Germany 1945
Major German resettlement area 1940-44
Expelled Germans (total 9,470,000)
The Iron Curtain dividing West & East Germany.

JAPANESE AGGRESSION
after PEARL HARBOUR
December 1941–July 1942
RUSSIA
CHINA
JAPAN
USA
CANADA
INDIA
AUSTRALIA
Bering Sea
Pacific Ocean
Indian Ocean
Coral Sea
Miles
0
1000
Harbin
Vladivostok
Mukden
Peking
Tokyo
Shanghai
Ledo
Chungking
Kohima
Calcutta
Akyab
MAY 1942
Rangoon
Hanoi
Hong Kong
25 DEC 1941
Bangkok
DEC 41
Saigon
Singapore
15 FEB 1942
Okinawa
FORMOSA
Manila
MAY 42
PHILIPPINES
Ceylon
APRIL 42
SUMATRA
JAVA
FEB 42
BORNEO
CELEBES
TIMOR
FEB–JUN 42
Darwin
NEW GUINEA
MAR 42
MARIANA IS.
(Japanese)
Guam
(US)
CAROLINE IS.
(Japanese)
Wake I.
(US)
MARSHALL IS
GILBERT IS.
SOLOMON IS.
JAN 42
JULY 42
MAY 42
NOV 42
St Cruz
(British)
NEW HEBRIDES IS.
(Anglo-French)
New Caledonia
(French)
FIJI IS.(British)
Samoa
(US)
Baker I.
(US)
Christmas I
(British)
Midway I.
(US)
JUNE 42
Pearl Harbour
HAWAII
(US)
ALEUTIAN IS.
Attu
Kiska
Dutch Harbour
3 JUNE 42
JULY 1942
JAPAN 1928
Occupied by Japan up to 1941
Occupied by Japan, 1941-1942
Japanese air attacks
Furthest extent of Japanese air cover in 1942.
Japanese sea victory
Furthest extent of U.S. air cover in 1942
Dates of Japanese attacks
U.S. sea victories
Furthest extent of Japanese conquest
Unconquered by Japan

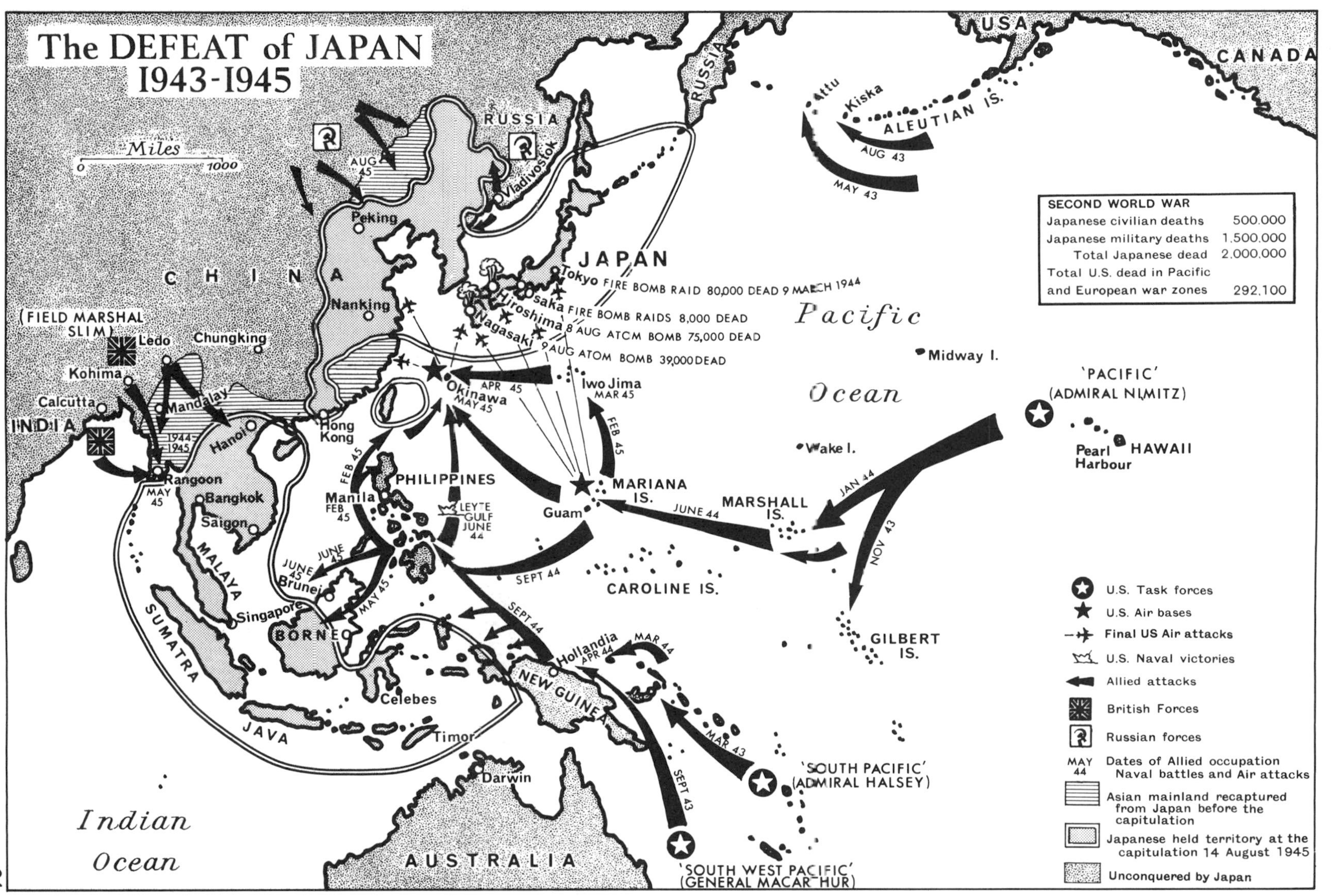

The DEFEAT of JAPAN
1943-1945
Miles
0
1000
CHINA
RUSSIA
USA
CANADA
JAPAN
INDIA
AUSTRALIA
(FIELD MARSHAL SLIM)
Ledo
Chungking
Kohima
Calcutta
Mandalay
Hanoi
Rangoon
Bangkok
Saigon
MALAYA
Singapore
SUMATRA
JAVA
BORNEO
Brunei
Celebes
Timor
Darwin
NEW GUINEA
Hollandia
Peking
Nanking
Hong Kong
Manila
PHILIPPINES
LEYTE GULF JUNE 44
Vladivostok
Tokyo FIRE BOMB RAID 80,000 DEAD 9 MARCH 1944
Osaka FIRE BOMB RAIDS 8,000 DEAD
Hiroshima 8 AUG ATOM BOMB 75,000 DEAD
Nagasaki 9 AUG ATOM BOMB 39,000 DEAD
Okinawa
Iwo Jima
MARIANA IS.
Guam
MARSHALL IS.
CAROLINE IS.
GILBERT IS.
Midway I.
Wake I.
Attu
Kiska
ALEUTIAN IS.
Pacific
Ocean
Indian
Ocean
'PACIFIC' (ADMIRAL NIMITZ)
Pearl Harbour
HAWAII
'SOUTH PACIFIC' (ADMIRAL HALSEY)
'SOUTH WEST PACIFIC' (GENERAL MACARTHUR)
AUG 45
MAY 45
1944-1945
FEB 45
JUNE 45
APR 45
MAR 45
SEPT 44
JUNE 44
JAN 44
NOV 43
MAR 44
APR 44
MAR 43
SEPT 43
AUG 43
MAY 43
SECOND WORLD WAR
Japanese civilian deaths 500.000
Japanese military deaths 1.500.000
Total Japanese dead 2.000.000
Total U.S. dead in Pacific and European war zones 292.100
U.S. Task forces
U.S. Air bases
Final US Air attacks
U.S. Naval victories
Allied attacks
British Forces
Russian forces
MAY 44 Dates of Allied occupation Naval battles and Air attacks
Asian mainland recaptured from Japan before the capitulation
Japanese held territory at the capitulation 14 August 1945
Unconquered by Japan

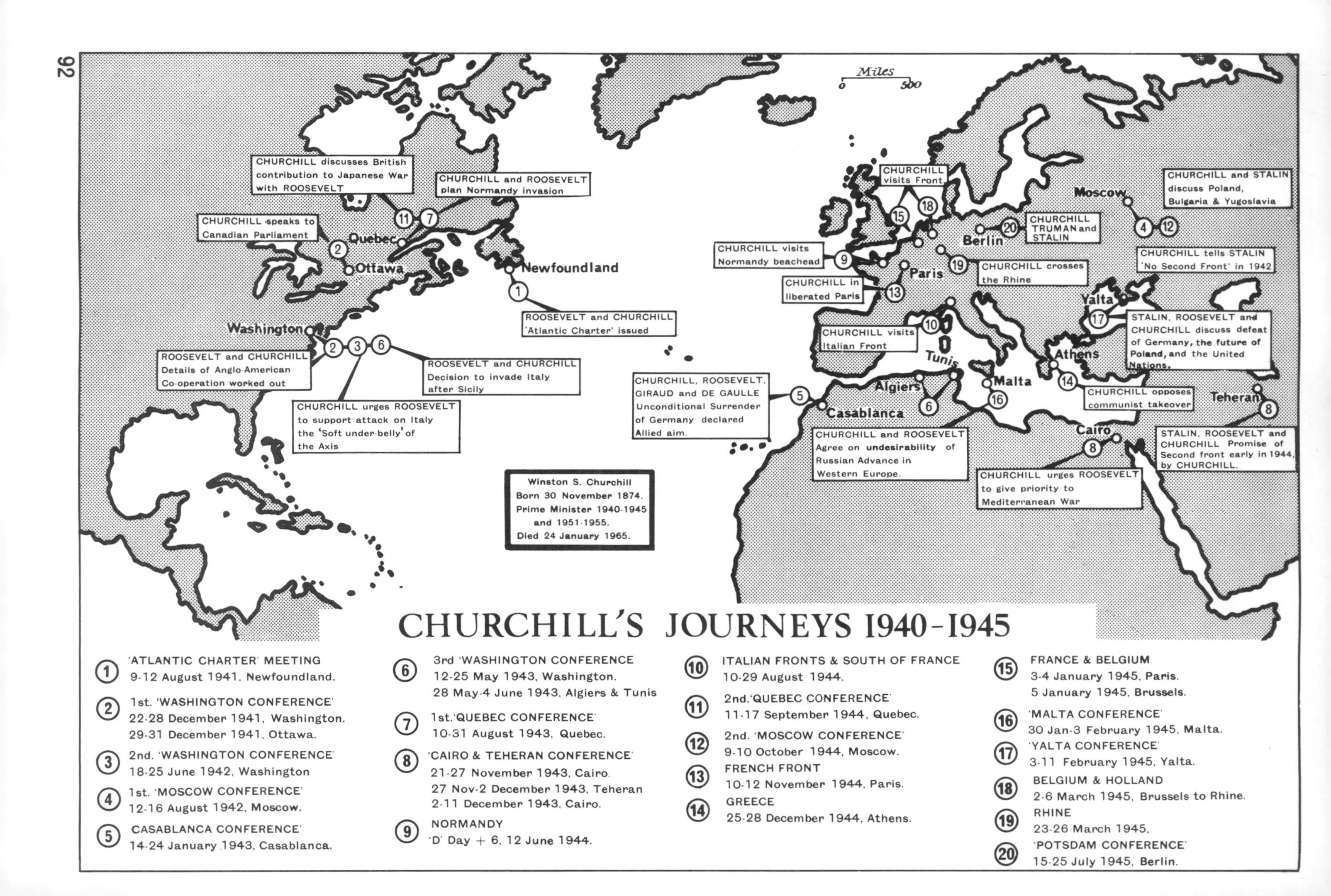
CHURCHILL'S JOURNEYS 1940-1945
Miles 0 500
CHURCHILL discusses British contribution to Japanese War with ROOSEVELT
CHURCHILL and ROOSEVELT plan Normandy invasion
CHURCHILL speaks to Canadian Parliament
Quebec
Ottawa
Newfoundland
Washington
ROOSEVELT and CHURCHILL 'Atlantic Charter' issued
ROOSEVELT and CHURCHILL Details of Anglo-American Co-operation worked out
ROOSEVELT and CHURCHILL Decision to invade Italy after Sicily
CHURCHILL urges ROOSEVELT to support attack on Italy the 'Soft under-belly' of the Axis
CHURCHILL, ROOSEVELT, GIRAUD and DE GAULLE Unconditional Surrender of Germany declared Allied aim.
Winston S. Churchill Born 30 November 1874. Prime Minister 1940-1945 and 1951-1955. Died 24 January 1965.
CHURCHILL visits Front
CHURCHILL visits Normandy beachead
CHURCHILL in liberated Paris
CHURCHILL visits Italian Front
Paris
Berlin
CHURCHILL TRUMAN and STALIN
CHURCHILL crosses the Rhine
Moscow
CHURCHILL and STALIN discuss Poland, Bulgaria & Yugoslavia
CHURCHILL tells STALIN 'No Second Front' in 1942
Yalta
STALIN, ROOSEVELT and CHURCHILL discuss defeat of Germany, the future of Poland, and the United Nations.
Athens
CHURCHILL opposes communist takeover
Teheran
Tunis
Algiers
Malta
Casablanca
Cairo
CHURCHILL and ROOSEVELT Agree on undesirability of Russian Advance in Western Europe.
STALIN, ROOSEVELT and CHURCHILL Promise of Second front early in 1944, by CHURCHILL.
CHURCHILL urges ROOSEVELT to give priority to Mediterranean War
1 'ATLANTIC CHARTER' MEETING 9-12 August 1941, Newfoundland.
2 1st. 'WASHINGTON CONFERENCE' 22-28 December 1941, Washington. 29-31 December 1941, Ottawa.
3 2nd. 'WASHINGTON CONFERENCE' 18-25 June 1942, Washington
4 1st. 'MOSCOW CONFERENCE' 12-16 August 1942, Moscow.
5 CASABLANCA CONFERENCE' 14-24 January 1943, Casablanca.
6 3rd 'WASHINGTON CONFERENCE 12-25 May 1943, Washington. 28 May-4 June 1943, Algiers & Tunis
7 1st.'QUEBEC CONFERENCE' 10-31 August 1943, Quebec.
8 'CAIRO & TEHERAN CONFERENCE' 21-27 November 1943, Cairo. 27 Nov-2 December 1943, Teheran 2-11 December 1943, Cairo.
9 NORMANDY 'D' Day + 6, 12 June 1944.
10 ITALIAN FRONTS & SOUTH OF FRANCE 10-29 August 1944.
11 2nd.'QUEBEC CONFERENCE' 11-17 September 1944, Quebec.
12 2nd. 'MOSCOW CONFERENCE' 9-10 October 1944, Moscow.
13 FRENCH FRONT 10-12 November 1944, Paris.
14 GREECE 25-28 December 1944, Athens.
15 FRANCE & BELGIUM 3-4 January 1945, Paris. 5 January 1945, Brussels.
16 'MALTA CONFERENCE' 30 Jan-3 February 1945, Malta.
17 'YALTA CONFERENCE' 3-11 February 1945, Yalta.
18 BELGIUM & HOLLAND 2-6 March 1945, Brussels to Rhine.
19 RHINE 23-26 March 1945,
20 'POTSDAM CONFERENCE' 15-25 July 1945, Berlin.

WAR DEAD 1939–1945
GREAT BRITAIN
(Military) 397,762
(Civilian) 62,000
DENMARK
(Military & Civilian) 3,000
SWEDEN
LATVIA
LITHUANIA
HOLLAND
(Military) 12,000
(Civilian) 198,000
BELGIUM
(Military) 12,000
(Civilian) 16,000
FRANCE
(Military) 210,671
(Civilian) 107,874
GERMANY
(Military) 3,500,000
(Civilian) 800,000
EAST PRUSSIA
Bomb plot against Hitler
20 July 1944
POLAND
(Military) 320,000
(Civilian) 3,000,000
CZECHOSLOVAKIA
(Military) 50,000
(Civilian) 220,000
RUSSIA
(Military) 7,500,000
(Civilian) 2,500,000
Over 2 million of the dead Russian soldiers were killed while they were prisoners of war
SWITZERLAND
AUSTRIA
(Military) 230,000
(Civilian) 104,000
HUNGARY
(Military) 410,000
(Civilian) 280,000
RUMANIA
(Military 300,000
(Civilian) 260,000
ITALY
(Military) 330,000
(Civilian) 80,000
YUGOSLAVIA
(Military) 410,000
(Civilian) 1,280,000
BULGARIA
(Military) 10,000
(Civilian) 10,000
ALBANIA
GREECE
(Military) 73,000
(Civilian) 140,000
TURKEY
Neutral until 23 February 1945
OTHER ALLIED DEAD
AUSTRALIA (Military) 29,395
CANADA (Military) 31,319
CHINA (Military & Civilian) 2,200,000
INDIA (Military) 36,092
NEW ZEALAND (Military) 12,262
NORWAY (Military) 6,000
(Civilian) 3,500
SOUTH AFRICA (Military) 8,681
USA (Military) 292,000
OTHER AXIS DEAD
JAPAN (Military) 1,500,000
(Civilian) 500,000
FINLAND (Military & Civilian) 85,000
These figures do not include over 5 million Jewish civilians murdered
See map 86
Miles
0
300

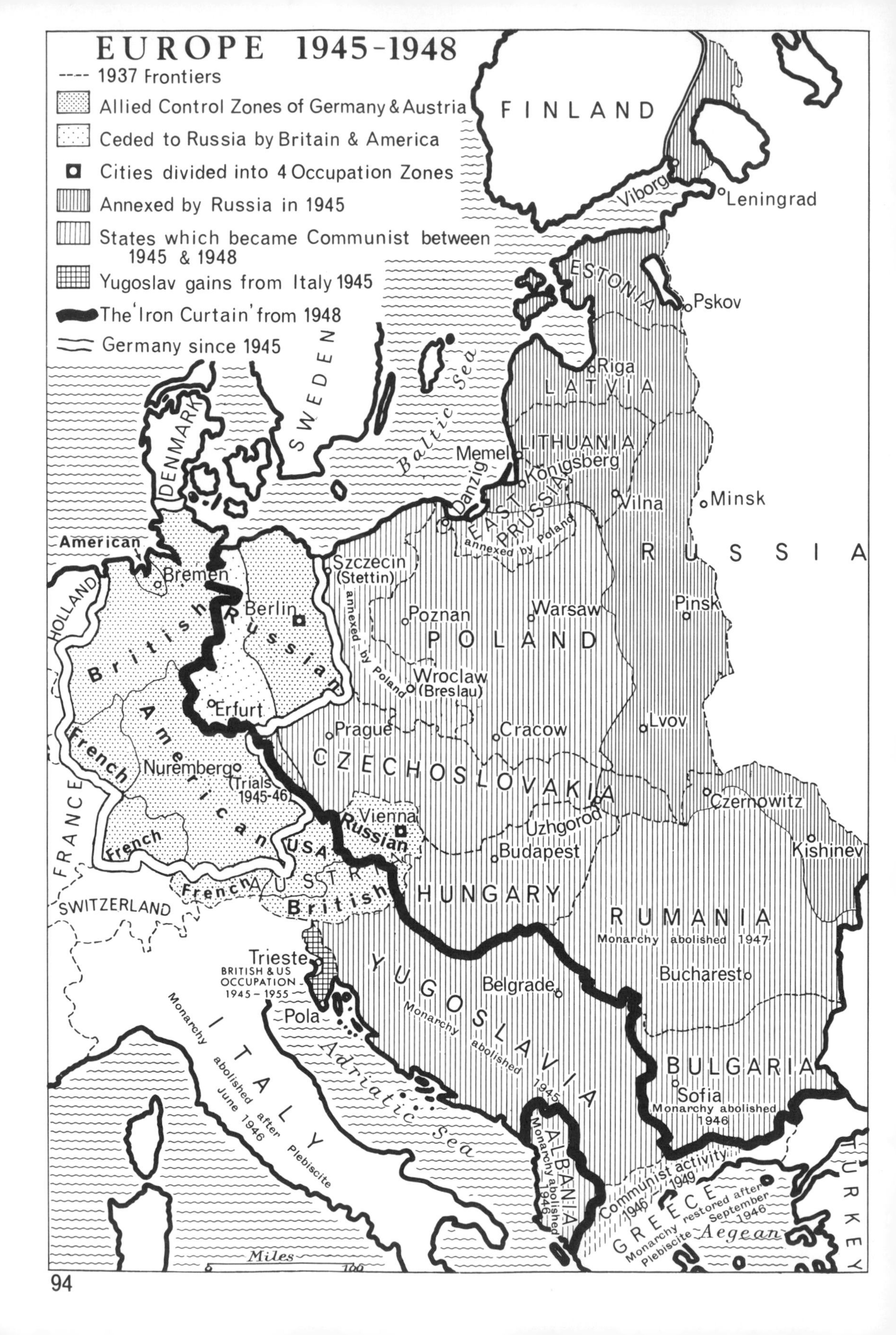
EUROPE 1945-1948
1937 Frontiers
Allied Control Zones of Germany & Austria
Ceded to Russia by Britain & America
Cities divided into 4 Occupation Zones
Annexed by Russia in 1945
States which became Communist between 1945 & 1948
Yugoslav gains from Italy 1945
The 'Iron Curtain' from 1948
Germany since 1945
FINLAND
Viborg
Leningrad
ESTONIA
Pskov
SWEDEN
Baltic Sea
Riga
LATVIA
DENMARK
Memel
LITHUANIA
Königsberg
Danzig
EAST PRUSSIA
annexed by Poland
Vilna
Minsk
RUSSIA
American
Bremen
Szczecin (Stettin)
annexed by Poland
HOLLAND
Berlin
British
Russian
Poznan
Warsaw
POLAND
Pinsk
Wroclaw (Breslau)
Erfurt
Prague
Cracow
Lvov
American
French
CZECHOSLOVAKIA
Nuremberg (Trials 1945-46)
Czernowitz
Vienna
Russian
Uzhgorod
Kishinev
FRANCE
USA
Budapest
French
AUSTRIA
British
HUNGARY
SWITZERLAND
RUMANIA
Monarchy abolished 1947
Trieste
BRITISH & US OCCUPATION 1945 – 1955
YUGOSLAVIA
Monarchy abolished 1945
Belgrade
Bucharest
Pola
ITALY
Monarchy abolished after Plebiscite June 1946
Adriatic Sea
BULGARIA
Sofia
Monarchy abolished 1946
ALBANIA
Monarchy abolished 1946
Communist activity 1946 - 1949
GREECE
Monarchy restored after Plebiscite September 1946
Aegean
TURKEY
Miles
0
100

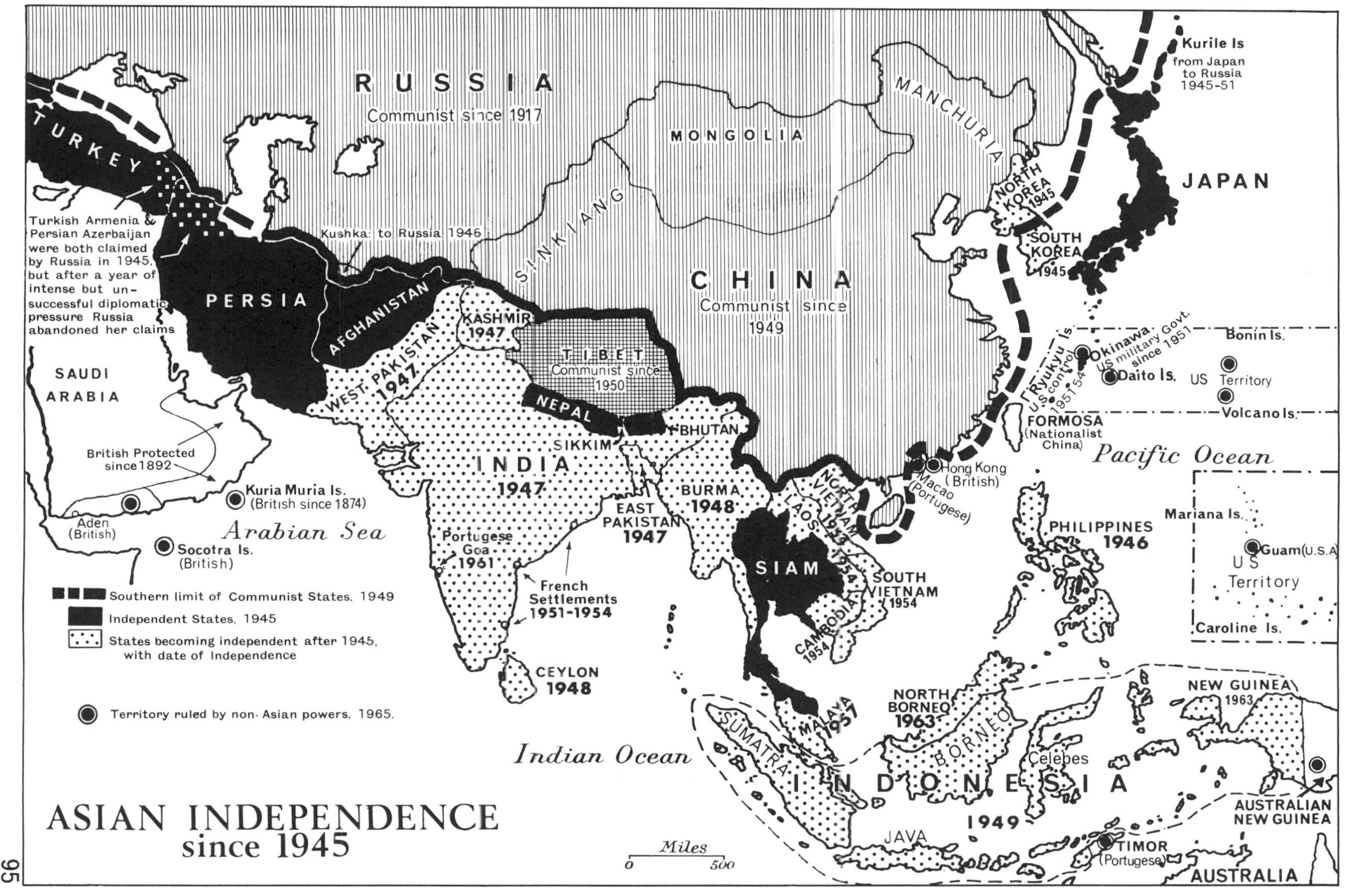

ASIAN INDEPENDENCE since 1945

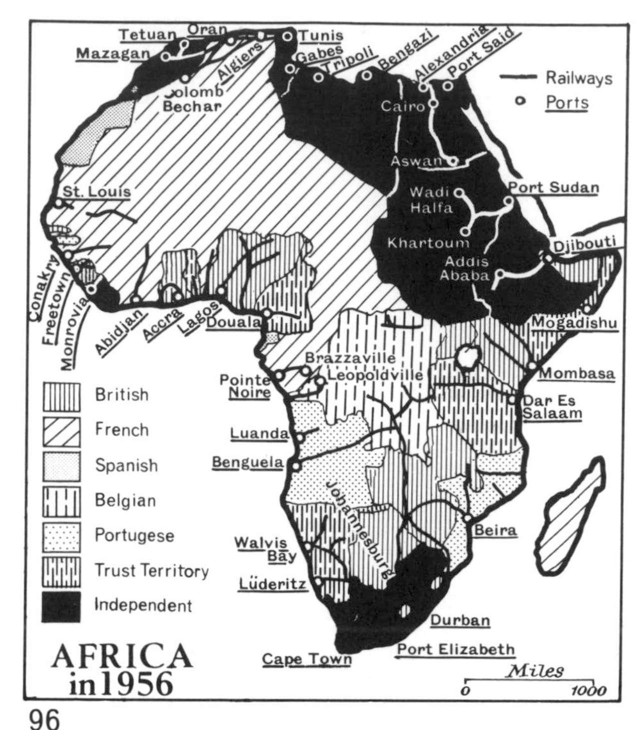
AFRICA in1956
Tetuan
Oran
Tunis
Mazagan
Algiers
Gabes
Tripoli
Bengazi
Alexandria
Port Said
Colomb Bechar
Cairo
Railways
Ports
Aswan
St. Louis
Wadi Halfa
Port Sudan
Khartoum
Djibouti
Addis Ababa
Conakry
Freetown
Monrovia
Abidjan
Accra
Lagos
Douala
Mogadishu
Brazzaville
Leopoldville
Pointe Noire
Mombasa
Dar Es Salaam
Luanda
Benguela
Johannesburg
Walvis Bay
Beira
Lüderitz
Durban
Cape Town
Port Elizabeth
British
French
Spanish
Belgian
Portugese
Trust Territory
Independent
Miles
0
1000

96

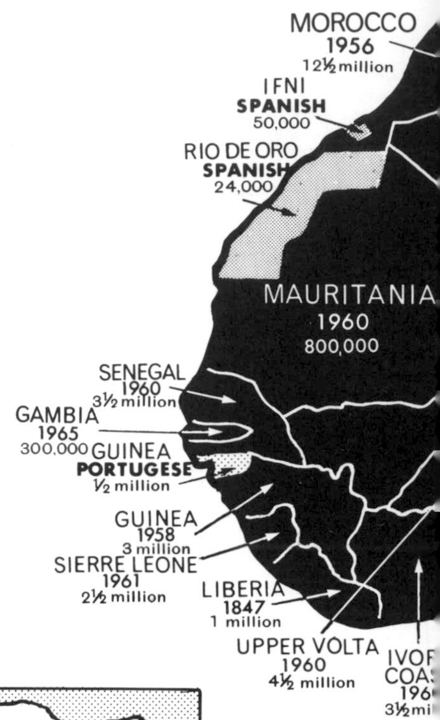
MOROCCO
1956
12½ million
IFNI
SPANISH
50,000
RIO DE ORO
SPANISH
24,000
MAURITANIA
1960
800,000
SENEGAL
1960
3½ million
GAMBIA
1965
300,000
GUINEA
PORTUGESE
½ million
GUINEA
1958
3 million
SIERRE LEONE
1961
2½ million
LIBERIA
1847
1 million
UPPER VOLTA
1960
4½ million

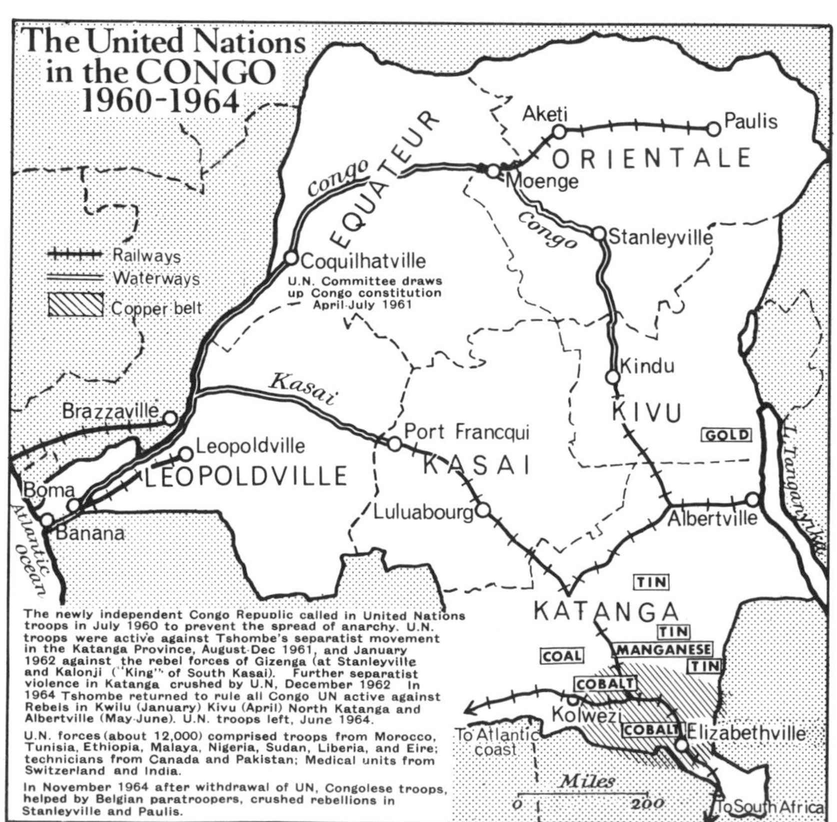
The United Nations in the CONGO 1960-1964
Aketi
Paulis
EQUATEUR
ORIENTALE
Congo
Moenge
Stanleyville
Railways
Waterways
Copper belt
Coquilhatville
U.N. Committee draws up Congo constitution April-July 1961
Kindu
Kasai
KIVU
Brazzaville
Port Francqui
GOLD
Leopoldville
KASAI
L. Tanganyika
Boma
LEOPOLDVILLE
Luluabourg
Albertville
Banana
Atlantic Ocean
TIN
KATANGA
TIN
MANGANESE
COAL
TIN
COBALT
Kolwez
COBALT
Elizabethville
To Atlantic coast
Miles
0
200
To South Africa
The newly independent Congo Republic called in United Nations troops in July 1960 to prevent the spread of anarchy. U.N. troops were active against Tshombe's separatist movement in the Katanga Province, August-Dec 1961, and January 1962 against the rebel forces of Gizenga (at Stanleyville and Kalonji ("King" of South Kasai). Further separatist violence in Katanga crushed by U.N, December 1962. In 1964 Tshombe returned to rule all Congo UN active against Rebels in Kwilu (January) Kivu (April) North Katanga and Albertville (May-June). U.N. troops left, June 1964.
U.N. forces (about 12,000) comprised troops from Morocco, Tunisia, Ethiopia, Malaya, Nigeria, Sudan, Liberia, and Eire; technicians from Canada and Pakistan; Medical units from Switzerland and India.
In November 1964 after withdrawal of UN, Congolese troops, helped by Belgian paratroopers, crushed rebellions in Stanleyville and Paulis.

97

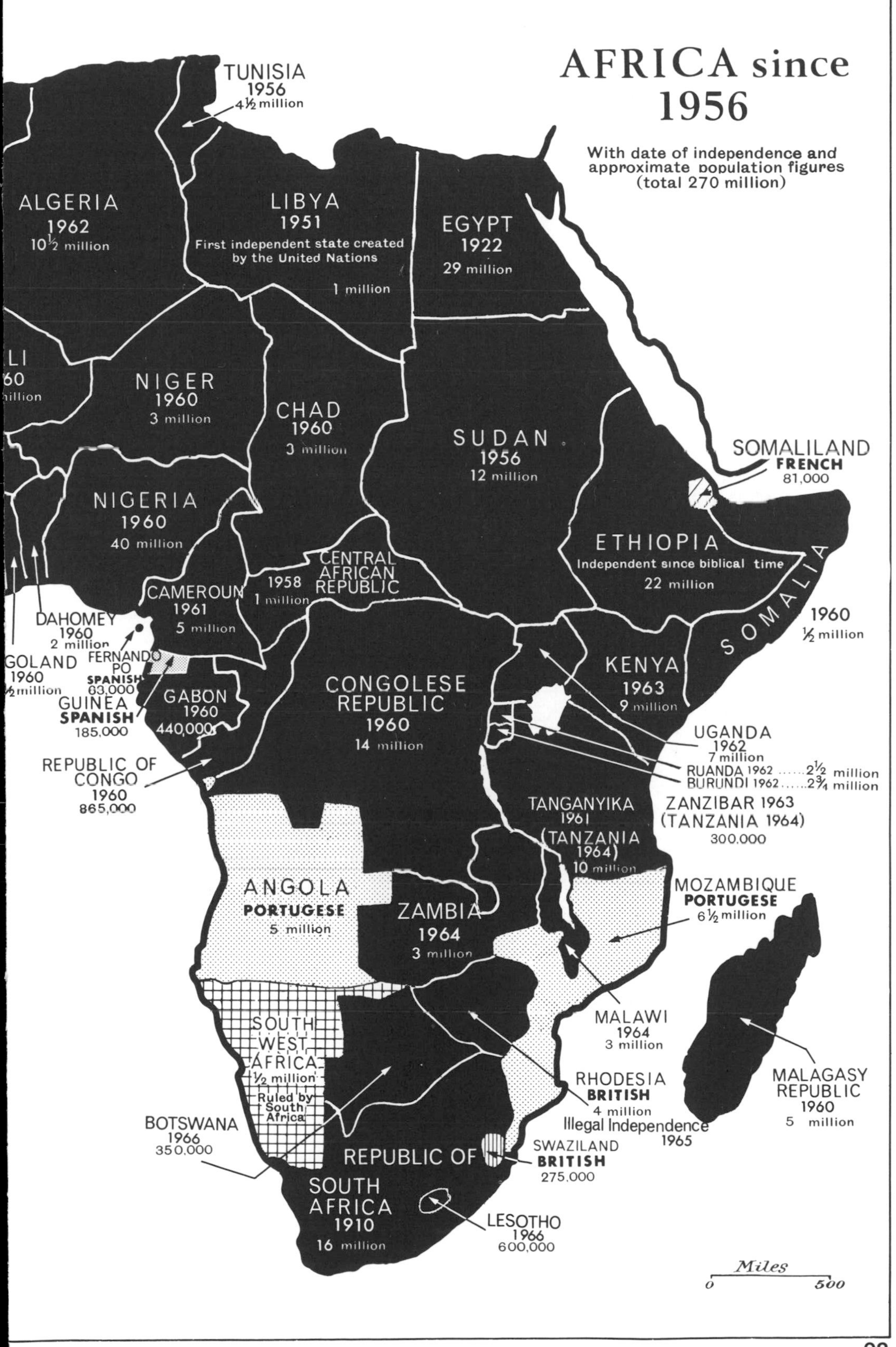

AFRICA since 1956
With date of independence and approximate population figures (total 270 million)
TUNISIA 1956 4½ million
ALGERIA 1962 10½ million
LIBYA 1951
First independent state created by the United Nations
1 million
EGYPT 1922 29 million
NIGER 1960 3 million
CHAD 1960 3 million
SUDAN 1956 12 million
SOMALILAND FRENCH 81,000
NIGERIA 1960 40 million
ETHIOPIA
Independent since biblical time
22 million
CENTRAL AFRICAN REPUBLIC 1958 1 million
CAMEROUN 1961 5 million
DAHOMEY 1960 2 million
SOMALIA 1960 ½ million
FERNANDO PO SPANISH 63,000
GUINEA SPANISH 185,000
GABON 1960 440,000
CONGOLESE REPUBLIC 1960 14 million
KENYA 1963 9 million
UGANDA 1962 7 million
RUANDA 1962 ...... 2½ million
BURUNDI 1962 ...... 2¾ million
REPUBLIC OF CONGO 1960 865,000
TANGANYIKA 1961 (TANZANIA 1964) 10 million
ZANZIBAR 1963 (TANZANIA 1964) 300,000
ANGOLA PORTUGESE 5 million
ZAMBIA 1964 3 million
MOZAMBIQUE PORTUGESE 6½ million
MALAWI 1964 3 million
SOUTH WEST AFRICA ½ million Ruled by South Africa
RHODESIA BRITISH 4 million
Illegal Independence 1965
MALAGASY REPUBLIC 1960 5 million
BOTSWANA 1966 350,000
SWAZILAND BRITISH 275,000
REPUBLIC OF SOUTH AFRICA 1910 16 million
LESOTHO 1966 600,000
Miles
0 500

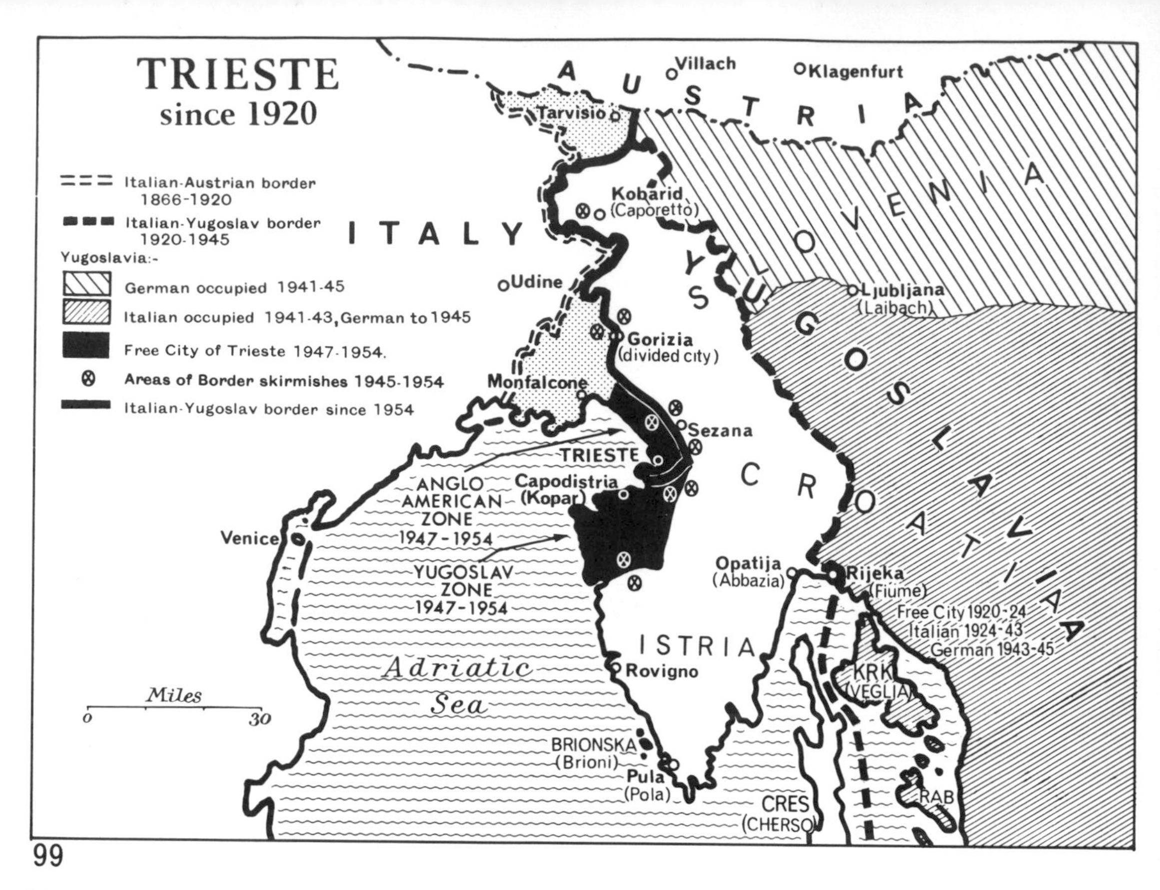

99

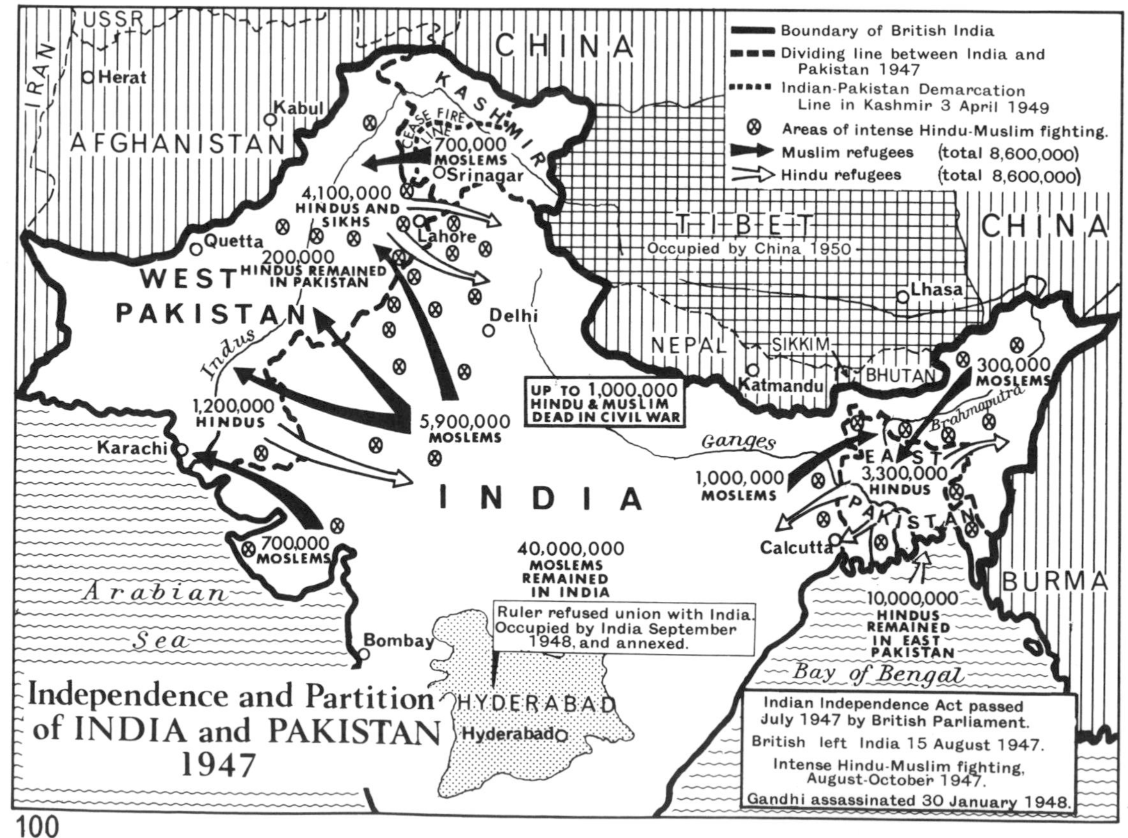

Independence and Partition of INDIA and PAKISTAN 1947

100

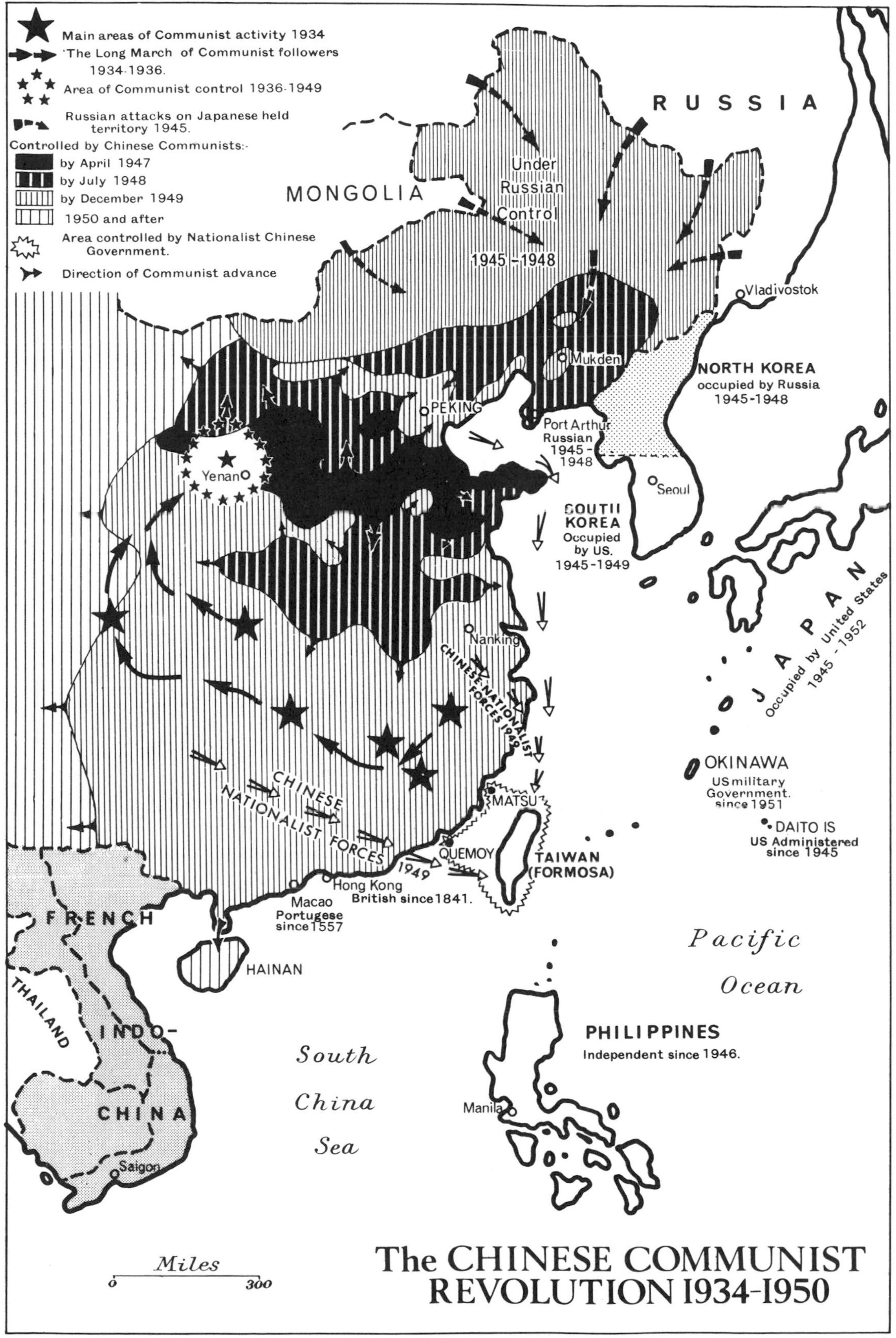

The CHINESE COMMUNIST REVOLUTION 1934-1950

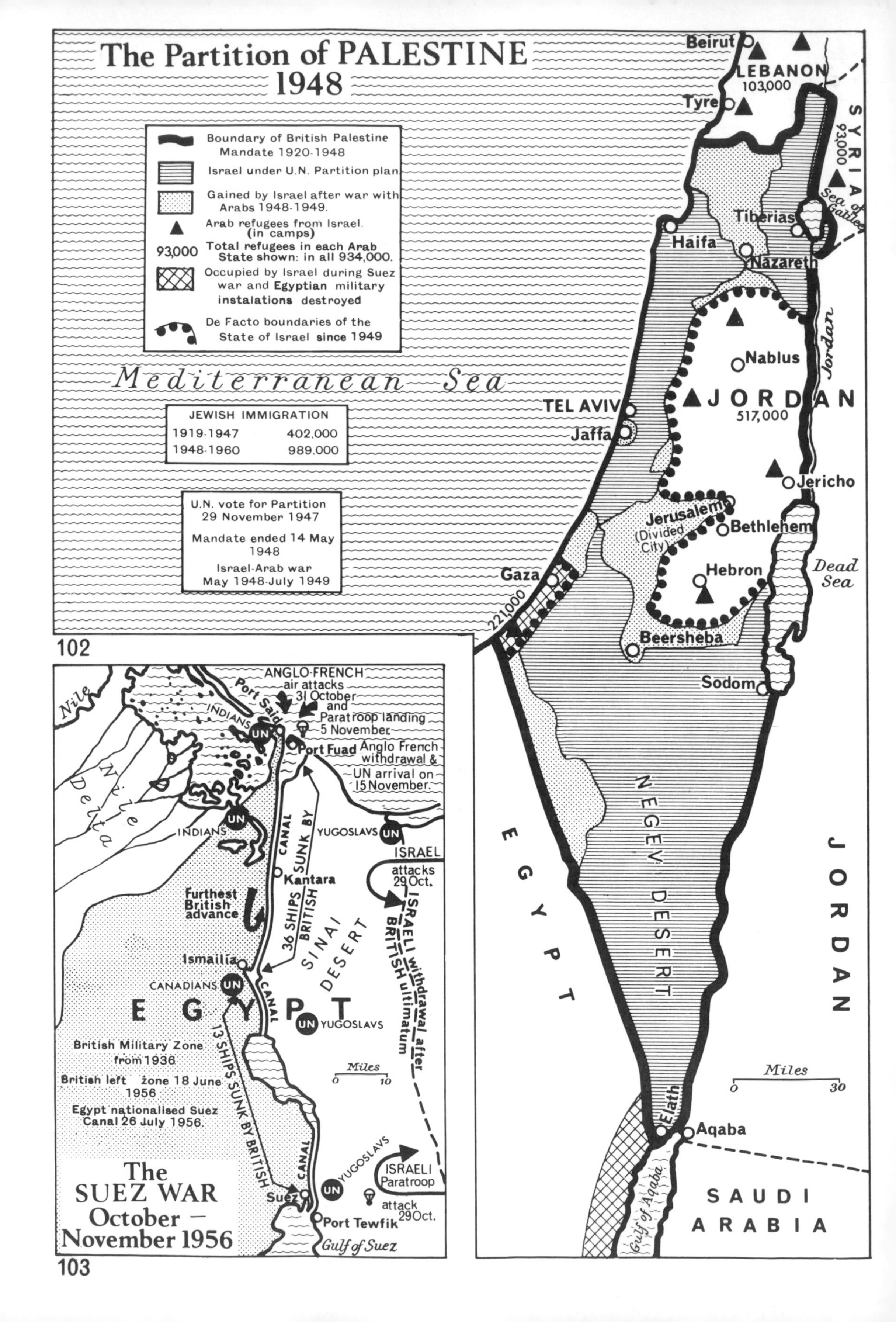

The SUEZ WAR October – November 1956

103

UNITED STATES activity in the CARIBBEAN 1895-1939
UNITED STATES
FLORIDA
Gulf of Mexico
Atlantic Ocean
Bahamas (British)
CUBA (Occupied 1898-1902, After war with Spain)
Guantanamo US base since 1898
DOMINICAN REPUBLIC (Occupied 1916-1924)
Virgin Islands (Purchased from Denmark 1916)
PUERTO RICO (Annexed 1898. After war with Spain)
Vera Cruz (Seized 1914)
MEXICO
BRITISH HONDURAS
Jamaica (British)
HAITI (Occupied 1914-1934)
Swan Island (USA)
Caribbean Sea
GUATEMALA
HONDURAS
EL SALVADOR
NICARAGUA (Occupied 1909-10, 1912-25, 1926-39)
Pacific Ocean
COSTA RICA
PANAMA
Panama Canal Zone (US Protectorate 1903-1939)
VENEZUELA
COLOMBIA
Miles
0
400

104

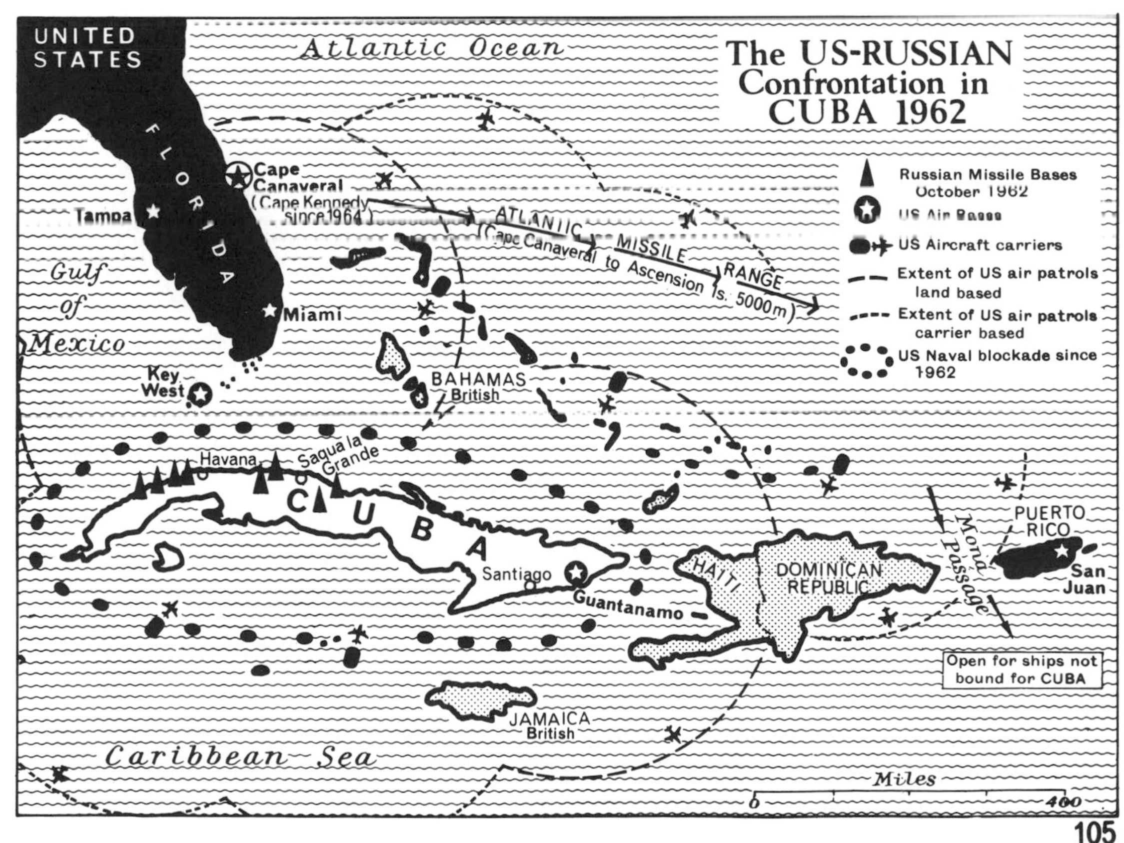
The US-RUSSIAN Confrontation in CUBA 1962
UNITED STATES
Atlantic Ocean
FLORIDA
Cape Canaveral (Cape Kennedy since 1964)
Tampa
ATLANTIC MISSILE RANGE (Cape Canaveral to Ascension Is. 5000m)
Gulf of Mexico
Miami
Key West
BAHAMAS British
Havana
Saqua la Grande
CUBA
Santiago
Guantanamo
HAITI
DOMINICAN REPUBLIC
Mona Passage
PUERTO RICO
San Juan
Open for ships not bound for CUBA
JAMAICA British
Caribbean Sea
Miles
0
400
Russian Missile Bases October 1962
US Air Bases
US Aircraft carriers
Extent of US air patrols land based
Extent of US air patrols carrier based
US Naval blockade since 1962

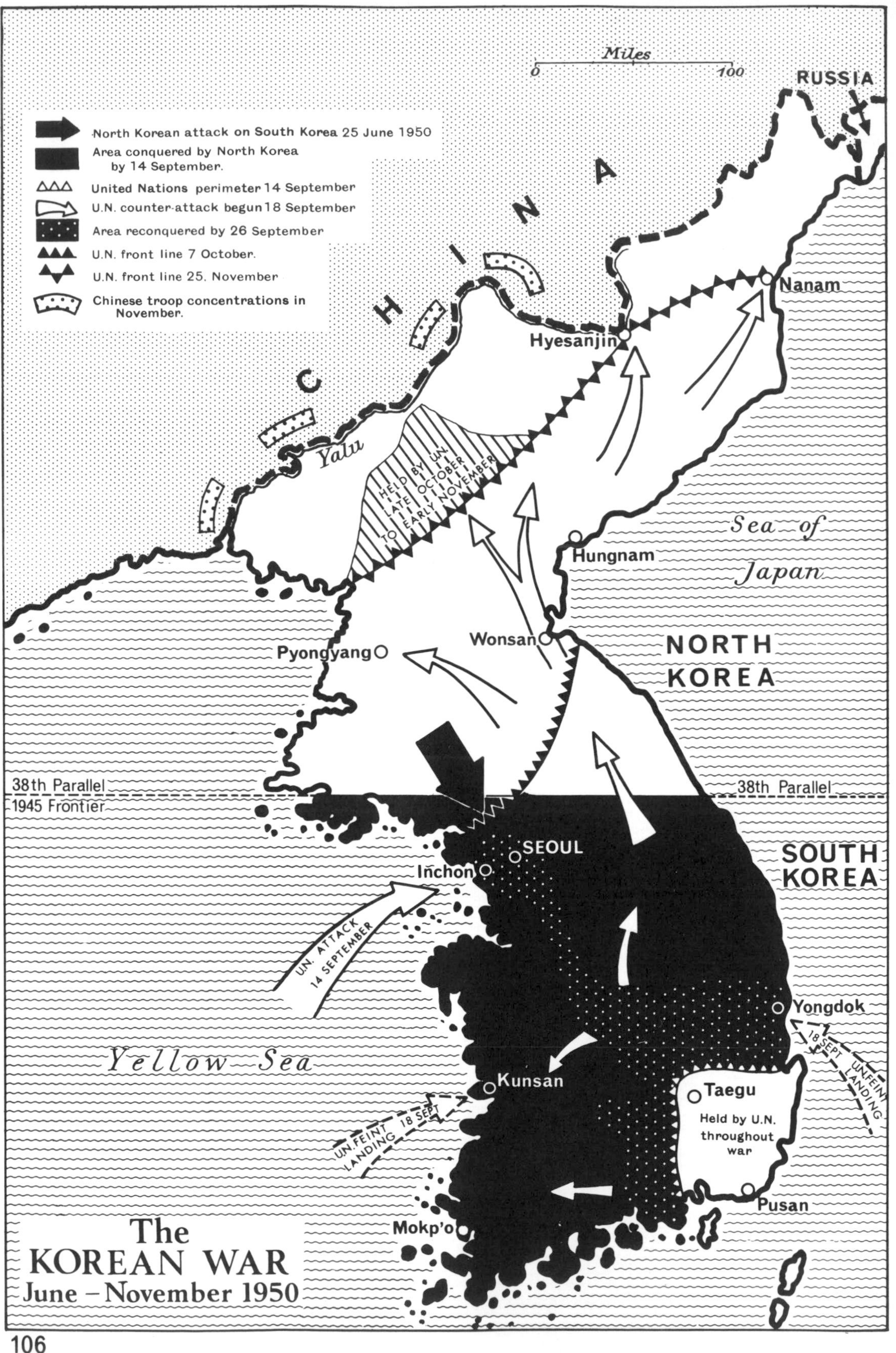

Miles
0
100
RUSSIA
North Korean attack on South Korea 25 June 1950
Area conquered by North Korea by 14 September.
United Nations perimeter 14 September
U.N. counter-attack begun 18 September
Area reconquered by 26 September
U.N. front line 7 October.
U.N. front line 25. November
Chinese troop concentrations in November.
CHINA
Yalu
Nanam
Hyesanjin
HELD BY U.N. LATE OCTOBER TO EARLY NOVEMBER
Sea of Japan
Hungnam
Wonsan
Pyongyang
NORTH KOREA
38th Parallel
1945 Frontier
38th Parallel
SEOUL
Inchon
SOUTH KOREA
U.N. ATTACK 14 SEPTEMBER
Yongdok
18 SEPT UNFEINT LANDING
Yellow Sea
Kunsan
Taegu
Held by U.N. throughout war
U.N. FEINT LANDING 18 SEPT
Pusan
Mokp'o
The KOREAN WAR June – November 1950

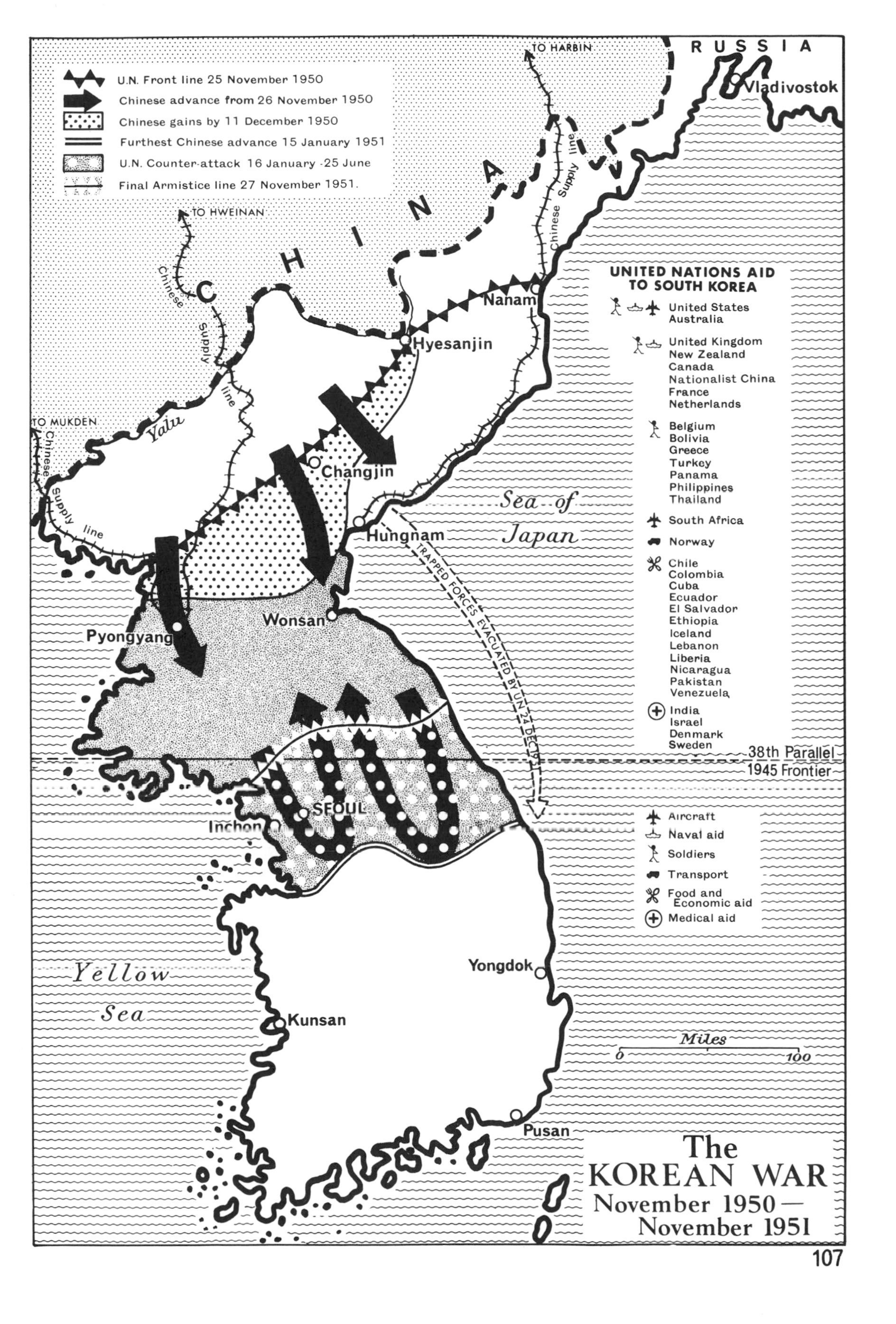

The KOREAN WAR November 1950 — November 1951

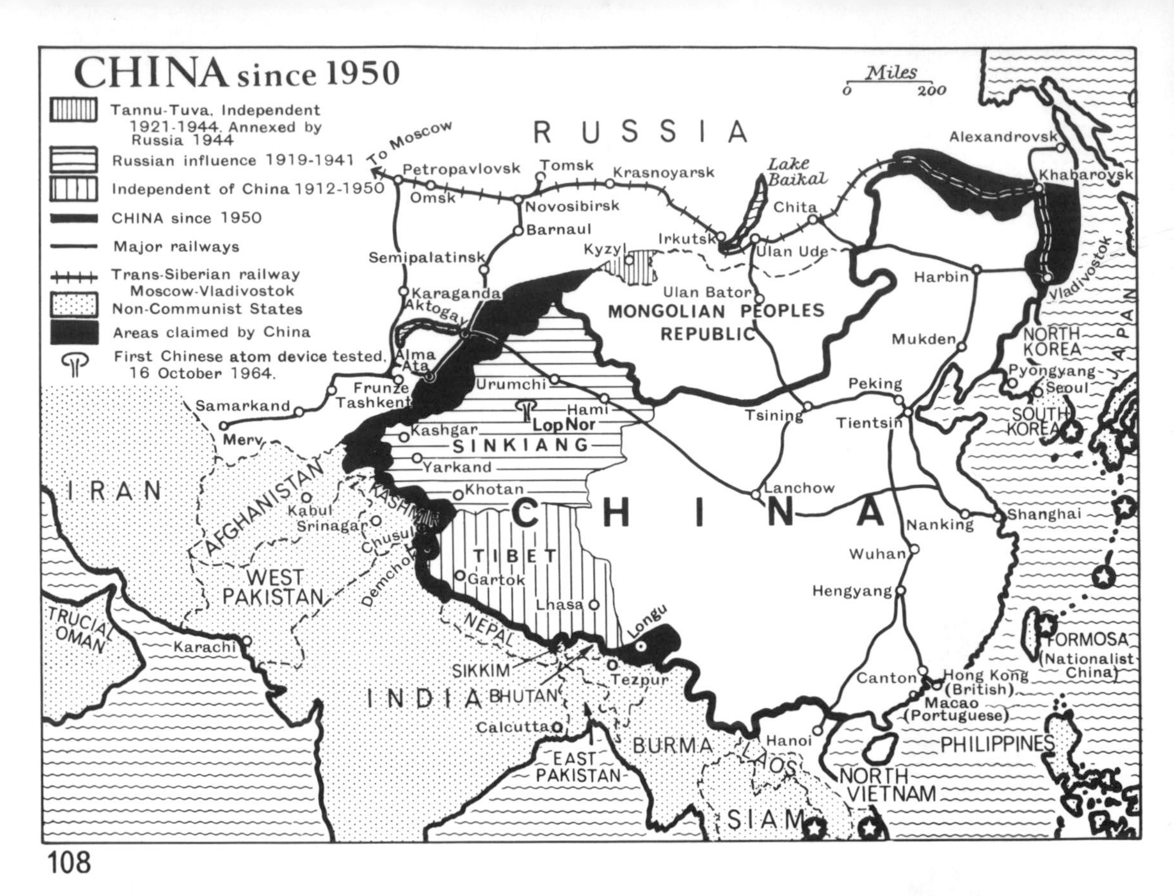

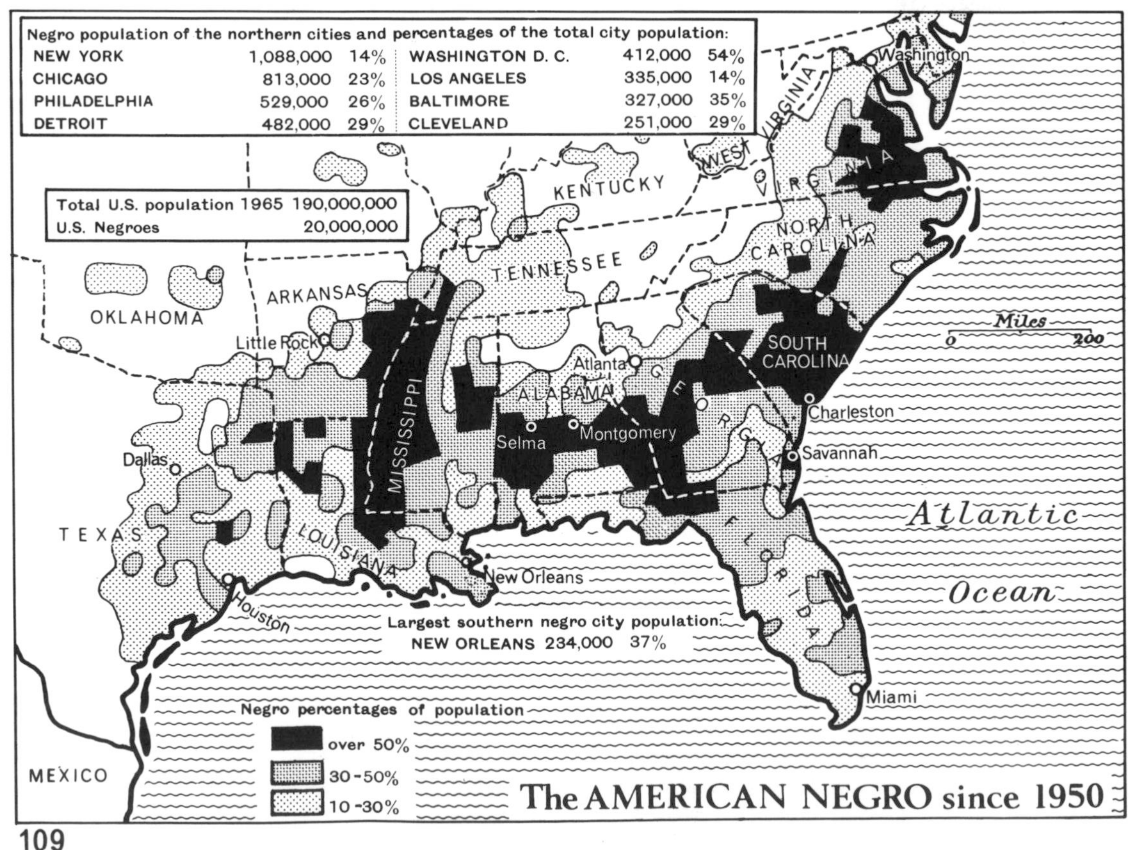

Negro population of the northern cities and percentages of the total city population:

NEW YORK	1,088,000	14%	WASHINGTON D. C.	412,000	54%
CHICAGO	813,000	23%	LOS ANGELES	335,000	14%
PHILADELPHIA	529,000	26%	BALTIMORE	327,000	35%
DETROIT	482,000	29%	CLEVELAND	251,000	29%

Total U.S. population 1965	190,000,000
U.S. Negroes	20,000,000

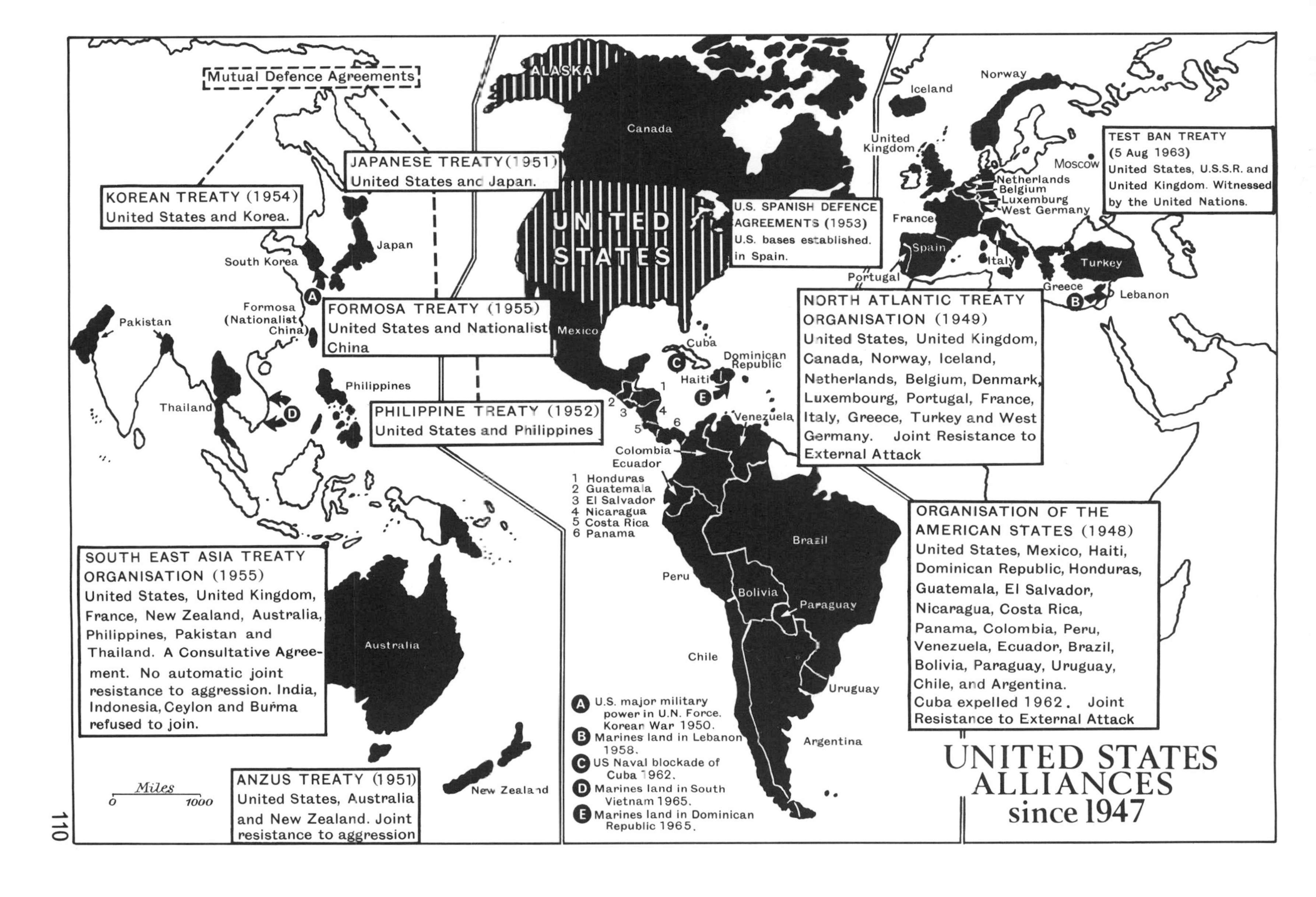
UNITED STATES ALLIANCES since 1947
Mutual Defence Agreements
KOREAN TREATY (1954)
United States and Korea.
JAPANESE TREATY (1951)
United States and Japan.
FORMOSA TREATY (1955)
United States and Nationalist China
PHILIPPINE TREATY (1952)
United States and Philippines
SOUTH EAST ASIA TREATY ORGANISATION (1955)
United States, United Kingdom, France, New Zealand, Australia, Philippines, Pakistan and Thailand. A Consultative Agreement. No automatic joint resistance to aggression. India, Indonesia, Ceylon and Burma refused to join.
ANZUS TREATY (1951)
United States, Australia and New Zealand. Joint resistance to aggression
U.S. SPANISH DEFENCE AGREEMENTS (1953)
U.S. bases established in Spain.
NORTH ATLANTIC TREATY ORGANISATION (1949)
United States, United Kingdom, Canada, Norway, Iceland, Netherlands, Belgium, Denmark, Luxembourg, Portugal, France, Italy, Greece, Turkey and West Germany. Joint Resistance to External Attack
TEST BAN TREATY
(5 Aug 1963)
United States, U.S.S.R. and United Kingdom. Witnessed by the United Nations.
ORGANISATION OF THE AMERICAN STATES (1948)
United States, Mexico, Haiti, Dominican Republic, Honduras, Guatemala, El Salvador, Nicaragua, Costa Rica, Panama, Colombia, Peru, Venezuela, Ecuador, Brazil, Bolivia, Paraguay, Uruguay, Chile, and Argentina.
Cuba expelled 1962. Joint Resistance to External Attack
A U.S. major military power in U.N. Force. Korean War 1950.
B Marines land in Lebanon 1958.
C US Naval blockade of Cuba 1962.
D Marines land in South Vietnam 1965.
E Marines land in Dominican Republic 1965.
1 Honduras
2 Guatemala
3 El Salvador
4 Nicaragua
5 Costa Rica
6 Panama
ALASKA
Canada
UNITED STATES
Mexico
Cuba
Haiti
Dominican Republic
Venezuela
Colombia
Ecuador
Peru
Brazil
Bolivia
Paraguay
Chile
Uruguay
Argentina
Iceland
Norway
United Kingdom
Moscow
Netherlands
Belgium
Luxemburg
West Germany
France
Spain
Portugal
Italy
Turkey
Greece
Lebanon
South Korea
Japan
Formosa (Nationalist China)
Pakistan
Thailand
Philippines
Australia
New Zealand
Miles
0
1000

EUROPEAN ECONOMIC BLOCS since 1947
Miles
0
300
FINLAND
NORWAY
SWEDEN
GT BRITAIN
EIRE
DENMARK
HOLLAND
EAST GERMANY
POLAND
RUSSIA
BELGIUM
WEST GERMANY
LUXEMBURG
CZECHOSLOVAKIA
FRANCE
SWITZ
AUSTRIA
HUNGARY
RUMANIA
YUGOSLAVIA
BULGARIA
ITALY
ALBANIA
GREECE
TURKEY
PORTUGAL
SPAIN
Benelux customs Union since 1947
Comecon Mutual Economic aid since 1948
European Coal and Steel Community since 1952
European Common Market Treaty of Rome 1957
European Free Trade Association since 1958

111

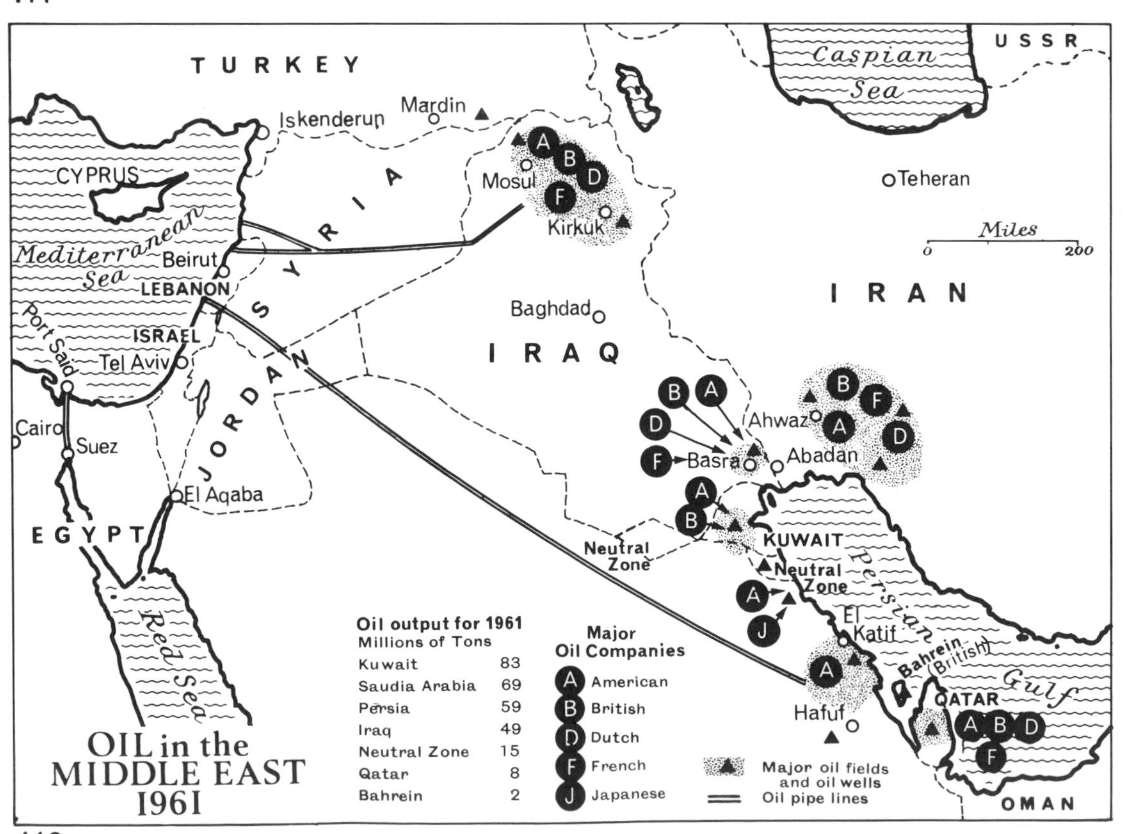
TURKEY
USSR
Caspian Sea
Mardin
Iskenderun
CYPRUS
Mosul
Kirkuk
Teheran
SYRIA
Mediterranean Sea
Beirut
LEBANON
Miles
0
200
IRAN
Baghdad
ISRAEL
Port Said
Tel Aviv
IRAQ
JORDAN
Cairo
Suez
Ahwaz
Abadan
Basra
El Aqaba
EGYPT
Neutral Zone
KUWAIT
Neutral Zone
Persian Gulf
Red Sea
El Katif
Bahrein (British)
Hafuf
QATAR
OMAN
OIL in the MIDDLE EAST 1961
Oil output for 1961
Millions of Tons
Kuwait 83
Saudia Arabia 69
Persia 59
Iraq 49
Neutral Zone 15
Qatar 8
Bahrein 2
Major Oil Companies
A American
B British
D Dutch
F French
J Japanese
Major oil fields and oil wells
Oil pipe lines

112

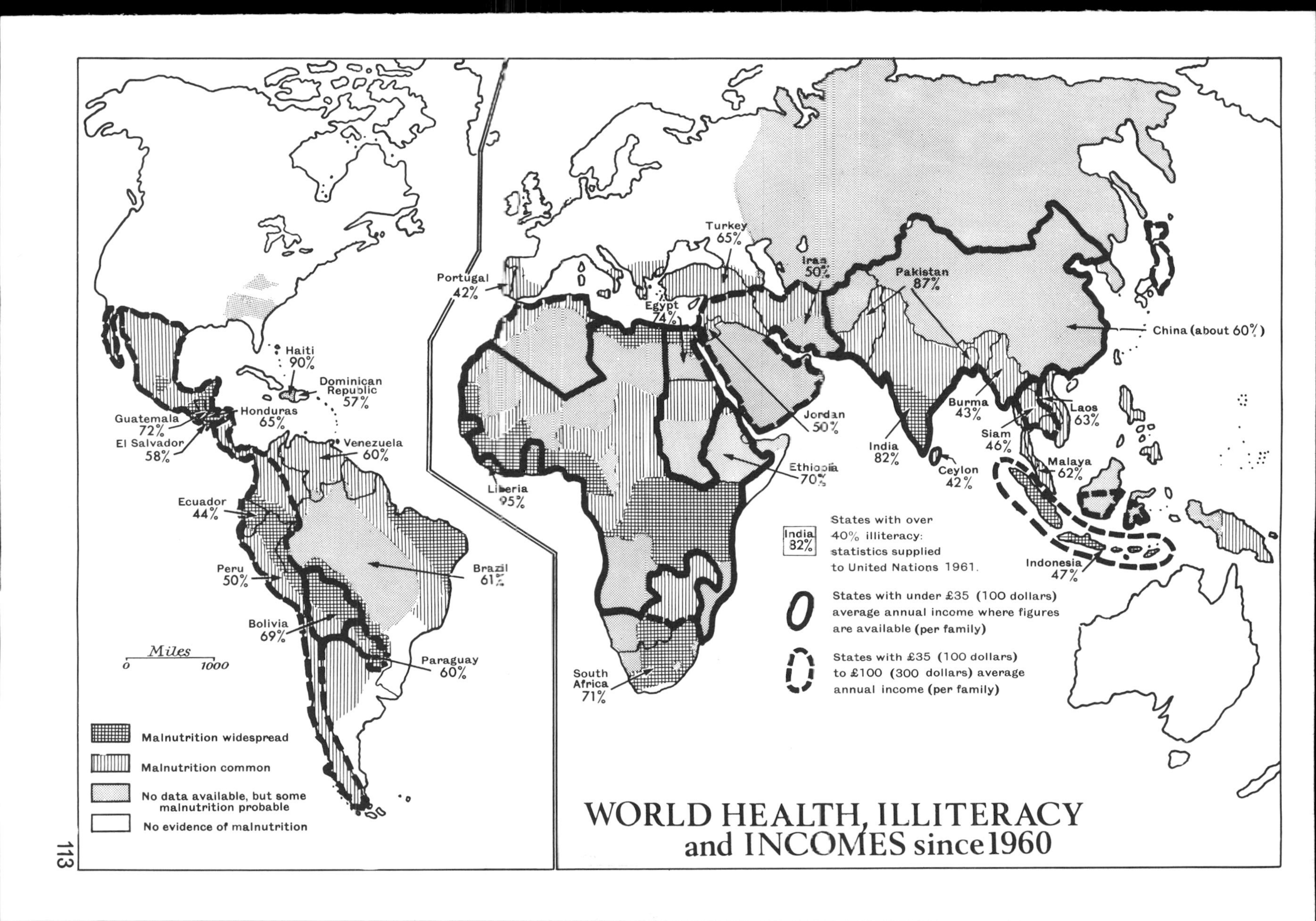
WORLD HEALTH, ILLITERACY and INCOMES since 1960
Malnutrition widespread
Malnutrition common
No data available, but some malnutrition probable
No evidence of malnutrition
Miles
0
1000
India 82%
States with over 40% illiteracy: statistics supplied to United Nations 1961.
States with under £35 (100 dollars) average annual income where figures are available (per family)
States with £35 (100 dollars) to £100 (300 dollars) average annual income (per family)
Haiti 90%
Dominican Republic 57%
Guatemala 72%
Honduras 65%
El Salvador 58%
Venezuela 60%
Ecuador 44%
Peru 50%
Brazil 61%
Bolivia 69%
Paraguay 60%
Portugal 42%
Turkey 65%
Egypt 74%
Iraq 50%
Pakistan 87%
China (about 60%)
Jordan 50%
Liberia 95%
Ethiopia 70%
India 82%
Burma 43%
Laos 63%
Siam 46%
Ceylon 42%
Malaya 62%
Indonesia 47%
South Africa 71%

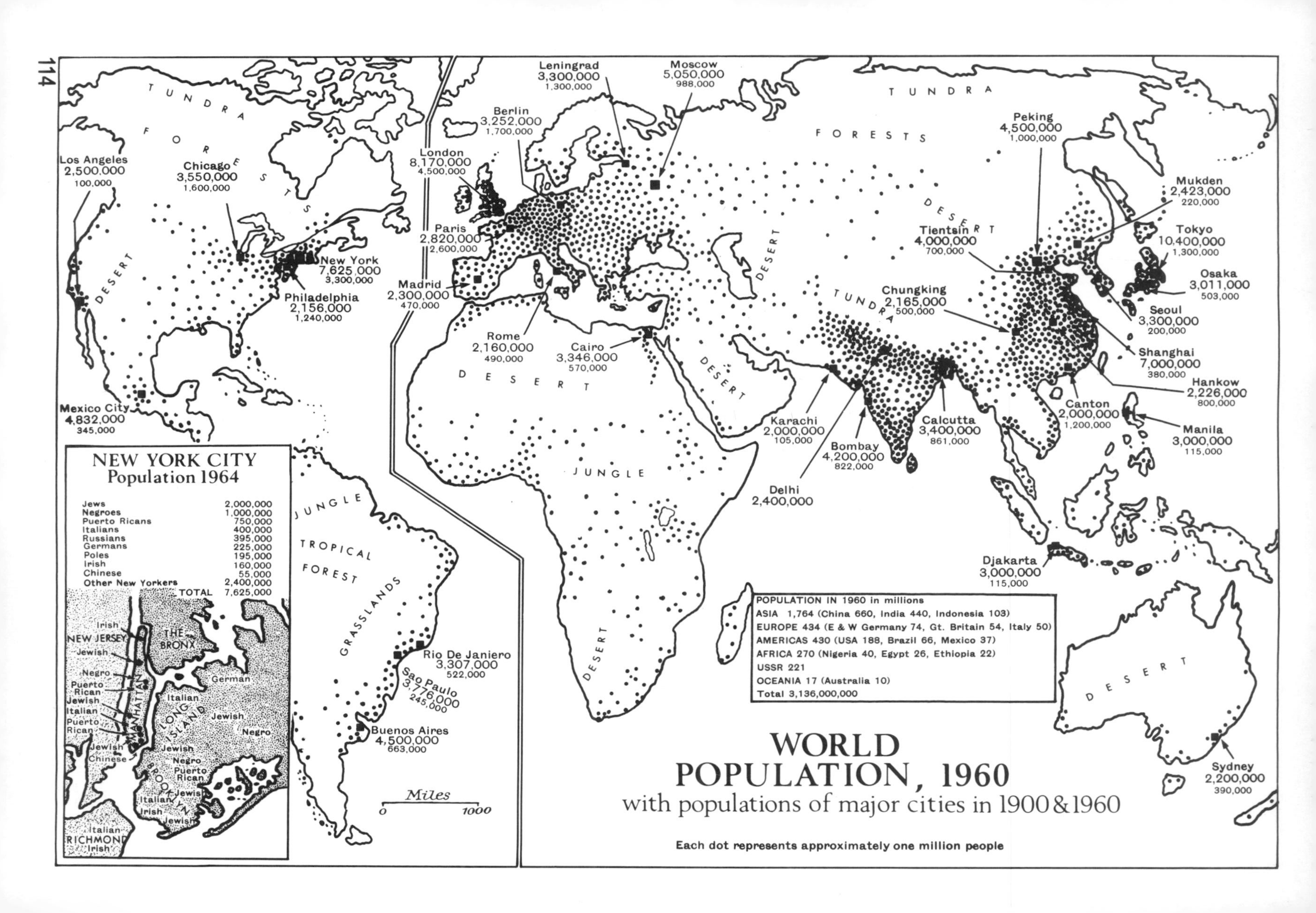

WORLD POPULATION, 1960

with populations of major cities in 1900 & 1960

Each dot represents approximately one million people

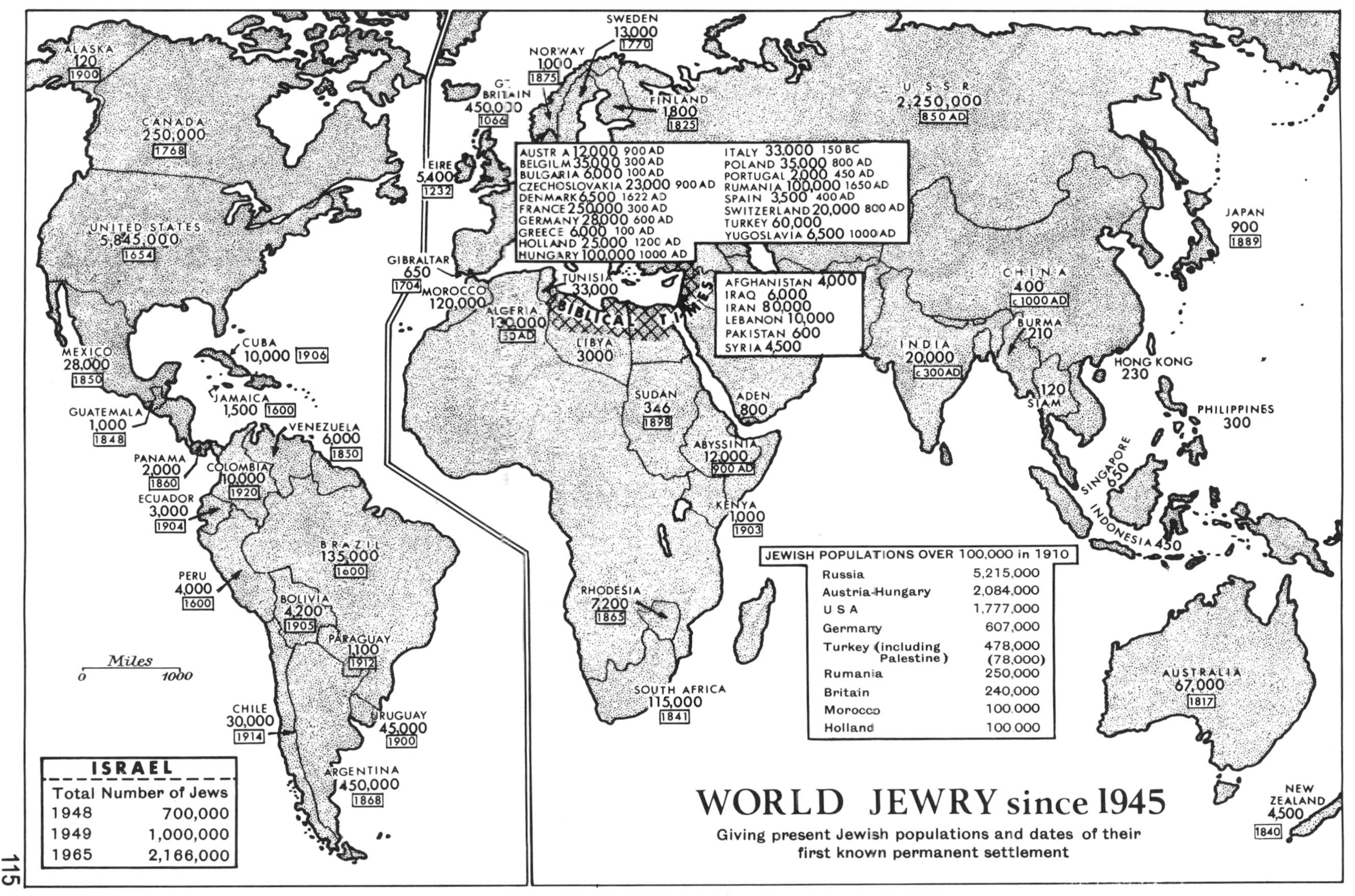

WORLD JEWRY since 1945
Giving present Jewish populations and dates of their first known permanent settlement
ALASKA 120 1900
CANADA 250,000 1768
UNITED STATES 5,845,000 1654
MEXICO 28,000 1850
GUATEMALA 1,000 1848
PANAMA 2,000 1860
COLOMBIA 10,000 1920
ECUADOR 3,000 1904
PERU 4,000 1600
CUBA 10,000 1906
JAMAICA 1,500 1600
VENEZUELA 6,000 1850
BRAZIL 135,000 1600
BOLIVIA 4,200 1905
PARAGUAY 1,100 1912
CHILE 30,000 1914
URUGUAY 45,000 1900
ARGENTINA 450,000 1868
Miles
0
1000
ISRAEL
Total Number of Jews
1948 700,000
1949 1,000,000
1965 2,166,000
EIRE 5,400 1232
GT. BRITAIN 450,000 1066
NORWAY 1,000 1875
SWEDEN 13,000 1770
FINLAND 1800 1825
U.S.S.R. 2,250,000 850 AD
AUSTRIA 12,000 900 AD
BELGIUM 35,000 300 AD
BULGARIA 6,000 100 AD
CZECHOSLOVAKIA 23,000 900 AD
DENMARK 6500 1622 AD
FRANCE 250,000 300 AD
GERMANY 28000 600 AD
GREECE 6,000 100 AD
HOLLAND 25,000 1200 AD
HUNGARY 100,000 1000 AD
ITALY 33,000 150 BC
POLAND 35,000 800 AD
PORTUGAL 2,000 450 AD
RUMANIA 100,000 1650 AD
SPAIN 3,500 400 AD
SWITZERLAND 20,000 800 AD
TURKEY 60,000
YUGOSLAVIA 6,500 1000 AD
GIBRALTAR 650 1704
MOROCCO 120,000
ALGERIA 130,000
TUNISIA 33,000
BIBLICAL TIMES
LIBYA 3000
AFGHANISTAN 4,000
IRAQ 6,000
IRAN 80,000
LEBANON 10,000
PAKISTAN 600
SYRIA 4,500
SUDAN 346 1898
ADEN 800
ABYSSINIA 12,000 900 AD
KENYA 1,000 1903
RHODESIA 7,200 1865
SOUTH AFRICA 115,000 1841
INDIA 20,000 c 300 AD
CHINA 400 c 1000 AD
BURMA 210
SIAM 120
HONG KONG 230
JAPAN 900 1889
PHILIPPINES 300
SINGAPORE 650
INDONESIA 450
AUSTRALIA 67,000 1817
NEW ZEALAND 4,500 1840
JEWISH POPULATIONS OVER 100,000 in 1910
Russia 5,215,000
Austria-Hungary 2,084,000
U S A 1,777,000
Germany 607,000
Turkey (including Palestine) 478,000 (78,000)
Rumania 250,000
Britain 240,000
Morocco 100.000
Holland 100.000

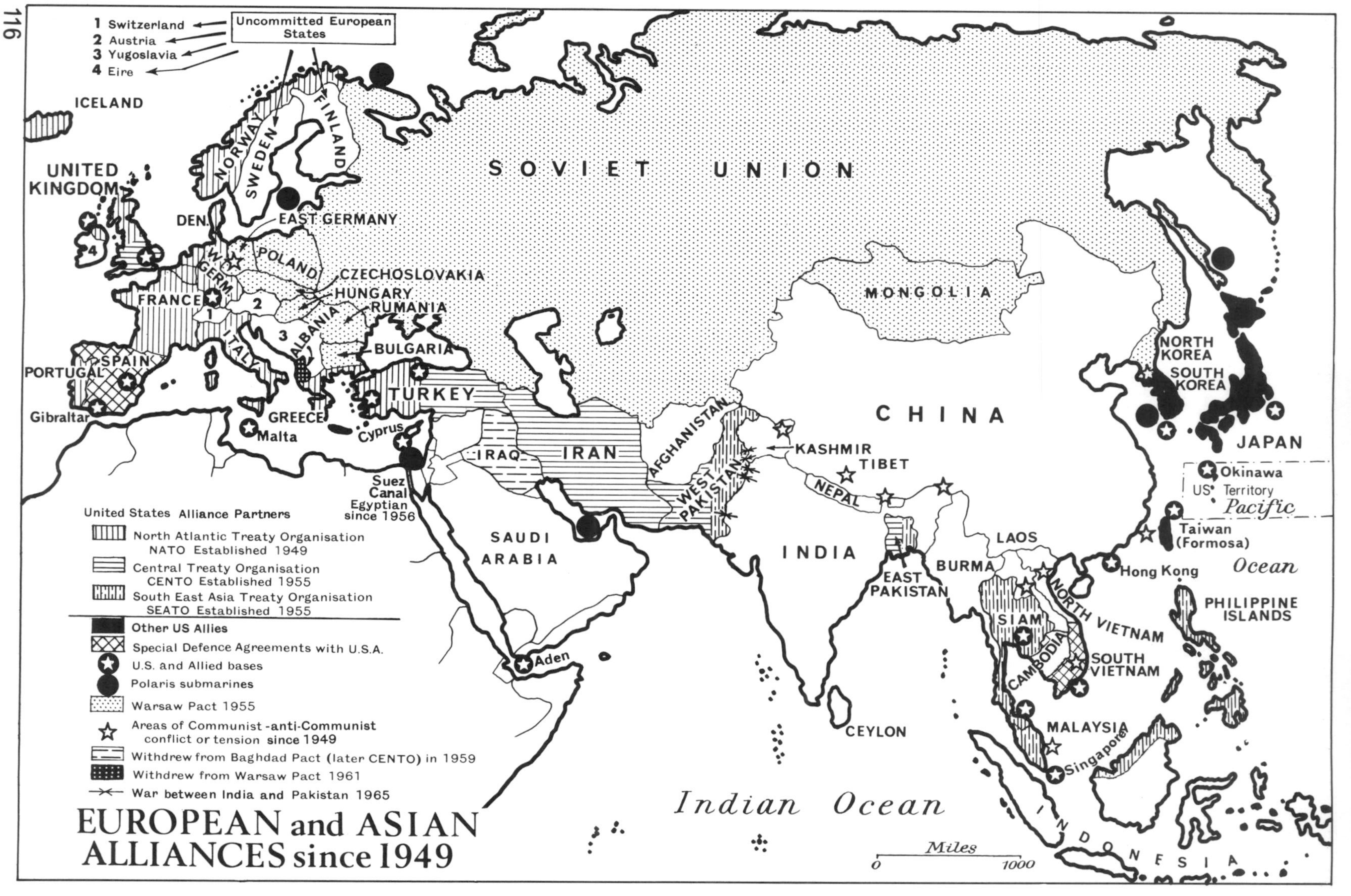

EUROPEAN and ASIAN ALLIANCES since 1949

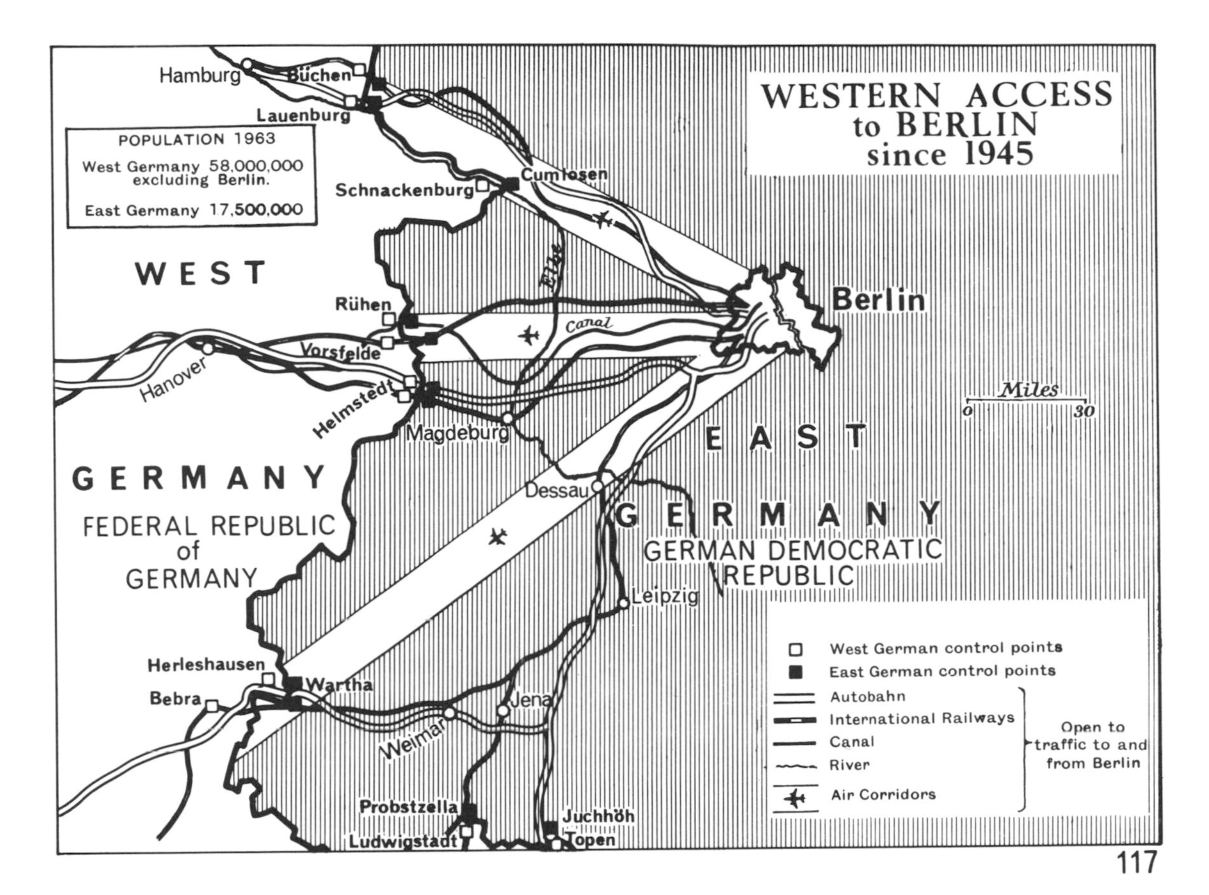
WESTERN ACCESS to BERLIN since 1945
POPULATION 1963
West Germany 58,000,000 excluding Berlin.
East Germany 17,500,000
Hamburg
Büchen
Lauenburg
Cumlosen
Schnackenburg
Elbe
Berlin
WEST
GERMANY
FEDERAL REPUBLIC of GERMANY
Rühen
Vorsfelde
Canal
Hanover
Helmstedt
Magdeburg
Miles
0
30
EAST
GERMANY
GERMAN DEMOCRATIC REPUBLIC
Dessau
Leipzig
Herleshausen
Wartha
Bebra
Jena
Weimar
Probstzella
Ludwigstadt
Juchhöh
Töpen
West German control points
East German control points
Autobahn
International Railways
Canal
River
Air Corridors
Open to traffic to and from Berlin

117

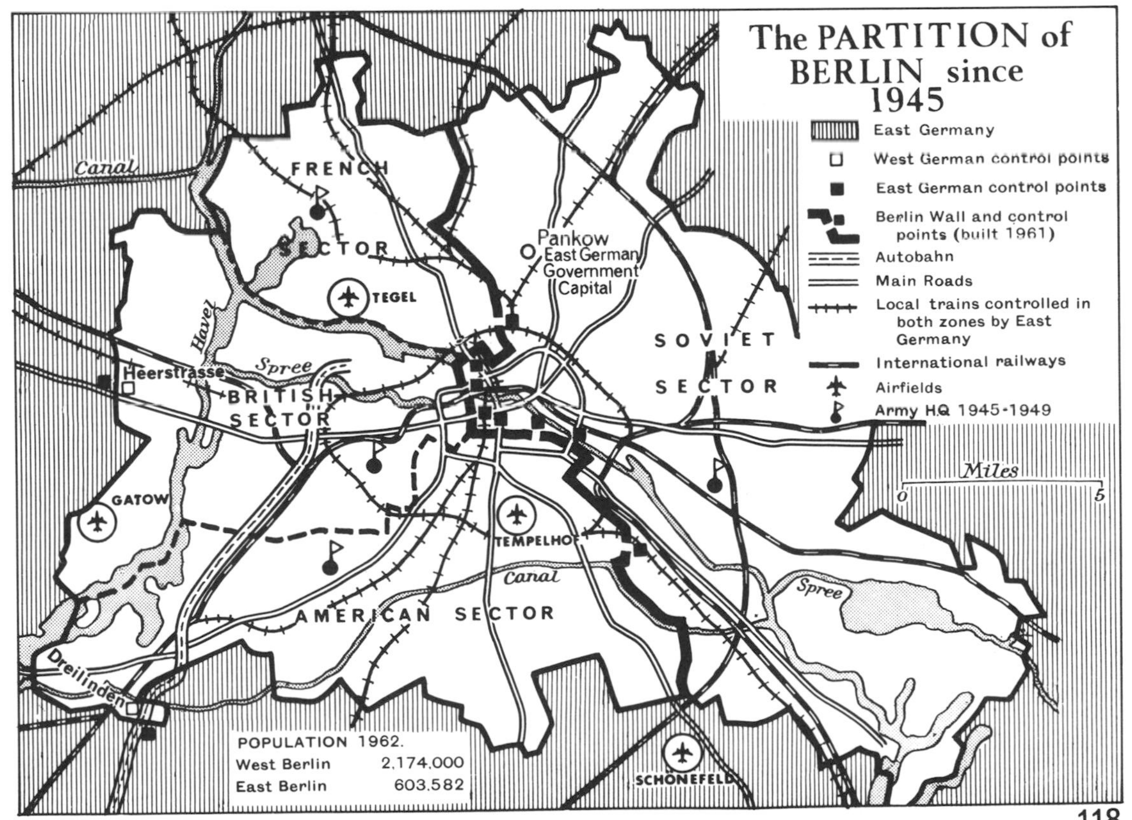
The PARTITION of BERLIN since 1945
East Germany
West German control points
East German control points
Berlin Wall and control points (built 1961)
Autobahn
Main Roads
Local trains controlled in both zones by East Germany
International railways
Airfields
Army H.Q. 1945-1949
Canal
FRENCH
SECTOR
Pankow
East German Government Capital
TEGEL
Havel
Spree
Heerstrasse
BRITISH
SECTOR
SOVIET
SECTOR
Miles
0
5
GATOW
TEMPELHOF
Canal
Spree
AMERICAN SECTOR
Dreilinden
POPULATION 1962.
West Berlin 2,174,000
East Berlin 603,582
SCHÖNEFELD

118

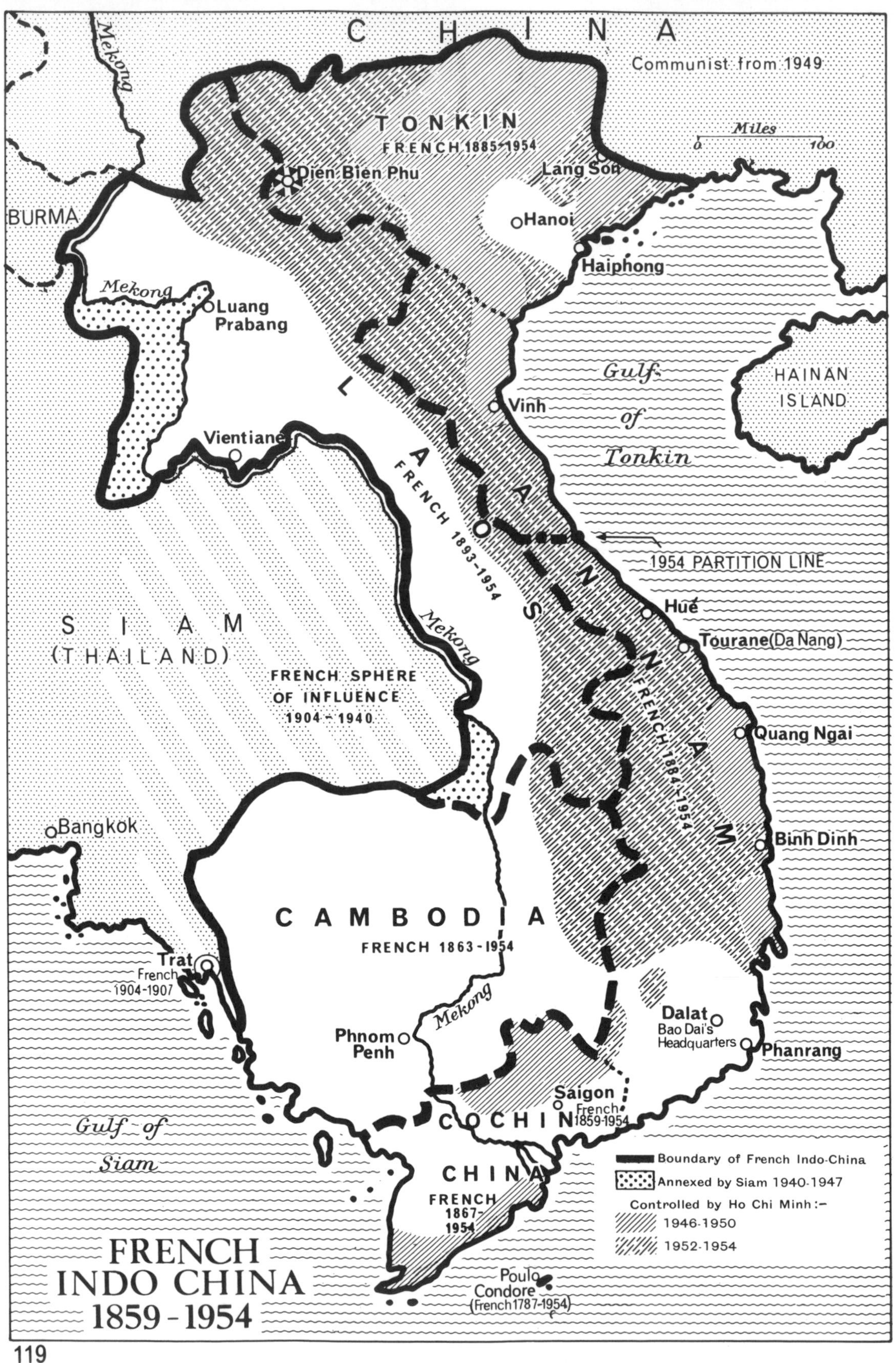
C H I N A
Communist from 1949
TONKIN
FRENCH 1885-1954
Miles
0
100
Dien Bien Phu
Lang Son
Hanoi
Haiphong
BURMA
Mekong
Luang Prabang
Gulf of Tonkin
HAINAN ISLAND
Vinh
Vientiane
LAOS
FRENCH 1893-1954
1954 PARTITION LINE
Hué
Tourane (Da Nang)
S I A M
(T H A I L A N D)
FRENCH SPHERE OF INFLUENCE 1904 - 1940
ANNAM
FRENCH 1884-1954
Quang Ngai
Binh Dinh
Bangkok
CAMBODIA
FRENCH 1863-1954
Trat
French 1904-1907
Dalat
Bao Dai's Headquarters
Phanrang
Phnom Penh
Saigon
French 1859-1954
COCHIN CHINA
FRENCH 1867-1954
Gulf of Siam
Boundary of French Indo-China
Annexed by Siam 1940-1947
Controlled by Ho Chi Minh:-
1946-1950
1952-1954
Poulo Condore
(French 1787-1954)
FRENCH INDO CHINA 1859-1954

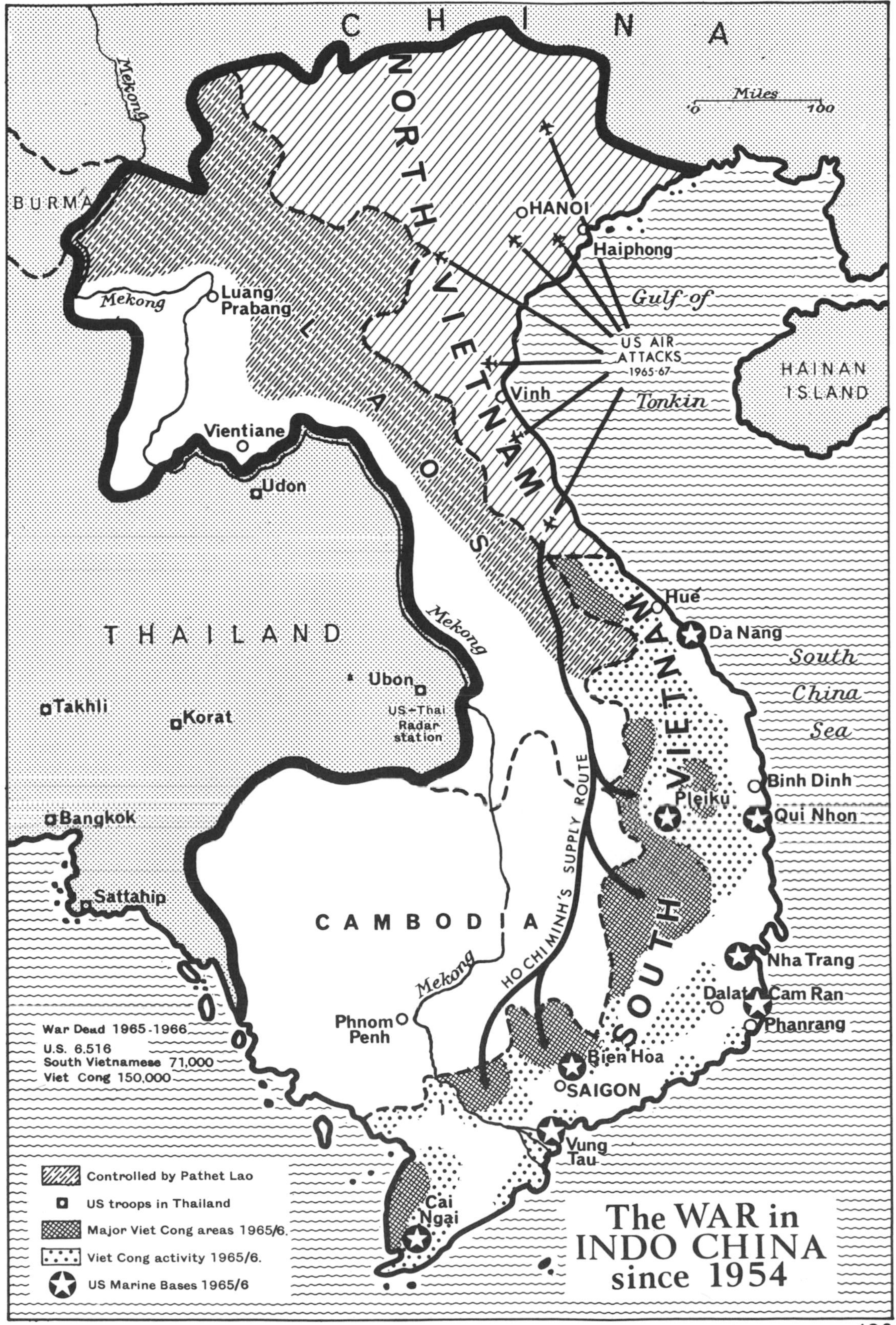

CHINA
NORTH VIETNAM
Miles
0
100
Mekong
BURMA
HANOI
Haiphong
Gulf of
Tonkin
US AIR ATTACKS 1965-67
HAINAN ISLAND
Vinh
Luang Prabang
LAOS
Vientiane
Udon
THAILAND
Mekong
Hué
Da Nang
South China Sea
Ubon
US-Thai Radar station
Takhli
Korat
Binh Dinh
Pleiku
Qui Nhon
Bangkok
SOUTH VIETNAM
HO CHI MINH'S SUPPLY ROUTE
Sattahip
CAMBODIA
Nha Trang
Mekong
Dalat
Cam Ran
Phanrang
Phnom Penh
Bien Hoa
SAIGON
Vung Tau
Cai Ngai
War Dead 1965-1966
U.S. 6,516
South Vietnamese 71,000
Viet Cong 150,000
Controlled by Pathet Lao
US troops in Thailand
Major Viet Cong areas 1965/6.
Viet Cong activity 1965/6.
US Marine Bases 1965/6
The WAR in INDO CHINA since 1954

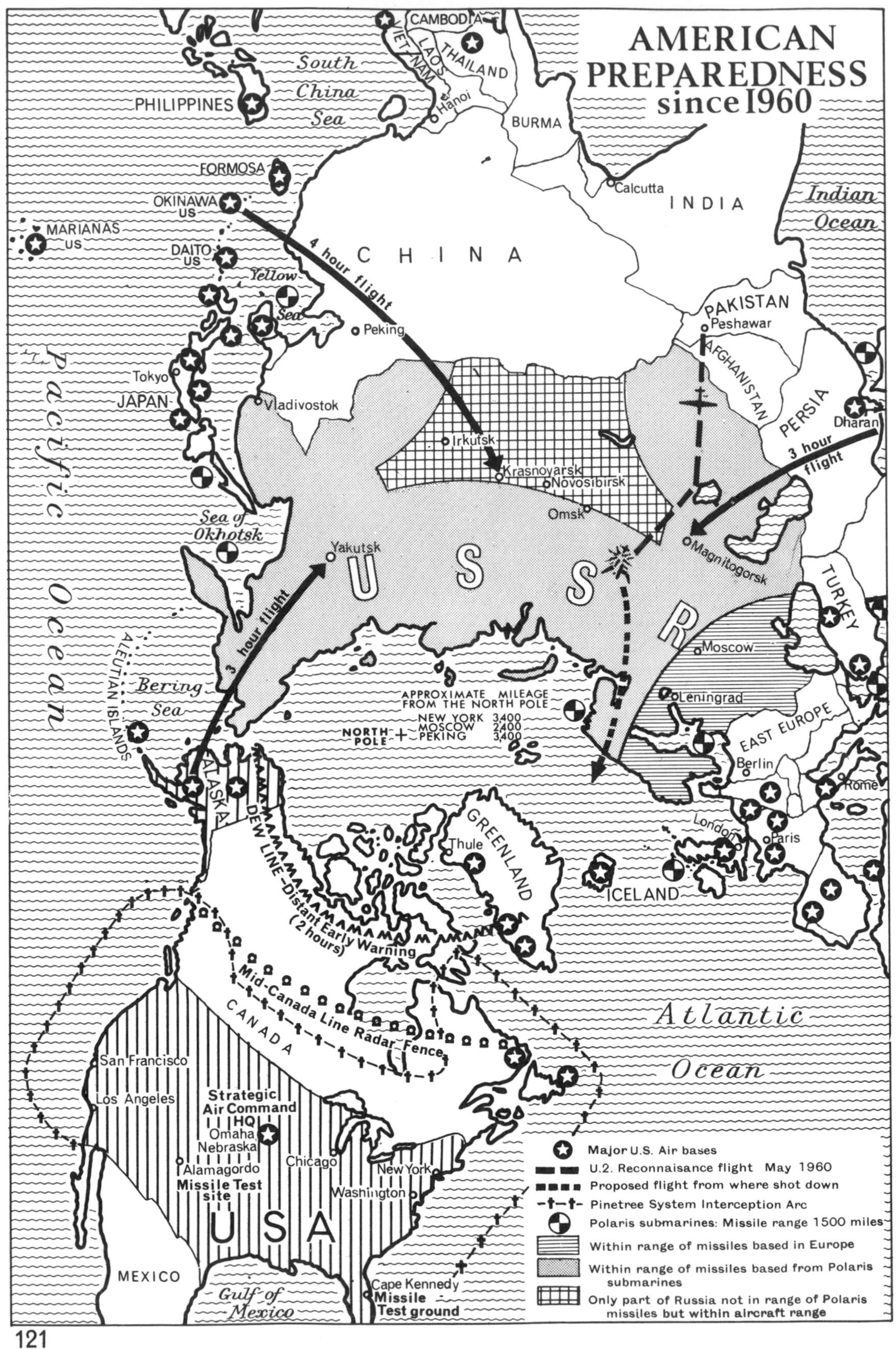

AMERICAN PREPAREDNESS since 1960
CAMBODIA
VIET NAM
LAOS
THAILAND
South China Sea
PHILIPPINES
Hanoi
BURMA
FORMOSA
Calcutta
INDIA
Indian Ocean
OKINAWA US
MARIANAS US
DAITO US
4 hour flight
C H I N A
Yellow Sea
PAKISTAN
Peshawar
Peking
AFGHANISTAN
PERSIA
Dharan
3 hour flight
Pacific Ocean
Tokyo
JAPAN
Vladivostok
Irkutsk
Krasnoyarsk
Novosibirsk
Omsk
Magnitogorsk
Sea of Okhotsk
Yakutsk
U S S R
TURKEY
Moscow
3 hour flight
ALEUTIAN ISLANDS
Bering Sea
APPROXIMATE MILEAGE FROM THE NORTH POLE
NEW YORK 3,400
MOSCOW 2,400
PEKING 3,400
NORTH POLE
Leningrad
EAST EUROPE
Berlin
Rome
ALASKA
DEW LINE–Distant Early Warning (2 hours)
GREENLAND
Thule
London
Paris
ICELAND
Mid-Canada Line Radar Fence
CANADA
Atlantic Ocean
San Francisco
Los Angeles
Strategic Air Command HQ
Omaha Nebraska
Alamagordo
Missile Test site
Chicago
New York
Washington
USA
MEXICO
Gulf of Mexico
Cape Kennedy
Missile Test ground
Major U.S. Air bases
U.2. Reconnaisance flight May 1960
Proposed flight from where shot down
Pinetree System Interception Arc
Polaris submarines: Missile range 1500 miles
Within range of missiles based in Europe
Within range of missiles based from Polaris submarines
Only part of Russia not in range of Polaris missiles but within aircraft range